MBA IN A BOX

How the Markets Really Work

Radical E
(with Glenn Rifkin)

Thought Leaders:
Insights on the Future of Business

The Death of Money:
How the Electronic Economy Has Destabilized the
World's Markets and Created Financial Chaos

The Decline and Crash of the American Economy

Futurecasting

RCDC:
Regional Cooperation Among Developing Countries

MBA IN

Practical Ideas

CROWN
BUSINESS
NEW YORK

A BOX

from the Best Brains in Business

Joel Kurtzman

with Glenn Rifkin
& Victoria Griffith

Grateful acknowledgment is made to the following for permission to reprint previously published material:

The Discipline of Personal Mastery (page 26), from *The Fifth Discipline* by Peter M. Senge. Copyright © 1990 by Peter M. Senge. Reprinted by permission of Doubleday, a division of Random House, Inc.

The Fall and Rise of Strategic Planning (page 119), from "The Fall and Rise of Strategic Planning" (January–February, 1994). Copyright © 1994 by the Harvard Business School Publishing Corporation. All rights reserved. Reprinted by permission of *Harvard Business Review*.

Location, Location, Location (page 134), from *On Competition*, chapter 7, *Clusters and Competition: New Agendas for Companies, Governments, and Institutions,* by Michael E. Porter. Reprinted by permission of Harvard Business School Publishing Division, October 1998.

When Bad Things Happen to Good Products (page 406), from *Apple Confidential: The Real Story of Apple Computer, Inc.,* by Owen Linzmayer. Copyright © 1999 by Owen Linzmayer. Reprinted by permission of No Starch Press, Inc.

Where Have All the Leaders Gone? by Bill George (page 305) was previously published in slightly different form in *European Business Forum* (Autumn 2003): Issue 15. Reprinted by permission of the European Business Forum, www.ebfonline.com.

Published by Crown Business, New York, New York.
Member of the Crown Publishing Group, a division of Random House, Inc.
www.crownpublishing.com

CROWN BUSINESS is a trademark and the Rising Sun colophon is a registered trademark of Random House, Inc.

Printed in the United States of America

DESIGN BY BARBARA STURMAN

Library of Congress Cataloging-in-Publication Data
Kurtzman, Joel.
   MBA in a box : practical ideas from the best brains in business / Joel Kurtzman with Glenn Rifkin and Victoria Griffith.—1st ed.
   1. Industrial management. I. Rifkin, Glenn. II. Griffith, Victoria. III. Title.
   HD31.K88   2004
   658—dc22   2003019647

ISBN 0-609-61088-0

10 9 8 7 6 5 4 3 2 1

First Edition

To my wife, Karen, with love and admiration.

C O N T

ENTS

INTRODUCTION

When I was the editor of the *Harvard Business Review*, I had a recurring fantasy (no, not *that* kind of fantasy). In my fantasy the dean of the Harvard Business School—my boss—would call me into his dimly lit, book-lined, wood-paneled office. He would sit me down, draw the shades, and lock the door. He would pace. In some version of the fantasy he would wring his hands, shrug, hem and haw. In others he would offer me a glass of port and a fine cigar. (I liked the second version better.)

In that fantasy, the dean—an enormous man with a raspy, conspirator's voice—would say to me that my job at the *Harvard Business Review* was to make business appear difficult to the readers. "Don't publish any smart-aleck articles about how Andrew Carnegie or Henry Ford never finished grammar school or how Bill Gates dropped out of college. Publish articles that talk about how difficult business is, how complicated it is to read a balance sheet, how many times you have to run a regression analysis to really understand your market, how the problems of strategy are intractable. Make it all seem *hard*," he would tell me with a scowl.

"Hard? Why?" I would ask rather meekly.

"Why? Why?" he would repeat, eyes narrowed into tiny slits. "Did you *really* ask me why, you nincompoop?"

"Yes," I would say, clearing my throat. "I did."

"Because it is. And besides, what would happen to *our* business if your readers thought business wasn't all that difficult? That any imbecile could do it? What do we do then?" the dean would bellow. "We sell business education, business books, business magazines, online business content, business videos, business case studies, lectures, degrees, research, class notes. The whole shebang. If people thought business was easy, we'd be wiped out. *Finito.* End of story."

My fantasy did not go on much after that. And in truth, I have great admiration for the dean, the school, the students, and the faculty. The Harvard Business School is a tremendous institution, and it has done an enormous amount of good for thousands of people and institutions on many, many levels. Even so, as I think about business, I have come to understand that my fantasy was in some ways right as well as wrong.

It was wrong because business isn't easy. At least it isn't at the moment. The forces governing competition today are very difficult to navigate. They are global, technological, financial, and human. The cycles of growth and decline—which many pundits in the 1990s said were no longer applicable—are back in full force. In fact, the same items—globalization and technology—that people said had ended the business cycle are now being viewed as making it worse. Globalization and technology, it is now said, have destroyed the ability of many companies to price their goods and services at a premium, which is hurting profits globally. (In the '90s, the same phenomenon was viewed the other way around. Globalization and technology would check inflation and keep prices low so that cost-conscious consumers would continue buying, fueling what some people at the time called the "long boom.")

But that's not all.

The forces governing business are large—very large. They range from sudden, short-term shifts in consumer buying habits—a two-season-long denim craze, a two-year Hula Hoop frenzy, a four-year-long cigar fad, for example—to slower, medium-term changes, such as the decade-long shift from conservative business attire to clothes for casual Fridays and then to clothes for (as my children might say) whatever.

And then there are the longer-term changes on top of these shorter-term shifts. In many countries since the 1960s there has been a slow growth of citizen movements (nongovernmental organizations, protest and pressure groups, business-oriented religious groups, human rights groups, antiglobalization groups, animal rights groups, and so on). Over the last three or four decades, these groups have become very sophisticated, professional, and well organized. Many are well funded and highly strategic in their approach. Many of their leaders have degrees from elite business and professional schools. These groups employ carefully thought-out strategies to achieve their overall goals. They ally themselves with political parties and labor groups.

I have had direct experience with several of these groups in the United States and in Europe. The leader of a French antiglobalization group told me that his organization would never compromise with business on their aims because they have a greater political agenda. The group—whose leaders include some well-respected French journalists and university professors—told me they will not negotiate. Their aim was to restrict outbound French investment (keep French jobs in France), create tougher environmental restrictions, and limit non-French cultural imports (movies, music, and books), among other things. The leader of the group said he was against markets and against American-style capitalism. When this group plans a demonstration, tens of thousands of people show up. As a result, the politicians listen and companies must cope.

Another group, an American environmental organization, explained to me why it had mounted a boycott against a certain Japanese automaker. The carmaker, the group's leader explained, was actually innocent when it came to the environmental offense in question. It did, however, have significant investment from, and shared directorships with, another Japanese company that was clear-cutting hardwood forests in Indonesia. By putting pressure on one company it could exert influence over the other due to their shared governance structure, the environmental leader explained. Over the last twenty-five years this organization has come to know as much about business as the best stock market analysts and investment bankers do.

There are other large, long-term changes as well—new technologies (broadband, for example) where the business *case* has been obvious for decades but the correct business *model* has yet to materialize.

In this category, difficult, long-term problems increased competition from nontraditional corporate and/or global rivals—the three-decade-long rise of China from economic backwater to high-tech manufacturing giant, the nearly three-decade move by several European governments to develop Airbus Industries into a powerful rival to Boeing for passenger jets, the growing threat to Microsoft from the so-called free (you still have to pay experts to install it and customize it) Linux operating system.

Competition from the margins moves to center stage in a familiar pattern written about by Harvard's Clayton Christensen, author of *The Innovator's Dilemma*. In this work Christensen recounts the story of Digital Equipment Company (DEC), which, until the late '80s, produced a market-leading minicomputer—the VAX—whose dominance was overturned by the PC, which began as an inferior product that wasn't even on DEC's competitive radar scope. He also recounts the story of how Big Steel suddenly found itself supplanted by the rise of mini-mills that produced far cheaper steel from scrap, while the big players were forced to smelt ore using higher-priced technologies and processes.

There is no question that business is complex. On that point, I have to hand it to the dean. But difficult does not mean *hard*, which I take to mean something akin to joyless toil. From my point of view, doing business is not the emotional equivalent of a sentence to San Quentin or Rikers Island. Nor is it drudgery. Business is one of life's great games, and it is exhilarating. In fact, calling business *business* is demeaning. I much prefer the words the French use for business, *les affaires,* which imply (at least to me) that the subject, in one way or another, applies to nearly everything; that it is encompassing, vast, integral to what we are and even who we are. Business is not just a job. It is so much more—goods and services, folly and delight, wealth and power, value and loss, money, dazzle, hype, dread, and exuberance, and of course *exchange*.

In the end—or rather the beginning—business is about exchange, which means that it is a game that cannot be played alone. A farmer can grow food enough for himself and his family, but it is not *business* until someone takes that food to market to trade it for something else. Business is a networking event. Business has no equivalent of a baseball pitching machine. It is not bowling alone, nor is it hitting a tennis ball against the garage door. Business is played with others and without a helmet.

The beauty and enticement of business is not just that it is so broad. People make a living from overseeing pharmaceutical research that takes decades and will save lives, just as they do from printing custom T-shirts with pictures of your dog. The beauty of business is that no part of it—from the gigantic pharmaceutical company to the little T-shirt entrepreneur—is ever risk-free. Big companies fail just like the little ones.

It is not exactly fair to say that people find business exciting for the same reasons that deep-sea divers or aerialists like their areas of endeavor. Yet the potential for a business washout does focus the mind. And if business is a game—as I believe it is—it is all the more exciting because the stakes are so high.

I don't mean to sound flip or inhumane in this short introduction to this big book. People losing their jobs, their savings, and their retirement accounts are not subjects to laugh about. When Enron, WorldCom, or Barings Bank failed, thousands of people's lives were devastated. Not only were their bank accounts lightened, their dreams were dashed, and worse.

Still, because business is played with only the barest of safety nets—at least in the United States—successes, when they occur, are that much sweeter.

Every business is built on Big Ideas. What do I mean by Big Ideas? I am not necessarily talking about complex ideas, flashy ideas, complicated ideas, or mathematical ideas, although they certainly have their place.

What I mean by Big Ideas are concepts that are practical, down-to-earth, and appropriate, and which in the end reduce the fog of complexity into something simple, solid, tangible, and most of all *workable*. Big Ideas are practical ideas. They are ideas that help people achieve their dreams, that serve as the pathways from one success to another. They help one group fulfill another group's needs.

You do not have to be the proverbial rocket scientist to be successful, unless your business is building rockets. A century and a half ago Levi Strauss founded the clothing company that continues to bear his name when he realized that miners in the California gold rush needed trousers far more rugged than anything they could buy at the time. True, it wasn't exactly the theory of relativity, and denim pants don't exactly cure cancer. But Levi Strauss' idea was imbued with great utility and—as we know—longevity. His idea was sufficient to support the development of a company that over time provided the livelihood of tens of thousands of workers in factories and in stores, all the while covering, protecting, and in some cases enhancing the bottoms of millions of customers. To put it in the vernacular, it was an idea with legs.

But that's not the end of the story, as we know. The wonderful and simple idea that begat the world's first blue-jeans maker, Levi Strauss, also begat a host of rivals worldwide. Many of those rivals had very short lives. But many found their own niches, taking away market share from the once-dominant player. What is the point of this story? Simply that the game of business is not just played on the offense. There is a defensive game as well. Great companies—and great business leaders—play both games equally well.

In this book I have asked some of the best minds in business to put down some of their best thoughts. I have asked them to be candid, open, and opinionated. I have asked them to tackle the subjects they love from perspectives that they know work. I have asked them to give readers a glimpse of how they think about what they do.

There are a number of different types of contributors to this book.

First, there are people we used to call "business practitioners" when I worked at the *Harvard Business Review.* This group includes people such as Dean Kamen, the inventor of dozens of high-tech medical devices, the developer of the Segway human transportation device, and the founder of many successful companies; Michael Milken, one of the world's most important, brilliant, and controversial financial minds, who raised hundreds of billions of dollars through the high-yield bond market to fund new and emerging companies worldwide; and James Champy, inventor of the term *reengineering* and author of the first book on the subject.

In addition, a number of journalists have contributed to this volume—people such as Glenn Rifkin, a frequent writer for the *New York Times,* and Victoria Griffith, a reporter for Europe's *Financial Times.*

And there are academics. Among this group are Harvard's Michael Porter and Benjamin Shapiro, both leaders in their respective disciplines of strategy and marketing, and Yale's Jeffrey Sonnenfeld.

And finally, there are the brilliant thinkers who defy categorization because they do so many different things. These include Sam Hill, whose understanding of "branding" is without equal; Adrian Slywotzky, who has developed new theories about profits and how to get your fair share; and Robert Eccles, one of the world's most profound thinkers on financial reporting and measurement. There are dozens more.

The aim of this book is simple—to help readers become more accomplished at what they do. Its goal is to help readers shift their vantage points, shake up their thinking, and stretch their minds. Its aim is to help people look at the world from new and unusual points of view.

But it has another aim as well. While this book is serious, thoughtful, and deep, it is also supposed to be fun. Consider this book a friend at the ready, one who is always there with something to say—sometimes analytical, sometimes opinionated, but rarely equivocating. Consider it to be a tool to freshen up your thinking whenever you come to a seemingly intractable problem. It is a book filled with big ideas, but it is also a book whose aim is practicality. It is a book you can open up at random or read all the way through. If you enjoy this book as you are being informed by it, it will have served its purpose.

How to Use This Book

Like almost everyone in the late '90s, I had an idea for a business-related Internet start-up company. The company would gather together great business content and organize it from the perspective of a business user. It would make that content easily searchable and accessible.

The idea was that when people get a new job, decide to start a company, are moved to a new division, or simply want to do their current job better, they need access to high-quality, highly focused information. In addition, teams, whether they're inside a company or are a group of consultants, are composed of people with different backgrounds and skills and need a way to quickly understand each other's disciplines and points of view.

To use a little jargon, the idea was that since so many companies are trying to become flatter and leaner—less hierarchical and more matrixlike—with fewer silos, people need to get a better understanding of how everyone thinks about life and business. To do this, they need knowledge that is not only *deep* and *specialized* but also *wide* and *general.*

To work in flatter organizations with less supervision, more individual responsibility is required. Organizations like these demand that employees make decisions about each other and about their customers with far less supervision. Organizations like these give each individual more freedom, but they also hold people to tougher standards of accountability. To function in organizations like these, people need to understand each other.

Enron and some of the other scandal-ridden organizations are very good examples of how this can all go awry. The Enron culture was built on loose levels of supervision, flat hierarchy, and a very tight adherence to revenue and profit numbers. One troublesome problem in a culture like that, as statements and testimony have subsequently shown, was that a lot of people in the company did not understand what their peers or even their subordinates were doing. As long as people were making money, they were left alone.

In hindsight, it appears that what was not understood by Enron's employees, senior management, and even its board of directors contributed to that firm's demise and to the subsequent destruction of so many people's lives and fortunes. Had the board of directors had *MBA in a Box* on hand, its members might have made better decisions.

Because business is more complex and organizations are flatter, people need to acquire information more quickly and understand the way others think. They need to know each other's areas of competence and business aims. They also need to develop—as an old Hollywood producer once told me—"world-class, bulletproof bullshit detectors."

People need knowledge not to impress each other but to work together. More than ever, marketing people need to know the way financial people think, financial people need to understand the way the technical people work, and technical people need to know how the sales force does its job. More than likely, in today's understaffed organizations, there is no in-house company guru with sufficient time to explain the lay of the land.

In the late '90s the Internet business I devised was supposed to provide this information to people in a convenient, even fun format. But after I did what every budding entrepreneur does—populate a spreadsheet model with lots of detailed business assumptions about how much it would take to start and run the business versus how much it would earn in years one through five—I realized something I should have known all along: rather than invest millions of dollars in an Internet company, why not begin by making everything available in a book? Not only would a book be cheaper to produce than a big, overstaffed Web site, but you can bring this handsome product to the beach confident you will not damage any of its sensitive parts.

In addition, if you put this book on your bookshelf behind your desk, it will always be there to serve you. Web services and Web content are powerful and useful, but—to paraphrase that old advertisement for a certain precious stone—a book is forever.

MBA in a Box is designed to be used hard and frequently. It is organized to reflect the way normal people do and think about business. It is peppered with short excerpts from some very important books.

Each of these sections contains novel thinking but also common wisdom and ideas about how to do business better. Each of these pieces is written by a person who is a true source of knowledge.

There are three good ways to use this book. The first way is to read it from cover to cover. The second way is to keep it handy and thumb through it whenever you need a creative idea or a new concept. Use this book to jog your imagination and your creativity. The third way is to keep it handy to solve your problems or brief you on a subject at hand. The first two ways of using this book are pretty self-explanatory. But the third way requires understanding your problem or conflict first and then going to the relevant section in this book to find some advice.

As you can see from the headings, each section looks at a problem in business from what I hope is something akin to your own point of view. For that reason, I've chosen to use the vernacular:

- Innovation: How Breakthroughs Happen
- Sustainability and the Environment: A Business That Makes Nothing but Money Is a Poor Kind of Business
- Finance and Accounting: "We're Not in Kansas Anymore"— Getting Real About Numbers and What They Mean

- Strategy: Make Sure You Take the Right Fork in the Road—On the Importance of Strategic Direction
- Managing Is Getting Paid for Other People's Home Runs
- Human Resources: Why Brains Trump Brawn
- How to Be a Leader and Live to Tell About It
- Marketing: "Find Out What They Want and How They Want It and Give It to 'Em Just That Way"
- Communication: "A Fool May Talk, but a Wise Man Speaks"
- There's Many a Slip 'Twixt the Cup and the Lip: Good Ideas Gone Awry

Let's say your problem is financial. Look at Section 3, which deals with money. Then go through the chapters until you find the one that fits. Begin by reading that chapter, and then when you really have it understood, read another chapter. That way you'll get at least two points of view on every topic listed in this book.

If you use this book in any of the three ways I have just indicated, I am confident that it will become your friend—augmenting what you know, providing advice, helping you become more creative.

If this book helps you in the ways I've just described, then it is bound to help you grow in business. If that is what happens, then this book will have fulfilled its purpose. And if this book helps *you* grow in business, then I will feel happy for having gathered together these contributions from such a brilliant, eclectic, talented, and insightful group of business thinkers. For once, it will have been gratifying to have "thought inside the box."

—JOEL KURTZMAN

1. Innovation

How Breakthroughs Happen

BACK IN THE DARK AGES OF MY YOUTH, WHEN I WAS a penniless graduate student, rather than spend money on a mechanic I undertook the challenge of rebuilding the carburetor of my car. The car was an inexpensive, entry-level import. And because most mechanics I had dealt with failed to impress me with their intellect, I theorized I could do the job myself.

Because I was a student and rather bookish, I went to the library first, found a manual on my car, and read about how to do the job. When I came to the part about the carburetor, I was stunned. During the year my car was built, the manufacturer, Nissan, had made four very significant modifications to the carburetor it used in the model I had. With each modification the car's fuel economy and power improved. But the rebuild kit for each of these carburetors was different! Until I took my car apart—which would leave me no way to get to the auto parts store—I would be unable to tell which kit I needed to buy.

At the time I remember being astounded by the fact that the manufacturer was continuing to modify—innovate, really—throughout the model year. In my naive way, I had assumed that once a car had been introduced, the automaker would leave it alone.

But innovation is a curious thing. True, many of us love to tinker with things. But the engineers at a major Japanese car company? Why were they tinkering?

Over time I began to appreciate what Dean Kamen, the inventor and author of the first piece in this section, takes for granted. Innovation for its own sake is not a very productive use of anybody's time or money. But innovation to improve a product's function, to make it fulfill a customer's or client's need, is a very smart use of capital.

This notion was brought into sharp relief to me by a historical example. During a visit with my son to Colonial Williamsburg, Virginia, we went to the magazine, where British troops stored their weapons. Our guide, dressed as a British soldier, explained to us that the primary British weapon of the day, a musket, stayed in production for nearly two hundred years. During that time, the gun, which was made by hand in cottages and small shops, continued to be produced almost unchanged. Then, sometime after the Revolutionary War, the musket was abandoned and a new gun was introduced.

The reason why the musket stayed in production so long was simply that it did its job. Until the Revolutionary War, accompanied by the American invention of mass production, the standard-issue British musket had no peer and the British Empire had little competition. So why tinker with success?

Today, in a world of intense competition, we are in a period where the customer's needs must be identified and fulfilled. To do that may mean refining the design of a carburetor, a fuel injector, or even a service offering four or more times in a year. The point is, nothing remains static for very long, least of all the way we please customers. Without innovation, the customer or client is likely to leave us in the dust.

J.K.

PEOPLE DON'T BUY INVENTIONS OR TECHNOLOGY, THEY BUY *INNOVATIONS* THAT SOLVE PROBLEMS

Dean Kamen

Perhaps no other corporate mandate has received as much attention over the past decade as innovation. In the ever-increasing competitive landscape brought about by globalization, companies have spent ceaselessly and exorbitantly in the search for the next best thing, be it product or service. "Innovate or die" has become the watchword for a vast number of industry sectors, and even in a soft economy most corporations continue to brag about their firm commitment to research and development.

Despite this crush of interest in innovation and the endless flood of new products and services into the marketplace, there remains a significant lack of understanding about innovation. The best businessperson in the world can't sell something the world isn't ready to use. People don't buy inventions. They don't buy technology. They buy a solution to a perceived problem. And if you have the greatest solution in the world and people don't perceive it as the answer to their problem, they are not going to buy it.

Indeed, throughout history there has been a great deal of confusion about the differences between invention and innovation. Misconceptions about the invention process track straight into the dearth of understanding about when an invention becomes an innovation.

As an inventor, I've always been amazed at people's misunderstanding of what I do. The public always loves the easy, one-shot answer. You can tell by their questions that they really believe I went to bed one night, got up the next morning, and instead of making toast invented the Segway Human Transporter or the IBOT Mobility System. I must have leaped out of bed with the concept completely defined in my head, right down to the decals.

Invention is a difficult, messy process, more an evolution than a revolution. Inspiration may be of the moment. But bringing the inspiration to reality is usually a long, painful, expensive process. You end up iterating again and again and again. You make five different wrong turns that get you to the same place you were at six months ago. And after all the conceiving, designing, building, refining, and polishing, an invention remains a great distance from an innovation.

In their best-selling book *Built to Last*, James Collins and Jerry Porras suggested, "Try a lot of stuff and keep what works." Having examined countless visionary companies known for innovation, such as 3M, Hewlett-Packard, and Johnson & Johnson, the authors were struck by how often these companies "made some of their best moves not by detailed strategic planning, but rather by experimentation, trial and error, opportunism and—quite literally—accident."

Most inventors aren't businesspeople. But the reason many fail is not because they aren't good businesspeople; some are, others aren't. They fail because they misunderstand the difference between invention and innovation. There is a big valley between the two, and it is the public, the cruel arbiter of history, that decides if an invention has the influence and sustainability to become a true innovation.

The day after Thomas Edison created the lightbulb, everybody read about it by the candles they had been using for thousands of years. Who had electricity to power the first lightbulb? It was fragile and didn't provide much light. It was expensive, people didn't trust it or believe in it, and there was no infrastructure to support it. Similarly with the airplane: the day after the Wright Brothers first flew at Kitty Hawk, people rode into town on their horseless carriages to buy a newspaper to read about it.

The airplane and the lightbulb may be the inventions, but the innovation is the process by which those inventions start to affect the way people live, think, and make use of the technology. What is often required is massive marketing and public relations, extensive positive reaction in the media, and word of mouth, along with accessibility. More than anything else, it takes a long time.

One reason it takes so long is that there is inherent risk in using something new and different. People don't like change. They don't like to fail. They don't like situations that make them feel uncomfortable. More often than not they were pretty happy doing things the way they were doing them before.

In fact, the invention might only slightly improve the ability to do what they were doing before. The significant potential, the key differentiation between invention and innovation, is that a true innovation allows someone to do something *they never thought about doing before.*

Ford built his first automobile, and for years people called it the horseless carriage because they had horses pulling carriages for transportation. To them, this was an analog to what they had been doing before, getting from one place to the other. But it wasn't a horseless carriage at all, it was a car, and it could do things a horse-drawn carriage could never do.

When personal computers first appeared, for example, people used word-processing software much like an electronic typewriter. It took a long time before people realized that the PC was not a souped-up electronic typewriter. They could do far more than type on a keyboard and

The Visible Hand: The Managerial Revolution in American Business

ALFRED D. CHANDLER JR.

■ The multiunit business enterprise, it must always be kept in mind, is a modern phenomenon. It did not exist in the United States in 1940. At that time the volume of economic activity was not yet large enough to make administrative coordination more productive and, therefore, more profitable than market coordi-

nation. Neither the needs nor the opportunities existed to build a multiunit enterprise. The few prototypes of the modern firm—textile mills and the Springfield Armory—remained single-unit enterprises. The earliest multiunit enterprise, the Bank of the United States, became extremely powerful and, partly because of its power, was short-lived. Until coal provided a cheap and flexible source of energy and until the railroad made possible fast, regular all-weather transportation, the processes of production and distribution continued to be managed in much the same way as they had been for half a millennium. All these processes, including trans-

have the letters appear on the screen. Now they could search entire documents, move blocks of text around with a mouse click, edit, copy, spellcheck, send and receive, and carry out hundreds of other functions that they had never been able to do or think of doing before. It takes people a long time to realize that this is not an analog to what they were doing before.

From a business perspective, companies must be prepared to ride a long learning curve to true innovation. They must be prepared for people to substantially undervalue what is being given to them at the outset because users will always compare it to something they've already been doing.

portation and finance, were carried out by small personally owned and managed firms.

The first modern enterprises were those created to administer the operation of the new railroad and telegraph companies. Administration coordination of the movement of trains and the flow of traffic was essential for the safety of the passengers and the efficient movement of a wide variety of freight across the nation's rails. Such coordination was also necessary to transmit thousands of messages across its telegraph wires. In other forms of transportation and communication, where the volume of traffic was less varied or moved at slower speeds, coordination was less necessary. There the large enterprise was slower in coming. When steamship and urban traction lines did increase in size, they had little difficulty in adapting procedures perfected by the railroads. And when the development of long-distance technology permitted the creation of a national telephone system, the enterprise that managed it became organized along the lines of Western Union. ■

From Alfred D. Chandler Jr., *The Visible Hand: The Managerial Revolution in American Business* (Belknap Press, 1977).

I can carry a notepad and a pencil in my shirt pocket and it costs a dollar. Why would I want a $500 Palm Pilot that fits into that same pocket? It certainly doesn't compete with my desktop PC. So what good is it? If all I am doing is keeping notes, why would I give up that pad and pencil? But wait, I can connect it to my computer at home and download my schedule every day instead of writing it down. I can update it on the fly. I can beam messages to my colleagues and receive messages as well. I can put games and an entire address book on it. Over time people decided they needed the Palm Pilot not because it was better at what a pencil and paper could do but because with it they could do things they hadn't done before. And since they hadn't done these things before, few realized they needed those capabilities, and even fewer desired them. So it takes not only great insight and invention on the part of the people who build the technology but a rethinking on the part of every potential user to decide that he or she understands and buys into the idea that this fills a need.

How innovation happens is the $64,000 question. Unfortunately, there is no formula or correct answer. It happens differently for different kinds of innovation. Medical innovation can be quite clear. If I tell the world, "This vaccine will prevent your child from ever getting polio," it is not surprising that in the space of a year fifty million people are immunized. Certain innovations happen because the public knew it was looking for a solution to a problem. When the solution is provided, there is a ready marketplace.

When I was an undergraduate in college, for example, I listened to my brother, who is a physician, complain about the lack of a viable way for patients to receive the proper dose of intravenous medicine. Nurses were required to manually oversee the process in every patient, a time-consuming and tedious procedure. So I set out to build the first wearable infusion pump. Because it filled a dramatic need, my Auto-Syringe gained rapid acceptance in such diverse medical specialties as chemotherapy, neonatology, and endocrinology. A short time later I left school and founded my first company, to manufacture and market the pump.

But inventions, with rare exceptions, end up being used in ways that are a small subset of what makes them a Big Idea. People may end up growing into them and turn them into an innovation. When historians write about great inventions, they tend to start at the point of innovation. In reality, innovation is subject to all sorts of pitfalls: the public's average state of competence, its imagination, the amount of risk the public is willing to take, and the amount of resources it collectively has to take on this change. The key question is: when will it happen? And, perhaps more important: who will find it, not just financially but philosophically and emotionally? Who will benefit from using it?

The window between invention and innovation is, in fact, the dark unknown valley in which typical inventors end up groping around in frustration. As an inventor, I can control the creation and development of a product. I can add or remove a feature, change my goals, tweak the technology, and finally produce something I am proud of. It's exciting, even if I fail. I can control the failure. But when I then take that product or idea out into the public, it is a very different experience. I spend a lot of time explaining to people that the Segway is not a scooter, that the IBOT is not a wheelchair, that the For Inspiration and Recognition of Science and Technology (FIRST) program is not a science fair.

It is not about supply but about demand. And if that aspect of the equation doesn't come to fruition, then all you have is an invention, a patent, an event in history. Conversely, if people accept it and use it and make it a part of our culture, it becomes an innovation and, quite often, a very big business.

"DOESN'T PLAY WELL WITH OTHERS":
THE ROLE OF DISRUPTIVE TECHNOLOGY

Victoria Griffith

Every now and then a new technology comes along that shakes up the business world. The innovation is so significant that it changes the face of an industry. Eventually the change causes established companies to die and new ones to be born.

Ever wonder why the makers of horse-drawn carriages didn't simply transform into automobile makers? Conventional wisdom has it that the managers of the deceased companies didn't know what hit them. They were dumb; they failed to foresee the change and suffered as a result.

In 1997 a book by Harvard Business School professor Clayton Christensen, *The Innovator's Dilemma,* challenged this notion. Christensen was skeptical of the conventional wisdom that executives at failed companies run into trouble because of their own stupidity. His circle of acquaintances included a number of managers in this category, and he knew them to be smart and capable.

So Christensen came up with a new theory: that companies fail not because managers are dumb but because the system doesn't allow them to succeed. These managers make good decisions within the organizational framework of their employers. It's the organization itself that is wrong.

Executives at successful companies are on the ball, says Christensen. They notice important developments in their industry—innovations the author calls "disruptive technologies." Yet although they recognize the threat, they are incapable of doing anything about it.

In their zeal to please shareholders, successful companies tend to do what's best for them in the short run, even though it could ruin them in the long term. Managers' primary goal is to maximize profit margins, because that's what makes stock prices go up.

Unfortunately, the desire for short-term returns can be their undoing. The fattest profit margins are usually at the top, so customers willing to pay a high margin for a superior product become companies' main focus. The lower-margin businesses at the bottom end receive less and less attention.

Yet the greatest threats usually come from the bottom—the very segment established groups are not interested in guarding. And there's the rub. Challengers are able to mount an attack on companies' weakest flank.

A disruptive technology is born when someone invents a way to do something more simply and cheaply. Major innovations often don't work very well when they are first introduced. The top-end customers don't want them. Entrepreneurs are able to sell them only for a very low price. They don't make much money, but since they're just a start-up, they don't care.

Eventually, though, those entrepreneurs get better at what they do. They move up the ladder to the middle market and finally challenge the established companies at the top end. By that time the established managers are ready to act; the trouble is, it is usually too late.

Christensen's office at Harvard is filled with his collection of disk drives, and the industry's failure is one of the author's favorite cautionary tales. In the 1970s the makers of 14-inch disk drives supplied manufacturers of mainframe computers. When new disk drive companies began making 8-inch drives, the manufacturers of the 14-inch drives asked the mainframe computer makers whether they were interested.

They were not. The 8-inch drives were not as good and held less data. The computer companies wanted to make better mainframes, because that was what their customers were demanding. The 8-inch-drive makers sold products instead to a new generation of minicomputer makers, including Digital Equipment and Wang. These companies became the new successes.

In the 1980s these groups too were swept aside as personal computers became the rage. The pattern was the same. Digital and Wang saw the personal computer coming, yet their customers did not want the new technology. By the time the personal computer rose to challenge them at the high end of their business, it was too late.

Christensen's theories enjoyed enormous popularity in the late 1990s as the Internet grabbed everyone's imagination. His thoughtful analysis seemed to explain why it was smart to gamble on companies that might generate big profits in the future, even though they were currently in the red.

Unlike many management theorists, Christensen even had specific advice for long-in-the-tooth companies: they should set up a separate corporation that could operate outside of the rules of the existing one. That way, when disruptive technologies came along, they would be incorporated into the break-off group. In the end, the entrepreneurial spin-off would rise like a phoenix from the ashes to take the corporation through to the next innovation cycle.

The bookstore Barnes & Noble, the office supply chain Staples, and other companies followed Christensen's advice in addressing the challenge from the Internet, the greatest disruptive technology of the past decade. They set up separate dot-com businesses, designed to attack the established organization from the outside. The bursting of the dot-com bubble, however, eventually poked holes in the strategy.

As the stock prices of Internet companies collapsed, it reminded managers of why they cared about profit margins in the first place: to guarantee they had enough cash to be in business tomorrow. Staples' former CEO Tom Stemberg remarked that setting up Staples.com was his biggest strategic mistake in Internet retailing.

Despite the mixed success of Christensen's prescription, his concepts still carry weight, and the phrase "disruptive technologies" has become a part of managers' everyday lexicon.

THE DISCIPLINE OF PERSONAL MASTERY: THE ART OF THINKING SYSTEMICALLY

Peter Senge

On a cold, clear morning in December 1903 at Kitty Hawk, North Carolina, the fragile aircraft of Wilbur and Orville Wright proved that powered flight was possible. Thus was the airplane invented. But it would take more than thirty years before commercial aviation could serve the general public.

Engineers say that a new idea has been *invented* when it is proven to work in the laboratory. The idea becomes an *innovation* only when it can be replicated reliably on a meaningful scale at practical costs. If the idea is sufficiently important, such as the telephone, the digital computer, or commercial aircraft, it is called a *basic innovation,* and it creates a new industry or transforms an existing industry. In these terms, learning organizations have been invented, but they have not yet been innovated.

In engineering, when an idea moves from an invention to an innovation, diverse component technologies come together. Emerging from isolated developments in separate fields of research, these components gradually form an ensemble of technologies that are critical to each other's success. Until this ensemble forms, the idea, though possible in the laboratory, does not achieve its potential in practice.

The Wright Brothers proved in 1903 that powered flight was possible, but the Douglas DC-3, introduced in 1936, ushered in the era of commercial air travel. The DC-3 was the first plane that supported itself economically. During the intervening thirty years (a typical time period for incubating basic innovations), myriad experiments with commercial flight had failed. Like early experiments with learning organizations, the early planes were not sufficiently reliable and cost-effective.

The DC-3, for the first time, brought together five critical component technologies that formed a successful ensemble: the variable-pitch propeller, retractable landing gear, a type of lightweight molded body construction called monocoque, the radial air-cooled engine, and wing flaps. To succeed, the DC-3 needed all five; four were not enough. In 1933 the Boeing 247 had been introduced with all of them except wing flaps. Boeing's engineers found that the 247 was unstable on takeoff and landing, and they had to downsize the engine.

Today, I believe, five new component technologies are gradually converging to innovate learning organizations. Though developed separately, each will, I believe, prove critical to the others' success, just as occurs with any ensemble. Each provides a vital dimension in building organizations that can truly learn, that can continually enhance their capacity to realize their highest aspirations.

Systems Thinking

A cloud masses, the sky darkens, leaves twist upward, and we know that it will rain. We also know that after the storm, the runoff will feed into groundwater miles away, and the sky will grow clear by tomorrow. All these events are distant in time and space, and yet they are all connected within the same pattern. Each has an influence on the rest, an influence that is usually hidden from view. You can fully understand the system of a rainstorm only by contemplating the whole, not any individual part of the pattern.

Business and other human endeavors are also systems. They too are bound by invisible fabrics of interrelated actions, which often take years to fully play out their effects on each other. Since we are part of that fabric ourselves, it's doubly hard to see the whole pattern of change. Instead, we tend to focus on snapshots of isolated parts of the system and wonder why our deepest problems never seem to get solved. Systems thinking is a conceptual framework, a body of knowledge and tools that has been developed over the past fifty years to make the full patterns clearer and to help us see how to change them effectively.

Though the tools are new, the underlying worldview is extremely intuitive; experiments with young children show that they learn systems thinking very quickly.

Personal Mastery

Mastery might suggest gaining dominance over people or things. But mastery can also mean a special level of proficiency. A master craftsperson doesn't dominate pottery or weaving. People with a high level of personal mastery are able to consistently realize the results that matter most deeply to them; in effect, they approach their life as an artist would approach a work of art. They do that by becoming committed to their own lifelong learning.

Personal mastery is the discipline of continually clarifying and deepening our personal vision, of focusing our energies, of developing patience, and of seeing reality objectively. As such, it is an essential cornerstone of the learning organization—the learning organization's spiritual foundation. An organization's commitment to and capacity for learning can be no greater than that of its members. The roots of this discipline lie in both Eastern and Western spiritual traditions, and in secular traditions as well.

But surprisingly few organizations encourage the growth of their people in this manner. This results in vast untapped resources. "People enter business as bright, well-educated, high-energy people, full of energy and desire to make a difference," says former Hanover Insurance CEO William J. O'Brien. "By the time they are thirty, a few are on the fast track and the rest put in their time to do what matters to them on the weekend. They lose the commitment, the sense of mission, and the excitement with which they started their careers. We get damn little of their energy and almost none of their spirit."

And surprisingly, few adults work to rigorously develop their own personal mastery. When you ask most adults what they want from their lives, they often talk first about what they'd like to get rid of: "I'd like my mother-in-law to move out," they say, or "I'd like my back problems to clear up." The discipline of personal mastery, by contrast, starts with clarifying the things that really matter to us, of living our lives in the service of our highest aspirations.

Here I am most interested in the connections between personal learning and organizational learning, in the reciprocal commitments between individual and organization, and in the special spirit of an enterprise made up of learners.

Mental Models

Mental models are deeply ingrained assumptions, generalizations, or even pictures or images that influence how we understand the world and how we take action. Very often we are not consciously aware of our mental models or the effects they have on our behavior. For example, we may notice that a coworker dresses elegantly, and we say to ourselves, "She's a country-club person." About someone who dresses shabbily, we may say,

"He doesn't care what others think." Mental models of what can or cannot be done in different management settings are no less deeply entrenched. Many insights into new markets or organizational practices fail to get put into practice because they conflict with powerful, tacit mental models.

Royal Dutch/Shell, one of the first large organizations to understand the advantages of accelerating organizational learning, came to this realization when they discovered how pervasive was the influence of hidden mental models, especially those that become widely shared. Shell's extraordinary success in managing through the dramatic changes and unpredictability of the world oil business in the 1970s and 1980s came in large measure from learning how to bring to the surface and challenge managers' mental models. (In the early 1970s Shell was the weakest of the big seven oil companies; by the late 1980s it was the strongest.) Arie de Geus, Shell's recently retired coordinator of group planning, says that continuous adaptation and growth in a changing business environment depend on "institutional learning, which is the process whereby management teams change their shared mental models of the company, their markets, and their competitors. For this reason, we think of planning as learning and of corporate planning as institutional learning."

The discipline of working with mental models starts with turning the mirror inward—learning to unearth our internal pictures of the world, to bring them to the surface, and to hold them up to rigorous scrutiny. It also includes the ability to carry on "learningful" conversations that balance inquiry and advocacy, where people expose their own thinking effectively and make that thinking open to the influence of others.

Building Shared Vision

If any one idea about leadership has inspired organizations for thousands of years, it's the capacity to hold a shared picture of the future we seek to create. One is hard pressed to think of any organization that has sustained some measure of greatness in the absence of goals, values, and missions that become deeply shared throughout the organization. IBM had service; Polaroid had instant photography; Ford had transportation for the masses; Apple had computing power for the masses. Though radically different in content and kind, all these organizations managed to bind people together around a common identity and sense of destiny.

When there is a genuine vision (as opposed to the all-too-familiar vision statement), people excel and learn, not because they are told to but because they want to. But many leaders have personal visions that never get translated into shared visions that galvanize an organization. All too often a company's shared vision revolves around the charisma of a leader or around a crisis that galvanizes everyone temporarily. But, given a choice, most people opt for pursuing a lofty goal, not only in times of crisis but at all times. What has been lacking is a discipline for translating individual vision into shared vision—not a cookbook, but a set of principles and guiding practices.

The practice of shared vision involves the skills of unearthing shared "pictures of the future" that foster genuine commitment and enrollment rather than compliance. In mastering this discipline, leaders learn that it's counterproductive to try to dictate a vision, no matter how heartfelt.

Team Learning

How can a team of committed managers with individual IQs above 120 have a collective IQ of 63? The discipline of team learning confronts this paradox. We know that teams can learn; in sports, in the performing arts, in science, and even occasionally in business there are striking examples where the intelligence of the team exceeds the intelligence of the individuals in the team, and where teams develop extraordinary capacities for coordinated action. When teams are truly learning, not only are they producing extraordinary results, but the individual members are growing more rapidly than they could have done otherwise.

The discipline of team learning starts with dialogue, the capacity of members of a team to suspend assumptions and enter into a genuine "thinking together." To the Greeks, *dialogos* meant a free flow of meaning through a group, allowing the group to discover insights not attainable individually. Interestingly, the practice of dialogue has been preserved in many so-called primitive cultures, such as those of the American Indians, but it has been almost completely lost to modern society. Today the principles and practices of dialogue are being rediscovered and put into a contemporary context. (*Dialogue* differs from the more common *discussion*, which has its roots in the Latin *discutere,* which means "to shake apart.")

The discipline of dialogue also involves learning how to recognize patterns of defensiveness, which often are deeply ingrained in how a team operates. If unrecognized, they undermine learning. If recognized and surfaced creatively, they can actually accelerate learning.

Team learning is vital because teams, not individuals, are the fundamental learning unit in modern organizations. This is where the rubber meets the road; unless teams can learn, the organization cannot learn.

If learning organization were an engineering innovation, the components would be called technologies. For an innovation in human behavior, the components need to be seen as disciplines. By *discipline,* I do not mean an enforced order or means of punishment, but a body of theory and technique that must be studied and mastered to be put into practice. A discipline is a developmental path for acquiring certain skills or competencies. As with any discipline, from playing the piano to electrical engineering, some people have an innate gift, but anyone can develop proficiency through practice.

To practice a discipline is to be a lifelong learner. You never "arrive"; you spend your life mastering disciplines. You cannot say "We are a learning organization" any more than you can say "I am an enlightened person." The more you learn, the more acutely aware you become of your ignorance. Thus a corporation cannot be excellent in the sense of having arrived at a permanent excellence; it is always practicing the disciplines of learning, becoming better or worse.

That organizations can benefit from disciplines is not a totally new idea. After all, management disciplines such as accounting have been around for a long time. But the five learning disciplines differ from more familiar management disciplines in that they are personal. Each has to do with how we think, what we truly want, and how we interact and learn with one another. In this sense, they are more like artistic disciplines than traditional management disciplines. Moreover, while accounting is good for keeping score, we have never approached the subtler tasks of building organizations, of enhancing their capabilities for innovation and creativity, of crafting strategy and designing policy and structure through assimilating new disciplines. Perhaps this is why, all too often, great organizations are fleeting, enjoying their moment in the sun, then passing quietly back to the ranks of the mediocre.

Practicing a discipline is different from emulating a model. All too often new management innovations are described in terms of the "best practices" of so-called leading firms. While such descriptions are interesting, I believe they can often do more harm than good, leading to piecemeal copying and playing catch-up. I do not believe great organizations have ever been built by trying to emulate another, any more than individual greatness is achieved by trying to copy a great person.

When the five component technologies converged to create the DC-3 the commercial airline industry began. But the DC-3 was not the end of the process. Rather, it was the precursor of a new industry. Similarly, as the five component learning disciplines converge they will create not *the* learning organization but rather a new wave of experimentation and advancement.

It is vital that the five disciplines develop as an ensemble. This is challenging because it is much harder to integrate new tools than to simply apply them separately. But the payoffs are immense.

This is why systems thinking is the fifth discipline. It is the discipline that integrates the disciplines, fusing them into a coherent body of theory and practice. It keeps them from being separate gimmicks or the latest organizational fads. Without a systemic orientation, there is no motivation to look at how the disciplines interrelate. By enhancing each of the other disciplines, it continually reminds us that the whole can exceed the sum of its parts.

For example, vision without systems thinking ends up painting lovely pictures of the future with no deep understanding of the forces that must be mastered to move from here to there. This is one of the reasons why many firms that have jumped on the vision bandwagon in recent years have found that lofty vision alone fails to turn around a firm's fortunes. Without systems thinking, the seed of vision alone fails to turn around a firm's fortunes. Without systems thinking, the seed of vision falls on harsh soil. If nonsystemic thinking predominates, the first condition for nurturing vision is not met: a genuine belief that we can make our vision real in the future. We may say, "We can achieve our vision" (most American managers are conditioned to this belief), but our tacit view of current reality as a set of conditions created by somebody else betrays us.

But systems thinking also needs the disciplines of building a shared vision, mental models, team learning, and personal mastery to realize its potential. Building a shared vision fosters a commitment to the long term. Mental models focus on the openness needed to unearth shortcomings in our present ways of seeing the world. Team learning develops the skills of groups of people to look for the larger picture that lies beyond individual perspectives. And personal mastery fosters the personal motivation to continually learn how our actions affect our world. Without personal mastery, people are so steeped in the reactive mind-set ("someone or something else is creating my problems") that they are deeply threatened by the systems perspective.

Lastly, systems thinking makes understandable the subtlest aspect of the learning organization—the new way individuals perceive themselves and their world. At the heart of a learning organization is a shift of mind—from seeing ourselves as separate from the world to seeing ourselves as connected to the world, from seeing problems as caused by someone or something "out there" to seeing how our actions create the problems we experience. A learning organization is a place where people are continually discovering how they create their reality—and how they can change it. As Archimedes said, "Give me a lever long enough, and single-handed I can move the world."

THE UNCERTAIN PATH OF BREAKTHROUGHS AND THE ROAD TO PROFIT: THE EXAMPLE OF PHARMACEUTICALS AND BIOTECHNOLOGY

Victoria Griffith

> *I get it. You guys do science. We technology guys know if we can get a product out; it's just a question of when and how much it will cost. But you guys, you don't really know, do you?*
> —DAVID PACKARD, cofounder of Hewlett-Packard, to fellow board members at Genentech

Even in ancient cultures, healing was good business. Witch doctors, who use herbs and other plants to treat the ailing, were among the most respected members of a tribe. Tribal healers would be envious of the wide array of medicines physicians have at their disposal today. Yet society remains frustrated by its inability to eradicate deadly diseases such as cancer, stroke, AIDS, and Alzheimer's.

The making of a drug is a long, hard road. It costs $800 million and takes ten years to bring a treatment to market, on average. And despite an explosion of medical knowledge in the last few decades, scientists have not yet gained control of the process. At every step, sheer luck plays a role. For every 5,000 to 10,000 substances researchers screen for potential new treatments, just 250 are thought promising enough to give to animals. Of those, five are tested in humans. Even after drugs are cleared for market, they may be withdrawn because of toxicity concerns.

So why does any company bother to come up with a new drug? Because pharmaceutical products are so profitable. Good drugs are scarce. New ones tend not to face a lot of competition. Pharmaceutical companies may operate as virtual monopolies in certain disease areas. The scarcity of the product means the pharmaceutical sector can charge what it likes for drugs, at least in the unregulated U.S. market, which is why the industry consistently ranks as the most profitable in the world.

Yet businesspeople don't like to leave a lot up to chance, and people in the drug industry are no exception. For decades they've struggled to make sense of the discovery process, to eliminate the element of chance from their plan of operations. So far they've had little luck.

Key scientific breakthroughs are often not recognized for centuries. Technologies seized upon as the Holy Grail of medical research have repeatedly been shown to be no such thing. Treatments that look promising end up having no impact on the targeted disease; others prove so toxic that they are deemed worse than the illness itself. The good news is that the number of medicines on the market has grown dramatically in recent years. That may reflect, in part, an increase in efficiency. It also likely shows the expanding resources thrown behind the search for medications.

Undoubtedly some progress has been made. In the 1800s researchers had little idea how to come up with treatments for any disease. Physicians still relied on folkloric beliefs, such as the idea that bleeding would somehow rid a patient of the harmful effects of an illness.

It's perhaps not surprising, then, that the pharmaceutical industry was formed not around a new medical treatment but around the commercialization of a very old one. Just as the automobile sector depended on Ford to turn the innovation into a moneymaker, the drug industry relied on the German company Bayer to make it profitable.

Somewhere around 400 B.C. the Greek physician Hippocrates wrote that a powder made from the bark and leaves of the willow tree helped cure headaches, pain, and fever. Not until 1829 did scientists identify the active compound in the powder—salicin. The trouble was that salicylic acid was hard on stomachs. Researchers began to search for a way to neutralize the acid.

In 1853 a Frenchman by the name of Charles-Frédéric Gerhardt came upon a way to buffer the drug by combining it with two other compounds—sodium and acetyl chloride. Although the treatment worked, Gerhardt decided not to market it. Not until 1899 did a German chemist named Felix Hoffman, who worked for a company called Bayer, come upon Gerhardt's formula and recognize the commercial potential of the product. Bayer named the drug aspirin, and the pharmaceutical industry was born.

It was off to a shaky start. Besides aspirin and a few antiseptic ointments, drug companies had little to sell. With a thin portfolio of treatments, morphine and heroin were sold as legitimate medicines. A turn-of-the-century Bayer advertisement even marketed heroin as a cure for infant respiratory troubles.

During the Roaring Twenties science took a double leap forward. In 1922 insulin was administered to diabetic patients. Healthy people make enough insulin on their own. Diabetics do not. Insulin is a naturally occurring protein—a "large molecule," in scientific terms. Fifty years later large molecules would form the basis for the biotechnology industry, but at the time, insulin was hailed only as a major step forward in treating a formerly fatal disease.

In 1928 another event would alter the shape of medicine. A Scottish doctor by the name of Alexander Fleming observed that the bacte-

ria he was growing in culture were being killed by a mysterious substance. That substance turned out to be penicillin, still the most important antibacterial in use.

Penicillin gave physicians the power to kill microbes inside the
body. It was a revolutionary discovery. Yet as with many such events,
it would take some time before the new technology would be widely
adopted. That's because penicillin couldn't be made in massive amounts.
Not until 1941 were researchers able to manufacture the substance as a
powder. That development changed the industry. Soon the Allies were
using the compound to treat wounded soldiers on World War II battle-
fields.

The next big event in the drug sector occurred in 1953, when
Francis Crick and James Watson elucidated the structure of DNA, the
building block of life. Even at the time, the discovery was recognized as
significant. But in the typical delayed reaction between academic discovery and product, it would be years before researchers could use that
information to develop medical treatments.

The pharmaceutical industry grew rapidly in the 1960s and 1970s.
In 1977 the once-feared disease smallpox was declared eradicated from
the face of the planet, a major scientific achievement. A year later the
first test-tube baby was born, an event that expanded scientists' control
over the reproductive process. The event would spawn an ethical debate
that remains unresolved.

Remember insulin? The substance saved the lives of many but
was very expensive because it had to be extracted from the pancreatic
tissue of animals. The push to cheaper manufacturing would spawn a
technological revolution, as it had so many times before. In the 1970s
scientists figured out that by transplanting DNA into bacteria, they
could coax those cells into excreting medically useful proteins. The technology was called recombinant DNA.

In 1976 the first biotechnology company, Genentech, was formed
to take advantage of the new production method. In 1982 the group got

clearance to sell its first product, Protropin, a growth hormone for children with growth hormone deficiency. Genentech—and its competitors—was soon making other drugs as well, including recombinant insulin. The biotechnology revolution had begun.

The public noticed. When Genentech went public in 1980 it kicked off an investment boom in the sector. It proved to be a bubble. Investors believed for a while that biotechnology would erase the element of uncertainty from drug discovery, but that didn't happen. In 1992 the biotechnology company Centocor failed to receive approval for its much-hyped drug for septic shock, a potentially lethal infection of the blood. Investors realized that biotechnology too was fallible. Stocks in the sector plunged, and the industry would not recuperate from the carnage for many years.

About this time the pharmaceutical sector began to question its own methods of drug discovery. Companies felt their research and development efforts were at the mercy of chance occurrences. Scientists relied on serendipity above all else in the search for new products. Medicines were developed based on lucky observations of chemical interactions. Those chance encounters were becoming more rare as the most obvious drug candidates were picked off.

The sector began to search for ways to place drug discovery under greater control. Mechanization helped. Companies began to use robots to test thousands of compounds at once, rather than the few a chemist could handle. But the most important change was a shift to using computers to organize data and orient product development.

The method was dubbed "rational drug design" because it relied on a logical train of thought, more than sheer luck, to come up with new products. Scientists began to build three-dimensional computer models of molecules to better envision the challenge. They stored massive amounts of data and in a process known as bioinformatics programmed computers to sort compounds by structure and reactive characteristics.

The new approach helped. The biotechnology company Vertex,

for instance, designed a protease inhibitor as a special key to turn off the action of the AIDS virus. Yet by and large, rational drug design fell short of its promise. Molecules that looked great on the computer failed to work in mice. And ones that worked in mice often failed in humans.

In the late 1990s the crusade to make sense of the drug discovery process turned to genomics. Scientists had long noticed that illnesses tend to run in families. Yet many scientists were stunned by the extensive role genes play. In 1993 the gene for Huntington's disease was located, a gene that determines with 100 percent certainty whether someone will eventually develop the disease.

The revelation set off a rush to discover the genetic foundation for other diseases, a quest that sometimes turned farcical. By the end of the millennium researchers were claiming to find genes for every human trait imaginable, from happiness to homosexuality. Much of that research proved bogus, but little could shake the faith of scientists—or the public—in the importance of genetic research in the battle against disease.

If only they had a complete catalog of human genes. That goal was, for the time being, out of reach. But the next best thing seemed close at hand. In the early 1990s the U.S. government had committed to funding the Human Genome Project, an international consortium of scientists who would identify all the pieces of DNA that make up the human genome. With that information, researchers would be a step closer to a comprehensive database of genes.

Genes are made up of DNA, and the human genome is made up of genes. You're probably thinking, "So if we analyze all the DNA, we'll automatically know about the genes, right?" Wrong.

Actually, the Human Genome Project provides little information on the genes themselves. Think of it this way: the DNA is the letters of a book and genes are the words. It's as if someone took the letters in a novel, sprinkled them with a lot of junk and errors, took out punctuation, and spewed the whole thing out again. Because you don't know where one word begins and another ends—or even if it's a word at all—the information is actually not that helpful.

Which is why, when the project began, it was rightly seen as an academic exercise. After all, a listing of chemicals would be unlikely to boost the drug discovery effort. What changed this attitude? A scientist named Craig Venter.

Venter, a former government researcher, had a reputation as a scientific maverick. His story captured the public's imagination. Venter had long been frustrated by the laborious process of DNA sequencing. The Human Genome Project assigned the sequencing to researchers in an orderly fashion, one strand of DNA at a time. But in 1998 Venter heard about a machine that could accomplish the task far more quickly. Made by a division of Perkin-Elmer, the machine was highly automated and could function twenty-four hours a day.

Venter was hooked. When the U.S. government failed to see the machine's potential, he left to head a new division of Perkin-Elmer, Celera, set on becoming the first to sequence the human genome. The race was on. The U.S. government lambasted Venter's work at first. The approach would yield a genome full of errors, said the National Institutes of Health (NIH). Yet NIH was nervous enough to accelerate its own timetable for sequencing the genome.

The competition soon became intense. Celera and the Human Genome Project would each periodically brag about its progress and criticize the other side. Celera's stock price soared. Biotechnology stocks were suddenly fashionable again, and billions of dollars poured into the cash-starved sector.

Eventually NIH had to admit that Venter had been right. The new DNA sequencing machines worked. In 2001 the two sides called a truce and published a joint rough draft of the genome. It was a hollow victory for Celera, however, for after Venter reached his goal, investors began to realize that the data had little immediate commercial application. Drugs, not data, were still the real moneymakers. Celera's stock price collapsed, and today the company's shares trade at just a small fraction of their peak price.

The biotechnology sector in general made out far better. The influx of cash gave the industry clout. For the first time, biotechnology appeared to be on an equal footing with pharmaceutical companies.

The genomics revolution, however, proved disappointing. The unveiling of the human genome gave researchers so little information that scientists are still unsure how many genes are in the human body. Before the publication of the human genome in 2001 estimates hovered at about 100,000 genes. Celera and the Human Genome Project set the number far lower, at about 35,000. That estimate too is being challenged by researchers.

Genes are one step removed from human biology. They can be turned on or off, for reasons not completely understood. One gene, moreover, may produce many proteins with complex roles in bodily function. A renewed interest in proteins has led to the birth of a new field of research: proteomics. Will it prove more valuable than genomics? That is questionable, for proteins, while they tell us much about specific diseases, are highly complex. Genes are static; proteins are not. Proteins appear and disappear; they change form or join forces with other proteins. It will likely take decades to build a full understanding of the way they work.

All of which means that drug discovery, despite the scientific efforts of a century of pharmaceutical research, is still riddled with uncertainty. Sometimes scientists find a drug in their test tubes; most of the time they come up empty. It's a kind of business lottery that will probably continue for many years to come.

Working with Mother Nature: Making Breakthroughs in the Business of Biology

WILLIAM HASELTINE

As head of the biotechnology group Human Genome Sciences, Bill Haseltine is at the cutting edge of drug discovery. Like all pharmaceutical companies, HGS is looking to find treatments for disease. But Haseltine wants to take drug discovery one step further—to identify ways not only to halt devastating illnesses but to repair the damage they have already done.

This is a radical departure from traditional models. If successful, this new science—called "regenerative medicine" by its adherents—would allow the victims of degenerative disease to regain full biological function. A stroke patient could once again converse without difficulty; the victim of a spinal cord injury could once again walk.

In this conversation with Victoria Griffith, Haseltine outlines his vision for a radical new type of science.

■ Regenerative medicine is the future of drug making. The concept that the body is a self-assembling, self-maintaining machine is gaining support. This is not about stem cells and cloning, which I think of as rejuvenative medicine—trying to make something old new again. Regenerative medicine draws on those technologies but is different.

The idea is to use our body's own ability to make repairs to take care of the damage that occurs over time. To do that, we need to rely on our own biological signals or, if that is not possible, rebuild organs outside the body for subsequent replants. We want to coax the body into performing better than it would if left to its own devices.

Scientists must learn to stimulate cells to rebuild. The signals in question are mostly proteins or small molecules such as steroids. There are well-known growth hormones, for instance, that do just that—stimulate growth. Such signals will become the new drugs.

Cells receive instructions from the outside to remain stationary, commit suicide, or reproduce. Our goal is to gain control over these messages in order to influence the body's behavior. The question is, how do we get hold of these signals?

At Human Genome Sciences we do this by collecting messenger RNA. (Messenger RNA, or mRNA, is copied from cells' DNA and controls cell behavior.) We already have ten thousand mRNA sequences. The job is to match these signals to a medical need. For example, if we want to stimulate the body to produce more antibodies, we systematically test the mRNA sequences to discover which signals have that effect.

That's how we came up with B-lymphocyte stimulator. Humans' ability to make antibodies diminishes as they get older, regardless of an individual's health. We thought it would be good to get more mileage out of our bodies, to get the immune system to work harder for a longer amount of time. B-lymphocyte stimulator is in clinical trials for people with common variable immunodeficiency, a serious defect of the immune system. We hope to use it for other indications as well.

Once we had success in stimulating antibody production, we moved on to another area. It's all about balance. What we want to do is rebuild, recraft, and restructure our bodies. Sometimes we get too little of a good thing—but other times we get too much. If you have an overactive immune system, for instance, you may get rheumatoid arthritis. If you have overly active cell growth, you may get cancer.

We saw some indications in animal trials, for instance, that if we stimulated B-lymphocytes too much, the animals got autoimmune diseases. That led to another product, Lymphostat-B, which is designed to inhibit the biological activity of the B-lymphocyte stimulator. The drug is in clinical trials for lupus, a severe autoimmune disease. If successful, we will try the drug on rheumatoid arthritis.

Again, it's about restoring equilibrium. If there's too little, we try to add; if there's too much, we try to subtract. This science has the potential to cure so many diseases. We could induce bone growth in osteoporosis patients, or stimulate the pancreas in diabetic patients.

There's a theory that Mother Nature gave us inadequate ability to repair our bodies so that we wouldn't overdo it. If we made too much growth factor, for instance, we would get tumors at a young age. We must repair ourselves poorly to prevent cancer. But what if we added just a little growth factor, precisely in the spot where it is needed? Then it would likely do more good than harm.

There's another part to all this—tissue engineering. If we can't control the environment inside the body, we may be able to do it from the outside. There's already been a lot of work in this area, building normal tissue around a structure. If we want to build a new bladder, for instance, we just take a small snippet of cells from an existing bladder, add a stimulus, and grow a new one. We've been able to grow blood vessels—three layers of tissue around a tube. Scientists are trying to build a heart.

Cloning comes in later. It can be used to replace older cells with younger ones, or older tissue with new tissue. We know this can be done. There are sixty-year-olds who have had bone marrow transplants from younger donors. What does this mean? The patient has the body of a sixty-year-old but the blood of a twenty-five-year-old.

Both regenerative and rejuvenative medicine lead to a longer, healthier life. That doesn't mean immortality. It's unlikely we'll be able to expand the natural life span beyond 125 years. What it does is level the playing field that today is influenced by genetic and environmental accidents. When regenerative medicine comes of age, everyone, regardless of their genetic profile or exposure to various health hazards, would have the same life expectancy. ∎

2. Sustainability and the Environment

A Business That Makes Nothing but Money Is a Poor Kind of Business

THE QUESTION "WHAT IS THE PURPOSE OF BUSINESS?" has many answers across many different domains. One of those answers has always been "To make the world a better place." For the most part, however, making the world a better place was something business leaders did after they retired. The much-reviled steelmaker Andrew Carnegie was later revered for putting his fortune to work building libraries, schools, and universities. Henry Ford, whose goons bashed the heads of union organizers, created a foundation that funded, among other things, the green revolution. Bill Gates, declared a monopolist by his detractors, has given billions of dollars of his fortune to fighting AIDS and vaccinating children in the developing world.

But wait a minute. Should good works simply be the province of the moguls? Or should companies do business in ways that contribute to the communities in which they operate?

What is often called "good business," "sustainable business," or "corporate social responsibility" has gained a strong foothold in much of Europe and is now making headway in the United States. These practices—which include good environmental practices—began largely in response to protests about the way in which many companies treated the ecosystem.

Companies that were responsible for oil spills, clear-cutting of forests, and water and air pollution were targeted for boycotts and organized protests, with good effect. Companies that employed children in sweatshops or in unsafe conditions at home or abroad were also singled out.

Whereas once companies argued strenuously that their products and processes were not harmful, now many of them have acknowledged the problems they have caused and have begun tackling them. They have done this because awareness, particularly about the environment, is growing, and because—not surprisingly—their customers and employees wish them to do so. People want to work for companies they are proud of; customers want to buy from businesses they trust.

Sustainable business practices—which means running a business not simply to satisfy your own needs or your own generation's needs, but to satisfy the needs of your grandchildren and their generation—has been catching on. In Europe, several countries ask companies to report each year what they do to preserve and protect the environment. Poor business practices—using child labor, requiring workers to do their jobs in unsafe or unhealthy circumstances—are increasingly viewed as indicators of bad companies. And, with the Internet and e-mail, news of a toxic spill in even the remotest part of the world can no longer be kept secret.

How should businesses think and conduct themselves? This section not only points the way but discusses how to measure failure and success.

J.K.

SUSTAINABLE BUSINESS IS
ACCOUNTABLE BUSINESS

Simon Zadek

To some people, "sustainable development" is a warm, fuzzy term that has something to do with planting more trees so we don't run out. In reality, the concept is much broader than that. Sustainable development means accountable business.

What is the role of business as a responsible entity? That's not up to a business; that's up to society. Businesses can't define their role, but they should be part of the conversation about what their role should be. Monsanto can't decide whether genetically modified seeds are safe; Nike can't decide whether child labor in the workplace is good or bad. But they can choose to engage in the discussion.

Businesses interested in a long-term future need to examine their behavior. Certain behaviors are unacceptable. This is not to say that companies can solve the world's problems. Nike can't do much about world poverty. Glaxo Wellcome can't provide cures for all the diseases in the world free of charge. Exxon can't solve the world's energy and environmental problems. But they should act within accepted guidelines.

The issues of sustainability affect society, clearly, but they affect companies as well. The case of Enron (the now-defunct U.S. energy group) illustrates how this can play out. It's not clear whether the off-the-books transactions registered at that company were legal or not. But what is clear is that they weren't adequately revealed to the investment community. The Enron debacle shows accounting principles in bad need of repair.

These financial concerns are becoming a key part of the discussion surrounding sustainability. Society needs to question how companies divulge information and predict financial performance. They need to question the valuation of intangible assets such as brands and come up with a new way of analyzing balance sheets.

Some of the solution may come from "social accounting." Social accounting tries to measure these intangibles and capture certain aspects of the relationship between the corporation and society. Investors should care about these social aspects because they make a difference in a company's performance. What we've thought of as traditional accounting issues are now part and parcel of sustainable development.

The trouble with today's accounting is that some of the biggest threats to a business are often ignored because there's nowhere to place them in the balance sheet or income statement. If you look at drug corporations' profit statements and analysts' reports from a few years back, you probably won't find many references to drug pricing. Yet that's one of the biggest challenges facing the pharmaceutical industry today.

Social accounting is an attempt to put some of these concerns on the radar screen of investors as well as society in general. To do that, we need to change the way information is brought to the investment community. Analysts are mostly ignorant of these issues—they need to be given an incentive to pay attention. We need to know what these numbers really mean.

In the past we've assumed that social responsibility and profits are worlds apart. They are not. I'm not talking about the extra marketing boost a company can get from presenting itself as ethical. I'm talking about the kinds of things that can put a company out of business. Again, Enron is a case in point.

I'm optimistic that things are changing. With the shift of the balance of power away from labor and toward knowledge workers, employees are having a bigger say. So are consumers, and they are becoming more demanding of companies.

The entire corporate community is reassessing its role in the wake of the September 11 tragedy, and that's a good thing. Concerns that once seemed so far away, such as world poverty and religious education, are now of immediate concern.

How is corporate responsibility likely to develop in the wake of the tragedy? Some are cynical and view executives' focus on global societal issues as fleeting. Others believe corporations will permanently take on a new role.

The jury is out on how companies will behave going forward, but one thing has changed for good: the way risk levels are being assessed. Risk now comes from many different directions and can include things seemingly far removed from the corporation.

Before September 11, companies had become sensitized to the concerns of their employees, customers, and investors. All of these groups pressured corporations into behaving more responsibly. Employees convinced managers to diversify their workforce, for instance, and customers and investors convinced managers to care more about the environment.

These are all good things, but now we're looking at something completely different: how companies will respond to the concerns of people with whom they have no direct connection—people who don't work in a corporation, buy its products, purchase its stock, or live anywhere near the group's operations. Thinking about poverty in the Middle East and Africa, for instance, takes sustainability to a new scale. It raises questions about what development should look like within the global community.

Is corporate responsibility the need to behave responsibly to the immediate community, or does it mean something bigger? The question is key. Offering health benefits to gay employees' domestic partners is a good thing to do, but it won't make any dent in the number of children dying from disease and poverty around the world.

We need to reframe our understanding of corporate stakeholders. Corporate stakeholders include people far from the company's backyard. Farmers in Africa, for instance, will be affected by the trade policies governing farmers in the United States. So they need to be included in the discussion.

We need to ask in what way the business community can make a greater difference. We need to find ways to influence the bigger rules of the game. I'm optimistic that this will happen. I may be wacky, but my feeling is this: if my ambitions appear to be slightly insane, I must be on to something good.

EARTH, WE HAVE A PROBLEM

Carl Frankel

A decade ago few people had heard of sustainable development. Today, it is on the agenda of virtually every corporation. The actual level of commitment varies from company to company. Some enterprises are genuinely trying to embed sustainability into the core of their operations, while others are content with lip service. Still, something fundamental has changed. Today sustainable development is very much on the radar screen. A decade ago it wasn't.

Sustainability, on its most basic level, means survival. Needless to say, staying in business—survival—is at the very top of every company's list of priorities. But our cultural understanding of what makes for survival is changing. The last decade has been characterized by a battle of worldviews. The old-style one is Darwinian. It holds that individual companies are locked in a competition, with only the fittest surviving. The emerging alternative is more systems-oriented and holistic. It conceives of businesses as participating in a web consisting of other enterprises, their customers, and the entire social polity, all of which rests on the substrate of the natural environment.

Under the model of sustainable development, businesses must embrace the counterintuitive: that through altruism they can actually become more viable, even more profitable. It's possible, of course, to understand this concept on a very basic level. If the earth were to go up in flames, for instance, companies would have difficulty selling their products. By failing to protect our global life support systems, companies put their own well-being—and our entire industrial culture—at risk. No planet, no profits, as the saying goes.

Yet, taking the argument one step further, some organizations have found that by doing the right thing, they can actually become more profitable. At the manufacturer 3M, a Pollution Prevention Pays program has saved the company well over $750 million since its inception in 1975. The group discovered that practices friendly to the environment can also be cheaper.

In a 1993 environmental report Baxter International concluded that savings from its environmental program had generated $48 million. This added eight cents per share to Baxter's profitability, and added to shareholder value.

So why are we doing such a wretched job of protecting the environment? All our natural systems are in decline, and the rate of decline is accelerating. Scientists are now talking seriously of widespread ecosystem collapses—dramatic declines in the planet's capacity to support life—in the 2020–2030 time frame. On top of that, according to some estimates, up to one-quarter or more of the world's species will have died off by 2030. The implications of this for ecosystem integrity aren't clear, but they plainly aren't good. And then there is climate change. In the 1990s natural catastrophes caused more than $600 billion in economic losses worldwide, more than the total for the previous four decades combined. CGNU, one of the world's largest insurance companies, has projected that climate change could bankrupt the global economy by 2065.

Earth, we have a problem.

These trends dramatically redefine the meaning of survival for corporations. Under the old Darwinian model, it was kill or be killed. Under the new, more holistic model, it is sustain the systems in which we participate, or die. This is the premise on which the sustainability-in-business argument rests—that the capacity to survive depends on system dynamics as well as individual acumen and that a company's potential to thrive therefore depends in large measure on its capacity to work for the collective good as well as its own private benefit.

On one level companies do compete with each other; at another level interdependence, not competition, is the rule. Thus partnership—with other corporations and with a company's customers—becomes as important to business success as old-fashioned conquest, and protecting the planet becomes the most basic of strategies. Practically, this translates into the notion that companies promote their own survival—both short- and long-term—by allocating resources to the strengthening of social and natural capital, which together make up the glue that holds together our industrial culture. By implication, this means corporations have a de facto governance function.

This proposition tends to generate resistance inside the corporate community. It is contrary to conventional thinking, which holds that "the business of business is business" and that a corporation fulfills its obligations to society by creating jobs—and, maybe, making a modest philanthropic contribution to a cause or community. The public and private sectors are separate for a reason, in other words.

Sustainability advocates who wish to overcome this bias have two basic lines of reasoning to work with. First, they can try to show that working to build social and natural capital fits into the traditional corporate raison d'être, that is, that there is a business case for sustainability. It proposes that once you cut through all the philosophy and fine sentiments, sustainability is really about new business opportunities, as defined by the standard profit model.

The second approach is more radical. It proposes that with the changing times, the rules have changed, too, and that under these circumstances it is no longer appropriate, or for that matter strategic, for companies to wear blinders about their duties vis-à-vis our social and environmental woes. There are three components to this argument: moral, practical, and "reality-based":

■ **Moral:** Corporate activities are contributing mightily to the deterioration of natural and social capital. Business has a duty to alleviate the harm it's causing.

■ **Practical:** Corporations need stability to thrive, and nothing is more harmful to business than unraveling social and natural capital. Patch the *Titanic* or go down with the ship.

■ **Reality-based:** To those who argue that business should not meddle with governance, there is a short answer: multinational corporations are already governance institutions. They prop up (and topple) regimes, define cultural values, and assume de facto governance roles in other ways as well. To suggest otherwise is wildly naive—or disingenuous. And since corporations are already governance institutions, they might as well do it applying their full attention and vaunted world-class skills.

Both approaches—the business case and the concept of expanded corporate citizenship—have made some headway in recent years. But the opposition is considerable. Despite all the management books about embracing innovation and thinking outside the box, business executives are basically a conservative lot. They embrace new ideas reluctantly— and only if there is an abundance of proof, or pressure. This is especially the case when the new idea defies the first law of corporate capitalism, which is that corporations must maximize return for shareholders.

In recent years an enormous amount of sweat has been poured into developing a business case for sustainability. The ways it creates value have been identified, and a steady stream of anecdotal case studies has been trotted out about how individual businesses have done well by doing good.

Taken as a whole, the data strongly suggest that sustainability is a sound business strategy. To date, though, that has not been enough to bring the entire corporate world on board.

For sustainability to be widely embraced, an airtight case must be put together. This has not yet happened. In part this is due to a Catch-22: Companies are reluctant to commit to sustainability because there isn't a conclusive business case; there isn't a conclusive business case because not enough companies have committed to it yet, and round and round we go.

As for the expanded corporate citizenship argument, when an activity doesn't have clear links to the bottom line, it tends to get second-class status inside a corporation. No amount of moral or philosophical proselytizing can change this reality. Or hasn't, yet.

Still, as noted earlier, something fundamental has changed. Many more corporations are tinkering with sustainability today than was the case a decade ago, and they are doing so in increasingly sophisticated ways. Similarly, the bar has been raised considerably in terms of what the public expects of companies regarding their corporate citizenship performance. There is a cultural imperative here—a cultural imperative born of underlying environmental and social circumstances—and it is slowly but inexorably overriding established ways of thinking. Is there resistance? Absolutely. But change happens.

Meanwhile, the definition of sustainable development has been expanding. A decade ago, *sustainability* was basically synonymous with *environment.* Companies that were ecologically responsible were viewed as fulfilling their sustainable-development duties. Then social equity came along, commensurate with the notion that sustainable development required the harmonization of the so-called three E's: environmental protection, economic growth, and social equity. Over the course of the 1990s, companies were increasingly expected to take into account social justice issues such as the widening gap between rich and poor, the rights of indigenous peoples, and so on.

There was also an increased focus on corporate accountability and transparency, on the principle that companies will act responsibly only if

On Helping the Poor
Capitalism and Freedom

MILTON FRIEDMAN

■ Two things seem clear: First, if the objective is to alleviate poverty, we should have a program directed at helping the poor. There is every reason to help the poor man who happens to be a farmer, not because he is a farmer but because he is poor. The program, that is, should be designed to help people as people, not as members of particular occupational groups, age groups, wage-rate groups, labor organizations, or industries. This is a defect of farm programs, general old-age benefits, minimum-wage laws, pro-union legislation, tariffs, licensing provisions of crafts or professions, and so on in seemingly endless profusion. Second, so far as possible the program should, while operating through the market, not distort the market or impede its functioning. This is a defect of price supports, minimum wage laws, tariffs, and the like.

The arrangement that recommends itself on purely mechanical grounds is a negative income tax. . . . The advantages of this arrangement are clear. It is directed specifically at the problem of poverty. It gives help in the form most useful to the individual, namely, cash. It is general and could be substituted for the host of special measures now in effect. It makes explicit the cost borne by society. It operates outside the market. Like any other measures to alleviate poverty, it reduces the incentives of those helped to help themselves, but it does not eliminate that incentive entirely, as a system of supplementing incomes up to some fixed minimum would. An extra dollar earned always means more money available for expenditure. ■

From Milton Friedman, with the assistance of Rose D. Friedman, *Capitalism and Freedom* (The University of Chicago Press, 1962).

their behavior is subject to public scrutiny. The Global Reporting Initiative, which produced a worldwide standard for corporate sustainability reporting, grew out of this belief in the critical importance of communications transparency.

From one perspective, this definitional expansionism is quite understandable. Sustainability is a system challenge and must be addressed as such. A silo approach that tackles one or a few issues will not do; the entire cluster of issues must be addressed. As people's understanding of the dimensions of the challenge has grown, so have their expectations vis-à-vis the corporate contribution. But executives can be forgiven for feeling shoved down a slippery slope.

It is operationally challenging as well. What gets measured gets managed, as the expression has it, and it is difficult to measure such things as a corporation's impact on social equity. The sustainability trajectory requires this, though, and metrics for these more qualitative aspects of corporate conduct are under development.

Perhaps the leading corporate environmental (as distinguished from social) strategy that emerged during the 1990s was eco-efficiency, essentially the notion that companies could save money by reducing their environmental inputs and outputs. When companies reduce their consumption of energy and natural resources, dollars drop directly from the bottom line. Similarly for the efficient use of materials, which reduces disposal costs on the output side.

There is a major weakness in the eco-efficiency argument, though. When companies save money through eco-efficiency, it is typically reinvested in other projects, which in turn use energy, consume natural resources, and so on. Thus eco-efficiency may produce few actual benefits at the system level. Still, this hasn't kept a good number of companies from embracing eco-efficiency, largely because it can fairly readily be understood and implemented. This is not the case with sustainability writ large, whose broad and murky contours invite confusion and paralysis.

Another prominent sustainable-business theme has been strategic environmental management (SEM). According to this view, companies can create value by passing their activities through an environmental filter. This purportedly produces such benefits as revealing new market opportunities and supporting breakthroughs in product design. While many companies have adopted SEM on a piecemeal basis, its uptake has fallen far short of other management strategies, such as Total Quality Management and Six Sigma. This is probably because SEM is too ideologically loaded—not objective enough, so to speak—and relatively unproven.

Of late a new set of expectations has found its way into the sustainability kitchen sink. One such issue is the need for companies to steer clear of corruption. In its weak form this means pay no bribes. In its strong form it means eschew business relationships with corrupt institutions.

This is a tricky issue. Exxon Mobil is a financial supporter of Transparency International, a Berlin-based nongovernmental organization that focuses on the issue of corruption, and its internal policy unequivocally bans any sort of graft, yet it does business with a Cameroonian government that Transparency International ranks as one of the most corrupt in the world. It is a matter of perspective whether that makes the company a hypocritical practitioner of "greenwashing" or an enterprise intent on mitigating corrupt practices through engagement and dialogue.

One sustainability "emergent" is so-called bottom-of-pyramid strategizing. About three-quarters of the global population survive on under $4 a day. In no sense of the term are these lives sustainable. But how does one integrate them into the market economy in ways that do not unsustainably accelerate the consumption of natural resources?

In recent years there has also been increasing pressure on corporations to proactively address the world's most pressing social and environmental problems. The United Nations Global Compact, launched in

1999, calls on companies to help "build the social and environmental pillars required to sustain the new global economy and make globalization work for all the world's people." The Global Compact has been well received by corporations, though it remains to be seen how much their expressions of good intentions will translate into concrete action.

In the years ahead the sustainability funnel will probably keep expanding. One increasingly prominent issue is power. Indeed, it is already hitting home as antiglobalization activists protest the scope of corporate power and the negative impacts of globalization on natural and social capital. This is a social justice issue and one that companies will have more and more trouble sidestepping.

Another emerging issue is meaning. Increasing numbers of people oppose corporate capitalism because they believe it imposes an empty consumerist version of meaning on the world. Worse still, this meaning system is antiecological in that it encourages people to get their meaning through buying more stuff. Thus meaning, globalization-style, and ecological well-being are largely incompatible. Increasingly corporations will have to confront this issue.

Ultimately, the issue sustainability advocates address is this: Do corporations have a duty to build social and natural capital? This is a variation on the ancient question "Am I my brother's keeper?" only with a planetary-system spin appropriate to our circumstances. Sustainability advocates answer this question with a resounding yes. They are firmly persuaded that corporations must proactively adopt policies and strategies that promote social justice and environmental health. They also believe—and the data support them—that this is no minor matter. Our prosperity, maybe even our survival, depends on it.

The challenge is to present this argument in ways that business can easily embrace. The obstacles are considerable. The process is ongoing.

WHY FOLLOWING YOUR PASSIONS LEADS TO PROFIT

Randy Komisar

The dot-com boom was bad for entrepreneurs. I know that sounds crazy. It was so easy to get funding that for many start-ups it seemed like heaven.

But for people who really wanted to create long-term, viable, legacy businesses, it wasn't a good time. They were hoping the crash would come so that they could talk not about turning the company around for a quick profit on Wall Street but about building products and a customer base.

Now that the downturn is here, it's a mixed bag for people who are passionate about their ideas for businesses. At least we don't see the mercenaries we saw in Silicon Valley a few years ago. On the other hand, people with good ideas are discouraged.

You might say, "Oh, but the truly passionate will stick with it." But it's difficult for passion to coexist with discouragement in the extreme. I see a lot of good ideas that are not getting funded right now. Entrepreneurs need enough encouragement to overcome cynicism. Right now there's a pall over the valley.

I'm still excited about projects. One company I'm working with is

FHP Wireless, a broadband technology company that promises to allow individuals in developing countries to take control of the telecom network. That's very appealing, as anyone who's dealt with high levels of bureaucracy would recognize. The company could change the dynamics of communication in the developing world. But not many people are summoning up that kind of enthusiasm.

It's funny, because since September 11, more people are looking at their lives and careers and asking where the passion went. A lot of people who got caught without a chair when the music stopped are reassessing their values. They wasted a lot of time during the dot-com boom working with people they didn't like for ideas they didn't believe in. It was fruitless.

But where do they take their lives and careers from here? Entrepreneurship is an answer for some. But the business of start-ups and innovation is not pretty. The norm is that 90 percent of the experiments you conduct (in the form of new companies) won't give you the results you want. Holistically we move toward success, but if you're at a company that didn't make it, it feels like failure.

The process of building ideas into companies isn't glamorous. It's the sleeves-rolled-up blocking and tackling that creates successes. It's not a televised event. It's not that interesting.

That's why you have to believe so deeply in what you're doing to want to face that every day. True entrepreneurs can't hold back their excitement. They won't stop talking about the customers they want to serve, about their product's tremendous technology and how it's going to change the world. They've got what it takes to make it through.

During the boom I heard a lot of excitement, but it was more about the money people could make than the companies they could build. The worst group was the venture capitalists. Venture capitalists manage money to finance a portfolio of experiments. They take a fee of about 2 percent of all the money under management and 20 to 30 percent on the upside if they manage to sell the company or it goes public.

Before the dot-com frenzy, the formula was pretty straightforward. You'd expect 70 percent of the experiments to go bust quickly. About 30 percent would struggle on, and 10 percent would be sold or go public. That's where you'd make your money.

Things got distorted during the dot-com boom. All of a sudden, you'd expect not 10 percent but 80 percent of the companies you started to be sold. And you'd make 30 percent of those profits. The funds grew too, so instead of making $2 million a year on $100 million under management, you'd make $20 million on $1 billion under management. Before, you were wealthy. All of a sudden you were filthy rich.

So people lost their passion for the business and switched their passion to the money. You could argue about whether that counts as passion at all. Drive, maybe, but not passion in the true sense of the word.

The practice of building the business hadn't changed, but venture capitalists and entrepreneurs were getting Wall Street to take their risk and pay top dollar for companies just a year or two old. That meant that you didn't have to really believe in anything except the mechanical process of bringing a start-up to market.

Is there a relationship between money and passion? Yes, in the sense that people who believe in the power of an idea and enterprise expect at some point to be compensated for their faith and hard work. But if that's the only thing you expect, the odds are against you. They weren't during the boom, but that was the anomaly.

You have to ask yourself, "If I spend ten years on this and don't make money, will it be okay?" You have to ask if your drive to earn money is dictating where you place your passion or if your passions are dictating how you make money. The latter is better.

THREE YARDS AND A CLOUD OF DUST:
THE SMALL-BORE APPROACH TO
GLOBALIZATION

Josh Mills

The world began shrinking a long time ago, as early civilizations took to the sea, invented the wheel, and over the millennia built roads and bridges. Each breakthrough in technology and design brought nations and continents closer together, and eventually they were linked directly by telegraph cable and the web of railways. But in the twentieth century the pace picked up, and by its end the global market-place and the global village were deeply embedded in the world of business and societies in which they operated.

Put simply, globalization is nothing more than capitalism played on a global stage. It is the search by businesses for markets around the world, the search for the least expensive commodities, supplies, and labor. It is the search for the ultimate economies of scale: why sell merely half the vehicles bought in the United States, as General Motors once did, when you can control more than 20 percent of the *global* auto market, as GM docs now? And as the giants lengthen their reach, smaller businesses seek ways to do the same. Why should businesses in Scandinavia, Switzerland, the Netherlands, Belgium, and the Baltic nations settle for the domestic or regional market when they can expand globally?

Economic development, the lowering of trade barriers, deregulation, privatization, and technology have all driven the global economy forward, each adding momentum to globalization and making it seem inevitable. As nations raise their standard of living, consumers have more to spend and demand more choices. Companies worldwide step up to meet this demand. Free trade makes it easier for them to do so, and to compete with local producers. Deregulation has lowered the cost of doing business in many sectors and regions, and it has empowered companies to choose more freely where and how they compete—the airline industry being the leading example. Privatization puts more players in the field and at the same time makes them more nimble; it seems widely regarded as a success (the breakdown of the privatized British railway system, once the proud British Rail, an apparent exception). And the overwhelming advances in technology are evident everywhere, from robotics and machinery that increases productivity to the networking, telecommunications, e-mail, faxes, and videoconferencing that facilitate communications and command and control from afar.

The temptations to globalize are too great to resist, the competitive pressures too strong to ignore. As globalization grows, its impact is felt everywhere. Residents of Detroit have learned that their city's prospects have much to do with what is happening in Stuttgart, Seoul, São Paulo, and Sweden. One broad aspect of globalization has been to increase the geographic literacy of business executives everywhere. In the 1990s Daimler-Benz bought Chrysler, Deutsche Bank acquired Bankers Trust, British Petroleum bought Amoco, Hoechst merged with Rhône-Poulenc of France, and Wal-Mart acquired Cifra, Mexico's largest retailer. Managements struggled to adapt to the broader playing fields, the new rules, and the strong possibility that many of their competitors would respond with comparable deals.

But the march of this capitalism writ large generated criticism and fierce, occasionally violent opposition. Just as many people in Britain stood by the pound and rejected the euro, and as the United States turned its back on the un-American metric system, many people in many different countries object to the international economic integration that globalization brings.

They see, as the historian Eric Foner said, "nothing more than capital scouring the globe in search of cheap labor," or what H. Ross Perot called, somewhat less elegantly, "that great sucking sound" of American jobs heading south. They see exploitation of smaller and poorer nations, oppression, a growing gap between rich and poor, injustice. And worst of all, they see globalization as "a race to the bottom": as multinational corporations search the globe exploiting workers and nations, they create pressure on their home nations to create a less expensive climate for doing business, eroding social benefits. This opposition to globalization cannot be dismissed as a nostalgic left-wing critique of capitalism. Alongside its fringe elements stand major components of organized labor, respected environmental organizations, and human-rights activists.

"From this level of protest, I can only conclude that we have not been very successful in communicating the benefits of globalization to some very important and legitimate groupings—including influential nongovernment organizations," Jürgen Schrempp, CEO of Daimler-Chrysler, said in response to objections at the group's integration of the U.S. carmaker.

The conventional wisdom of the global marketplace is that companies need heft and the economies of scale it provides. That view has powered acquisitions, mergers, and alliances, from the brand-name manufacturers down through the vast supply chain that supports the vehicle industry. Shared development costs can produce savings of hundreds of millions of dollars, while manufacturing parts in vastly greater numbers drives down unit costs.

Few industries have embraced globalization to the extent the auto industry has. In 1999 the global market for vehicles had twenty-three major players. Just three years later only nine remained, the drive for consolidation surging across borders and over oceans. Daimler-Benz acquired Chrysler in 1998 and took a controlling share of Mitsubishi; Ford bought Jaguar, Volvo, and Land Rover and gained control of Mazda; Renault took control of Nissan. And the biggest automaker of them all, General Motors, bought a 20 percent stake in Fiat, took control of Saab, and formed alliances in Asia with Isuzu and Suzuki.

In search of these savings, the automakers have sought to develop vehicles, common platforms, and parts modules that can be used around the globe—Ford's "world car," the Focus, or the "world engine" that DaimlerChrysler, Mitsubishi, and Hyundai are hoping to develop jointly. GM and Fiat plan to share engines and gearboxes in Europe and South America; Nissan and Renault will eventually build all their cars with the same parts.

Other automakers (including Nissan, Honda, and BMW) developed global strategies that pioneered "transplants"—building manufacturing plants in other countries that served several purposes: sidestepping limits on imports, bringing production closer to key markets, and evading organized labor. The most popular region for such plants is the American South, a bastion of antilabor sentiment. BMW, for example, has most of its twenty-one factories in Europe but built a plant in South Carolina to produce a sport utility vehicle sold in a hundred countries.

For all the extensive and expensive commitments to globalization, progress has not always come easily: the auto industry has always been more fragmented than many other consumer-products industries. While television sets and personal computers are roughly the same in most parts of the world, despite some differences in circuitry, car tastes have been far more diverse. Against the industry's desire for "world cars" stands a broad range of local tastes—Americans' desire for gigantic sport utility vehicles in which to sit in traffic or navigate the parking lots of suburban malls, Europeans' and Asians' appetite for tiny little cars to wedge into congested streets—and a host of national and local regulations on pollution control, fuel consumption, and safety.

The industry has also been plagued by worldwide overcapacity. Many older, inefficient plants that employed thousands of workers enjoyed the political protection of regional and national governments, especially in Europe. They have proven difficult to shut.

Yet the appetite for global markets remains, and many of the giants continue to gaze covetously at and dip their toes into China and other untapped markets, awaiting the day when more wealth and consumer spending, better roads, and distribution networks will allow markets to swell. Noticing how much of their profit comes from financing the purchase of their vehicles in established markets, automakers are globalizing those operations too. Volkswagen, for instance, created Volkswagen Leasing Thailand to finance vehicle sales there and is creating similar operations in Taiwan and Australia.

Most, perhaps all, industries have now been transformed by globalization. Some, by their nature, have always had a broad international component—oil, pharmaceuticals, airlines. Strikingly, many businesses and sectors of the economy that were once regarded as regional, such as water companies or power generation companies, or even neighborhood-based, such as funeral homes, have gone global as well. The forces for globalization are much the same—the demand for growth, the opportunity for economies of scale, the power of technology to make long-distance operations easier.

Thirty years ago virtually every funeral parlor was a family-owned business. Service Corporation International, with its global view, changed that: it now owns more than 4,400 funeral homes in the United States, Canada, Britain, France, and Australia, as well as cemeteries and other related businesses. It has demonstrated that the same broad principles that General Motors relies on can apply to a business with a neighborhood face. SCI and its competitors have grown and profited by sharing personnel, vehicles, and preparation services (shrewdly, they leave the familiar family name on each funeral home as they acquire it—no branding here).

The power sector also embraced globalization, taking advantage of broad trends toward liberalization and deregulation. Some U.S. companies, for example, found they had more opportunities as Britain and the Netherlands opened their markets than they did at home; among the prominent deals was Entergy's acquisition of London Electricity in 1996. At the same time, various local water companies in England and Scotland were snapping up their counterparts in the United States.

Some of the strongest global competitive pressures have fallen on the pharmaceuticals industry. Nine pharmaceutical products rank among the two dozen most successful brand names in the world, and the number of medications with more than $1 billion in annual sales grew to more than forty in 2000 from seven a decade earlier. Within seven months of introducing Vioxx, the pain-reducing anti-inflammatory, Merck was selling it in fifty countries; Pfizer launched Viagra, the erectile dysfunction medication, in sixty countries in its first year. While technology has made communication, command and control, and customization far easier than in the past, the pharmaceutical companies have had to learn to deal with local and regional regulations, local cultures, and patient attitudes. They have been forced to *globalize.*

Different pharmaceutical makers—and, for that matter, consumer products companies—have developed different business models. Eli Lilly and Procter & Gamble have tried, wherever possible, to develop global brands (Lilly's Prozac antidepressant; P&G's Pampers diapers, Tide detergent, and Crest toothpaste). Pfizer and Unilever have preferred regional brands. Other companies have kept each national market in a silo. The more a company decides to brand globally, the greater the extent to which its operations must be integrated.

All these globalizing industries have a strong secondary effect—as the primary players expand, so too must the many industries that serve them. Law firms that specialize in the energy business, for example, have expanded from their traditional bases in Houston and London to Asia, Africa, and western Canada. Accounting, consulting, and other support services have done likewise. News-and-information companies that provide coverage of and data to global businesses have had to expand to keep pace—and so Reuters, Dow Jones, Bloomberg, McGraw-Hill, and other companies have operations around the globe.

An early example of companies with global vision was the alliance formed by Xerox and Fuji Photo Film in 1962. Xerox's global view was that it needed strong bases in markets outside the United States; Fuji's was that it needed to diversify beyond photo film and get involved in emerging technology and imaging businesses. The result was Fuji Xerox, whose mission was to market Xerox's copiers in Japan and to use that base to market to Indonesia, the Philippines, South Korea, Taiwan, and Thailand. Because Xerox placed its 50 percent stake in the hands of Rank Xerox, an earlier alliance it had formed with the Rank Organization of Britain, from the outset Fuji Xerox reached from Asia to North America to Europe.

Fuji Xerox had marketing responsibilities and, at the insistence of the Japanese government, a manufacturing role as well (the government wanted alliances that would build Japan's knowledge base). In the alliance's early days Xerox's copiers were dominating the marketplace, but by the 1970s Xerox was in jeopardy. While it focused on Eastman Kodak and IBM, which were threatening its lucrative middle-level and high-end markets, Japanese competitors were assaulting the low end. "The Japanese were selling products in the United States for what it cost us to make them," said David Kearns, Xerox's CEO at the time. To the astonishment of Xerox, Fuji Xerox came to the rescue.

From the very start the Japanese engineers at Fuji Xerox were trying to develop technology that would make them less dependent on the parent companies. By 1970 they had created a compact, inexpensive copier whose manufacturing costs were projected at half those of the smallest Xerox machines. It became a best-seller, securing Xerox's base in Asia and Fuji's reputation in the United States and Europe.

Another American technology company that found global solutions in Japan was Hewlett-Packard. For decades HP management was so intent on controlling its own fate that it even manufactured the screws it needed for its hardware. But under the pressure of globalization HP reached out and formed an alliance with Canon, with which it competed vigorously in the market for inkjet and laser printers (counterintuitively, more than half of strategic alliances bring together competitors).

As the alliance was constructed, Canon furnished the "engines" that powered HP's laser printers. HP provided the software and microprocessors and handled marketing. Both companies flourished in markets worldwide.

As more companies engage in more global activities, different models of doing business emerge, and some original premises are being challenged. Does all the world want the same car or the same refrigerator? Is one big monolith the way to go? Wal-Mart learned in the course of its alliance with and then acquisition of Cifra that Mexican consumers had different expectations than those in the United States; Tesco, the British supermarket chain, learned the same lesson and began customizing its stores in foreign markets.

Citibank decided it could tap into new markets overseas and a different customer base by using a fresh approach. It targeted midsize Indian companies, persuading them to open accounts for their employees with relatively low minimum balance requirements. Within a few years Citibank had acquired more than two hundred thousand retail customers in India. Whirlpool, the American appliance maker, decided that its "world platform" for a washing machine should be limited to about 70 percent of the parts, with the balance customized for local needs and tastes.

This small-bore approach to globalization, rather than trying to put a bottle of Coca-Cola in every hand or an IBM computer on every desktop, has several benefits. To cultivate diverse and smaller markets, companies are forced to work closely with local government officials, entrepreneurs, even community groups. Not only does this help the companies custom-develop products for local markets, but it offsets political objections to domination by multinationals.

Indisputably, the worldwide momentum for free trade and the consequent lowering of trade barriers has greatly increased the world's wealth and simultaneously driven down the prices of many consumer goods. At the same time, great pockets of poverty remain untouched, particularly in the Southern Hemisphere. Expecting globalization to solve the world's problems and correct the generations of political and social conditions as well as its own missteps is a great deal to ask.

Rich countries that have led the way and responded most quickly to globalization have benefited greatly. But they have left in place certain restrictive policies that, equally without question, harm the poor countries of the world. Nowhere is this clearer than the always contentious realm of agricultural policy. The continuing subsidies to farmers (in the United States, Japan, and Germany, just to start with the three largest economies) discriminate against other farmers everywhere. Similar barriers in many nations restrict global competition in textiles. The insistence of some wealthy nations on propping up uncompetitive industries—most notably steel—damages emerging economies. The inability of the enormously wealthy American society and its government to make available health care to many of its citizens raises questions around the world about the social costs of capitalism.

Most business executives and economists agree that the benefits of globalization and international economic integration are clear—and in any case inevitable. But they have not yet won the public debate, nor effectively confronted concerns about the social costs of such progress.

3. Finance and Accounting

"We're Not in Kansas Anymore"— Getting Real About Numbers and What They Mean

THE CAPITAL MARKETS—WHERE COMPANIES GO TO raise money and investors go to buy stock—are really communities of people with different perspectives on the world and different skills. In this vast and global community, where trillions of dollars change hands every day—the community includes money managers, traders, chief financial officers, analysts, bankers of all varieties, brokers, accountants, lawyers, salespeople, government regulators, idiots, and savants.

That community, working together and linked electronically, provides money to people with dreams. The capital markets are where big and small companies go when they need money to build new plants, finance expansion, sell their receivables, take on debt. It is where your bank bundles your mortgage together with others and sells them to pension fund investors from around the world. Because it traffics in assets and liabilities—and is highly adept at packaging, parceling, selling, and buying them both—the capital markets community is the world's most sophisticated tool for managing risk.

In this community theory and practice come together, reality and statistics collide. One risky bond that has the potential to pay off handsomely can spoil a person's day if it goes bad. But math and science applied to the markets can come as close to defying gravity as anything on earth. Instead of buying one risky bond, people buy into mutual funds, which are portfolios made up of dozens of bonds, each chosen to counter the others' risk and each selected to add to the potential for reward. By doing so—on average—the bias is to the upside with protection against the downside. The result: slightly lower highs with slightly higher lows.

Timing and information are critical to everything that happens in this community. Lies in one corner throw off all the others. Investors must be able to understand how borrowers intend to pay back their loans, how stock issuers intend to pay their dividends. When companies such as Enron and WorldCom issue false or misleading reports, the entire capital markets community is thrown off balance. Markets can tumble globally if trust in one country is breached.

The language of this community is mostly spoken with numbers. For the community to operate well, those numbers have to be a pretty good approximation of reality. That requires standards, standard setting, and verification. It requires groups of people willing to do the detailed work of ensuring that what is said on a balance sheet is right.

This section looks at timing, trust, and information.

J.K.

FINANCE IS THE ART AND SCIENCE OF SUSTAINING GROWTH, BUILDING WEALTH, AND CREATING JOBS

Michael Milken

Most people approach corporate finance the way scientists deal with problems in the physical world: plug in the right formula and you'll come up with the solution. But as any surgeon will tell you, at the very highest levels even the most technical pursuit becomes an art. In the same way that artists select from an infinite palette of colors, financiers choose from a broad range of financial technologies and securities to build the correct capital structure for a business. As conditions change over time, they modify the structure to keep the business strong.

There is no optimal capital structure—X percent equity and Y percent debt—that can be applied to different organizations, or to the same corporation at different points in time. Just as you can't make real money by putting a dollar bill on a copying machine, you can't successfully copy the financing technique that once worked for a particular company and transfer it to another time or another company. That's why I have always said that finance is a continuum with infinite variations and hybrids. It takes deep understanding of a company, its environment, and the financing tools available to build sustainable growth that will reward shareholders and create jobs.

Within a few years of my start on Wall Street in the late 1960s my department included more than a dozen divisions, each with special expertise in different types of assets. Collectively we employed scores of financial instruments to help clients grow. One way we measured success was our ability to free management from unnecessary concern about short-term financing so they could concentrate on what they did best—running their businesses for long-term success. The management of MCI, for example, had to devote a major portion of their time for more than a decade to raising capital. Then in 1983 the company was able to issue a hybrid security—$1 billion in ten-year bond warrant units with a coupon substantially below what U.S. Treasury bonds were paying. Because it created the optimal capital structure at the time, it turned out to be a good security for investors and for the company. Over the next ten years management spent little time raising capital. They could focus on building a revolutionary fiber-optic network that changed the face of communications in America. (Although, two decades later, MCI faced major problems under new management following its acquisition by another company, it was a remarkably agile and successful competitor in the 1980s.)

Building the right capital structure can be as important as managing other parts of a business. This was true for many of the growing companies that I had the opportunity to work with over the past thirty-five years. Companies such as McCaw Cellular, Turner/CNN, and TCI went through plenty of ups and downs in their basic businesses. But because they made the right capital structure decisions, they had the staying power to survive and were later sold for a total of well over $100 billion. Other companies, such as Safeway, Barnes & Noble, MGM Mirage, and Occidental Petroleum, had established franchises but still needed strong balance sheets to stay competitive.

This begs the question of what makes a balance sheet strong. Traditional hard assets—land, buildings, machinery—can lose value even as less tangible factors—human capital, management information systems, digital distribution networks—strengthen a company's ability to succeed. That kind of disparity between book value and real prospects sometimes contributes to popular myths. Any number of newspapers will tell you that the decade of the 1980s was dominated by debt. In fact, the 1970s was the decade of debt, because the value of equities declined, and the 1980s was the decade of equity. Industrial companies ended the 1980s *less* leveraged than they entered it.

In the mid-1970s, as interest rates were stabilizing and stock market values had declined relative to replacement values, many corporations used debt-oriented securities to extend maturities and finance growth. Because of the higher real replacement values, they often acquired existing assets rather than build from scratch. Thus, during the '70s debt made up more than half the capital structure of the typical industrial corporation, reversing the trend of the 1960s, when equity exceeded debt. By the late 1980s, with equity values for most companies above replacement costs, it made sense to invest in new plants and equipment and to reduce capital risk by selling equity-related securities. During the 1980s debt relative to book value for many companies was still fairly high. But that wasn't the correct ratio for determining how to finance future growth. The better measure was market-adjusted debt ratios, a concept I had developed during my studies in the 1960s and advocated in a series of research papers in the early 1970s. Looking at finance this way, it becomes apparent that leverage can be declining even as debt is increasing. For example, Exxon's equity market value in 1979 was $24 billion and its long-term debt was about $4 billion. During the 1980s Exxon repurchased more of its common stock than any other public company—some $16 billion worth—and increased its long-term debt to more than $8 billion. Despite this large debt increase, the rise in equity market value to $63 billion was ten times the added debt.

The Corporate Financing Cube

As important as financial ratios are to effective capital structure decisions, they are only the starting point. There is a broader environment that will affect how the decisions play out over time. One way to grasp this environment is to visualize the six faces of a simple cube labeled with the words *Company, Industry, Capital Markets, Economy, Regulation,* and *Society.*

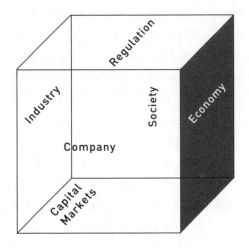

The Company

Is the company an established national supermarket chain, a high-tech start-up, or something in between on the continuum of risk? Although there is growing competition in the supermarket industry, grocery companies can usually be leveraged with a higher debt-to-equity ratio because they have more predictable revenue (people always have to eat) and a stable business model. A technology company, on the other hand, should rarely sell debt because of inherent business volatility and competitive risk. In such industries it's difficult to predict revenue or to say with confidence that cash flow will be sufficient to service the debt. Yet technology companies have often made the mistake of issuing convertible bonds, weakening their balance sheets to the point where they couldn't survive a cyclical business slowdown. If these companies have realistic business plans and qualified management, they should be able to meet their capital needs by selling equity to private investors, venture capitalists, and the public.

Qualified management, of course, is a key to determining capital structure. It's not enough to have smart people at the top; you need to understand exactly what their talents are. If, for example, the CEO is skilled in finance, more leverage may be appropriate than for a company headed by a former sales executive. Assuming equivalent financial skills, however, the simple rule of thumb is that risk in capital structure should vary inversely with volatility and risk in the basic business. To paraphrase the late Harold Geneen of ITT, you can make a lot of mistakes in business, but you can't run out of cash. For some companies, even a dollar of debt is too much. This was as true of the airline, aerospace, and technology companies of the late 1960s as it was of telecommunications, networking, and Internet companies of the late 1990s.

The Industry

Before deciding how to raise capital, managers and their advisors need to conduct exhaustive research on the structure of the industry. Some of the factors to consider are:

■ **Competition.** Is it local, regional, national, or global? If you lack wide geographic distribution, you may be vulnerable.

■ **Concentration and financial strength.** A small company about to launch a software product that will compete head to head with

Microsoft faces a different challenge than a manufacturer in an industry with less concentration and no companies with strong balance sheets.

■ **Cyclicality.** For the baby products industry, cycles take decades to play out; for semiconductors, things can change in a few months.

■ **Competitive R&D levels.** What percentage of revenue do companies in the industry spend on research and development? What is your risk of being severely hurt if that spending produces a new technology?

■ **Barriers to entry**. How easily and quickly can new entrants take market share?

■ **Volatility.** In the 1960s (and again in the 1990s) many technology companies were misfinanced, and ultimately failed, because they didn't adequately consider the ups and downs of the industry.

■ **Capacity.** New competitors entering the telecommunications industry in the late 1990s built far more capacity than was needed, driving down prices and leaving almost all players with insufficient cash flow to service their debt. Despite this overcapacity and demand that failed to materialize, these companies would have had more staying power if they had put more equity into their capital structures.

■ **Quality.** Where does your company rank in the quality spectrum of your industry? The effect of a change in customer demand will play out differently across the industry. While a recession might mean a 50 percent drop in revenue for low-end companies, industry leaders often suffer milder effects.

If your competitors are financially strong and your customers count on you to keep them operating, you might need excess liquidity. In the late 1970s MCI was a tiny company competing against an industry colossus, AT&T, with AAA credit, a strong balance sheet, and a 98 percent market share. Facing that kind of competitor, they needed to show staying power. By the early 1980s the company planned to build an advanced network that would require large amounts of capital. In arranging what was then the largest debt financing in history, I advised management to put an extra $500 million in cash on their balance sheet so that customers, suppliers, and investors would know they were financially strong. Over the ensuing years the company's growth allowed it to create more than fifty thousand jobs for American workers.

Capital Markets

A primary management goal should be maximal operational flexibility. This requires close attention both to the type of security used and to the timing of its issuance. Generally companies should build capital structure from the bottom up, selling equity and junior subordinated debt when markets are strong. Just as you'd hold back your highest cards until you need them in a card game, you'll want to reserve the most senior securities at the top of your capital structure for a rainy day. The time to raise capital is when the market is most receptive, not when you most need the funds. Remember, you're not just raising capital; you're enhancing the company's staying power and increasing its flexibility.

The Economy

Changes in the overall economy affect perceptions of individuals and corporations, making them feel more or less confident and willing to spend. A "wealth effect" came into play in the seventeen-year period between 1983 and 2000, when stocks compounded at almost 15 percent a year, not counting dividends. That contrasts sharply with the 1 percent annual growth before dividends in the seventeen years from 1965 to 1982. These cycles affect the optimal capital structure for any company.

In addition to the overall economic cycle, there are always sub-economies that follow their own rhythms. Every month some industries are on the way up, while others are declining. Every day, no matter what the broad stock market indicators say, some stocks hit new highs and others new lows. Sometimes the disparity is driven by regional variations, such as the slump in the "oil patch" states in the early 1980s; sometimes the driver is demography, which has created growing demand in such industries as pharmaceutical products and financial services as baby boomers age; and sometimes a specific event will send an industry up or down—the end of the Cold War drove down defense stocks, but they moved up following the September 11 terrorist attacks.

Regulation

No company and no industry can operate independent of regulation. In 1993 a new government health plan proposal would have led to sweeping changes in the pharmaceutical industry, including what some feared would be regulation of rates of return on investments. This could have had a major impact in an industry where it can take as long as fourteen years to bring a new drug to market. The ten largest companies in the industry lost a staggering $70 billion in market capitalization in only fourteen months because of the mere possibility of regulation. Tragically but logically, pharmaceutical companies responded by cutting research and development budgets in a necessary realignment of risk and return. While we'll never be able to measure what medical breakthroughs may have been lost or delayed, one thing is certain: corporate managements can never afford to ignore regulatory developments.

In the late 1980s Congress passed the Financial Institutions Reform, Recovery and Enforcement Act (FIRREA), which typified a brief period of overregulation that targeted insurance companies, bondholders, banks, and other lenders. Well-meaning but ill-advised, FIRREA banned investments by savings and loan institutions in non-investment-grade companies and forced the S&Ls to sell existing loans that had been made to these enterprises—the very companies that create all the new jobs in America. (When corrected for job losses among the big companies over the last thirty years, more than 100 percent of the net new jobs created in the United States have come from small and medium-sized companies that don't qualify for an investment-grade credit rating. During the same period, the eight hundred or so investment-grade companies have actually *shed* a net four million workers, while smaller companies created sixty-two million jobs.) At the time, there was only a handful of investment-grade companies headed or controlled by African Americans, Hispanics, women, or unions.

Thus, as recently as the late twentieth century, the Congress of the United States effectively, albeit unknowingly, said it was *illegal* to provide capital to businesses headed by minorities and women or to any company that would create jobs. It was okay to make a mortgage loan that would build a building, but you couldn't finance the company that provided jobs for the people inside the building. That's why I called FIRREA and similar regulatory acts "neutron legislation"—like a neutron bomb, they left buildings standing but eliminated the people, or at least their jobs. Because only a handful of our fifty states have more than a few dozen investment-grade companies (some states have no such companies), Congress effectively redlined most regions of the country, reducing asset values and employment.

Society

This is in some ways the most important face of the cube. Businesses always need to understand which way society is going on the key issues that affect their products. If you are perceived as part of the solution to current social concerns, then you're well positioned. But if you're part of the problem, you may want to exit the business. At the very least you'll need a more conservative financial structure. As recently as 1986 the most valuable brand name in the world was Marlboro. Yet its value was about to begin a long and steady decline that can be attributed almost entirely to changes in our society and its view of smoking as a social rite. These changes did not come without plenty of warning. As early as 1939 the surgeon general of the United States suggested that smoking could be bad for your health, and a surgeon general's report in the 1960s concluded that there was a direct link between smoking and cancer. Congressional hearings in the 1990s raked tobacco company executives over the political coals and encouraged massive lawsuits against the industry.

Just as smoking became an epidemic in the twentieth century, today a new epidemic—obesity—presents a growing threat to the health of our nation. More than half of Americans are overweight or obese, which leads to some three hundred thousand unnecessary deaths each year and costs our economy more than $100 billion. In much the same way that tobacco marketers were eventually held responsible for promoting unhealthful products, the new epidemic will undoubtedly encourage litigation in search of judgments against those purveying unhealthy food. Whether or not this is justified is a matter for the courts. The key for investors and corporate managers is risk analysis.

Where is society heading in the twenty-first century? The two largest sectors of the U.S. economy, health care and education, are poised to expand and become an even larger share of gross domestic product. In 1950 there was not a single health care or pharmaceutical company among the one hundred U.S. corporations with the largest market capitalizations. As this new century began, twelve pharmaceutical, biotechnology, and medical products companies were already on the list, and more health care firms seem sure to join it before long. Health care already accounts for about 15 percent of U.S. GDP, and its slice of the national economic pie continues to grow. Education may well follow a similar path. No education company is currently listed among the top one hundred, but several are growing fast and could be there within a decade as private enterprise responds to the growing need for lifelong learning.

The Importance of Human Capital

Finally, any analysis of capital structure should recognize that most balance sheets are dramatically inaccurate because (with the exception of professional sports franchises) they fail to include the value of human capital. Gary Becker, the Nobel prize–winning economist, calculates that human capital—the knowledge, skills, experience, and earning power of people—accounts for more than three-quarters of the asset value on the national balance sheet. It may sound like a platitude to say that people are the most important asset, but in fact they are. The market capitalization of many companies has changed by billions of dollars within hours of a change in CEO. And with good reason. The right leader can make or break a company. With every passing year, however, the people at *every* organizational level grow in importance. In the 1920s, when automobiles became a huge industry, 60 percent of the cost of producing a car was in raw materials and energy. For today's computer chips it's less than 2 percent of the cost. Brainpower has become the "raw material" for building companies. This human capital, combined with the social capital of democracy, open markets, and the rule of law is the basis of a prosperous economy.

Ultimately, the importance of finance in society lies in its ability to unlock the potential in people. As an undergraduate at Berkeley in the mid-1960s, I was surrounded by people who wanted to change society. "Unlike other crusaders from Berkeley," I wrote a few years later, "I have chosen Wall Street as my battleground for improving society because it is here that government institutions and industries are financed." In my first talk to the Wall Street community, I suggested that the best investors are social scientists. Such investors see beyond financial statements and physical assets to the changing needs and tastes of people. They respond to the opportunities created by change. In doing so, they create value for society. The opening of our capital markets to people of broader backgrounds over the last thirty years has allowed far more individuals with a dream to test themselves in the marketplace. That has strengthened our economy, to be sure. Equally as important, it has strengthened our democracy.

FACT, NOT FICTION: FINANCIAL STATEMENTS FOR THE REAL WORLD

Les Livingstone

Financial statements reveal financial condition, earning power, and cash flow. They are our business report cards and are indispensable for important transactions. For example:

- Apply for a mortgage on a home, and the lender will ask for your personal financial statements.
- A business wanting a loan from a bank, or credit from a supplier, will be asked for its financial statements.
- A corporation wishing to issue stock or bonds to investors will be required to present its financial statements.

The importance of financial statements is illustrated by the fact that all corporations who sell securities to the public in the United States are required by law to issue quarterly and annual financial statements in a timely fashion. These financial statements become public record and can be accessed through the Internet and in hard copy form through the SEC.[1]

The financial statements of an entity are usually compared with its financial statements for prior periods, in order to track the growth and progress (or lack thereof) of the entity. Also, the financial statements of an entity are often compared with those of similar entities in the same line of business. In order for these comparisons to be valid, the financial statements being compared must be prepared on a mutually consistent basis. For example:

- One entity records a sale as soon as an order is received. Its revenue is not consistent with the revenue of an entity that records a sale only after the goods have been delivered and payment has been received.

- One entity treats research and development costs as an asset. That is not consistent with another entity that writes off research and development costs as an expense.

- One entity has tax losses that can be deducted from future income if and when it might be earned, and reports this prospective tax saving as a current benefit. That is not consistent with another entity that recognizes a benefit only when future income is actually earned and the past tax losses in fact reduce the currently payable taxes.

As these few examples show, accounting is not by any means as cut-and-dried as it may appear to the uninitiated. There are many different ways to record assets, liabilities, revenues, and expenses. The possibilities of inconsistency are limitless.

Meet the Twins: GAAP and GAAS

Since consistency and comparability of financial statements are important, there are numerous rules about how financial statements must be prepared. The purpose of these rules is to ban as many as possible of the different ways to record assets, liabilities, revenues, and expenses. The rules narrow the options and are compulsory. The collected rules are known as *generally accepted accounting principles* (GAAP).

Although GAAP are compulsory, how is the user of financial statements to know that the GAAP rules have actually been followed and applied in the proper manner to the financial statements prepared by the management of an enterprise? This assurance is provided by an independent audit. All corporations that sell securities to the public in the United States are required by law to subject their annual financial statements to an independent audit.

An independent audit is an examination of the financial statements that have been prepared by the management of an entity. The independent audit is performed by a firm of certified public accountants, which is considered independent because it is separate from, and unrelated to, the entity being audited. The audit consists of collecting evidence from inside the entity (such as invoices, paid checks, purchase orders, and other business documents) and outside the entity (from customers, suppliers, bankers, attorneys, and others who do business with the entity). This collected evidence is used to determine whether the financial statements (and the underlying books of account and financial records) are in conformity with GAAP and free of material misstatements.

If the audit firm is satisfied with the financial statements, it issues a clean audit report, which is attached to the financial statements. If the audit firm is not satisfied and management refuses to bring the financial statements into line, the audit firm is not permitted to issue a clean report. Instead, it must issue a modified audit report, which explains why it has been modified, and which is attached to the financial statements. In short, the auditor is a watchdog, and the way the watchdog barks is by issuing a modified audit report. When an auditor issues a clean audit report, it is taken for granted that the watchdog has faithfully patrolled the territory, found that all is well, and therefore has no need to bark.

The U.S. Supreme Court has stated: "By certifying the public reports that collectively depict a corporation's financial status, the independent auditor assumes a *public* responsibility transcending any employment relationship with the client. The independent public accountant performing this special function owes ultimate allegiance to the corporation's creditors and stockholders, as well as to the investing public. This 'public watchdog' function demands that the accountant maintain total independence from the client at all times and requires complete fidelity to the public trust."[2]

For an audit report to be meaningful, the audit process must be consistent from year to year and from one audit firm to another. An audit would be meaningless if the examination was thorough one year and cursory the next year. It would also be meaningless if one audit firm's examination was thorough and another's was cursory. For these reasons, there is a set of compulsory rules to make the audit process consistent and reliable. This set of compulsory rules is known as *generally accepted auditing standards* (GAAS).

It is GAAP and GAAS that lend credibility to corporate financial statements and give confidence to investors that their funds are properly employed in profitable and legitimate pursuits and under the trustworthy stewardship of principled corporate executives. This investor confidence in corporate financial statements means that investors face little risk of management fraud and therefore are willing to accept lower returns by way of interest and dividends on their invested funds. Otherwise investors would demand higher rates of interest and dividends to cover the risk of false financial statements designed to conceal fraud by crooked corporate executives. Investor confidence and the resulting low cost of capital are vital to the efficiency of U.S. financial markets in raising capital from investors and channeling it into corporations with profitable opportunities to expand their operations.

Trouble in the Placid Paradise of Accounting

Until the late 1990s very few scandals rocked the placid scene of U.S. corporate financial reporting. True, there had been a few major corporate frauds and audit failures over the years:

- McKesson & Robbins (1940)
- BarChris Construction (1968)
- Continental Vending (1969)
- National Student Marketing (1975)
- Equity Funding (1978)
- The savings and loan debacle of the late 1980s and early 1990s

But these scandals were isolated events, and the CPA profession retained the trust of the investment community. Investors had faith in the financial statements of our largest corporations because they carried the blue-chip imprimatur of one or another of the respected Big 5 auditing firms, which became the Big 4 with the demise of Arthur Andersen in the wake of the Enron collapse.[3]

In the late 1990s U.S. stock markets soared to new heights on the rosiest of expectations. Few, if any, observers would have predicted the coming carnage that was soon to devastate U.S. financial markets. The symptom of trouble ahead was the increasing number of restatements of previously issued audited financial statements by U.S. corporations. A financial statement restatement is required when it is found that the previously issued financial statements have been materially misstated. By law, the previously issued financial statements must be withdrawn and the restated financial statements issued.

The restatement of financial statements does not necessarily indicate that there was fraud or that the audit failed. For example, there might have been material error that was accidental and not fraudulent. Further, no audit is absolutely guaranteed to detect material error or fraud. The auditor is not an insurer, and its job is to provide reasonable (but not absolute) assurance that the financial statements are free of material misstatement. An audit that is thorough enough to absolutely guarantee the absence of material misstatement would be prohibitively expensive. Therefore, the occasional restatement is not a smoking gun that points to audit failure. But when restatements happen more than occasionally, they become suspicious. Coincidence can stretch only so far.

The U.S. General Accounting Office (GAO) made a study of restatements by publicly listed companies and reported:

> The number of financial statement restatements identified each year rose from 92 in 1997 to 225 in 2001. The proportion of listed companies on NYSE, AMEX, and NASDAQ identified as restating their financial reports tripled from less than 0.89 percent in 1997 to about 2.5 percent in 2001 and may reach almost 3 percent by the end of 2002. From January 1997 through June 2002, about 10 percent of all listed companies announced at least one restatement. The 689 publicly traded companies we identified that announced financial statement restatements between January 1997 and March 2002 lost billions of dollars in market capitalization in the days around the initial restatement announcement.[4]

Meet Some of the Bad Boys

There have been an alarming number of restatements in recent years, often accompanied by accounting scandals involving huge sums. Some examples are as follows:

■ **Adelphia** filed Chapter 11 bankruptcy in June 2002. This cable TV operator and several related individuals were sued in July 2002 by the SEC and charged "in one of the most extensive financial frauds ever to take place in a public company" with fraudulently excluding from its annual and quarterly financial statements from mid-1999 to end of 2001 over $2 billion in debt by systematically recording those liabilities on the books of unconsolidated affiliates, which violated GAAP. The Rigas family, who founded Adelphia, collected $3.1 billion in off-balance-sheet loans backed by Adelphia. Three Rigas family members have been arrested on allegations of fraud. Adelphia has sued its independent auditor for malpractice.[5]

■ **Baptist Foundation of Arizona** was an audit client of Arthur Andersen, which paid $217 million to settle lawsuits alleging malpractice in the Baptist Foundation audit.

■ **Enron Corporation** filed for Chapter 11 bankruptcy in December 2001, setting a record for the largest corporate bankruptcy to date. Enron announced restatements that reduced reported net income by a total of $586 million and increased reported debt by $2.6 billion for 1997–2001. Enron's auditor, Arthur Andersen, was convicted in August 2002 of obstruction of justice through destruction of audit work papers and is no longer permitted to audit public companies in the United States. Andersen offered $750 million to settle civil lawsuits filed against that firm—an offer that was turned down. Soon after that, Andersen collapsed.

■ **Qwest Communications** admitted inflating reported sales by $1.16 billion in its financial statements and is restating results for 2000–2002.

■ **Rite Aid Corporation** announced restatements that reduced reported retained earnings by a total of $1.6 billion due to overstated net income for 1998 and 1999. Rite Aid did not restate 1996 and 1997 financial statements because it would require "unreasonable cost and expense," but it reported that the financial data for 1996 and 1997 should not be relied upon. Rite Aid's auditor, KPMG, resigned in November 1999 and withdrew its audit reports for 1997–1999, stating that it was unable to continue to rely on management's representations (a polite way of saying that they no longer could believe what management told them).

■ **Sunbeam Corporation** filed for Chapter 11 bankruptcy in February 2001. Sunbeam announced restatements that improved its reported 1996 net loss by $20 million, reduced reported 1997 net income by $71 million, and increased reported 1998 net income by $10 million. This strange pattern resulted from Sunbeam's creation of improper reserves in 1996, which were used to inflate 1997 reported income and give the false impression of a rapid turnaround. Sunbeam's auditor, Arthur Andersen, and other Sunbeam parties (including ex-CEO Al "Chainsaw" Dunlap) were sued, and settled in 2002 for $141 million, the largest portion of which was paid by Arthur Andersen.

■ **Tyco International** has lost more than 75 percent of its market value. All of its directors have resigned, and its three most senior executives are accused of looting the company by taking hundreds of millions of dollars in secret, unauthorized, and improper low-interest loans from 1996 through June 2002.

■ **Waste Management** restatements reduced reported net income for the period between 1992 and the first quarter of 1999 by more than $1.1 billion. Its auditor, Arthur Andersen, had issued clean audit opinions for those financial statements. Waste Management has paid out $220 million to settle some, but not all, of the lawsuits filed against it.

■ **WorldCom** is accused of overstating income by $9 billion (mainly in 2000), and it gave founder Bernard Ebbers a staggering $400 million in off-the-books loans. The company has stated that it may have to take a charge of $50 billion to write off loss of goodwill. Two former WorldCom executives have been arrested on allegations of fraud. WorldCom has since superseded Enron as the largest corporate bankruptcy. WorldCom's auditor? Arthur Andersen.

■ **Xerox Corporation** went through not one but two series of restatements. The first restatements reduced reported net income by a total of $207 million for 1998 and 1999. The second restatements reduced reported net income by a total of $1.4 billion (52 percent) for 1997–2000. The Xerox auditor was KPMG through October 2001, when it was replaced by PricewaterhouseCoopers.

As a result of these accounting scandals, the once impeccable reputation of the CPA profession has been severely tarnished. In fact, the media now constantly refer to the "accounting industry" rather than the "accounting profession." In the past CPA's were stereotyped as passive, boring, and unimaginative, but unquestionably honest. That is probably still true for the vast majority of CPA's. But a significant minority of CPA's have shown unsuspected imagination, unbelievable aggression, and a remarkable absence of ethics.

Asleep at the Switch

There is plenty of blame from the corporate scandals for the failures of all the gatekeepers responsible for safeguarding the integrity of large corporations: namely:

- ■ Boards of directors
- ■ The audit committees of the boards of directors
- ■ Regulators, such as the SEC
- ■ Bond rating agencies

Every Business Is the Same Inside

RAM CHARAN

■ Most people can understand cash on a small scale, in their own everyday life. If the bills are due before the paycheck arrives, what happens? In a large company, however, some people lose sight of cash. Many think that's the responsibility of the finance department.

But everyone in a company must be aware that his actions use cash or generate cash. A sales representative who negotiates a 30-day payment from a customer versus 45 days is cash wise. The company gets the money sooner, and that frees up cash—that is, makes the cash available to use for other things. A plant manager whose poor scheduling results in the accumulation of a lot of inventory consumes cash.

The decision to build a new plant clearly affects cash generation. Take the case of Miller Brewing Company. Philip Morris purchased Miller in 1970 and set the regional brewery onto a major growth trajectory. Market share rose quickly from 8 percent to 20 percent. Encouraged by this momentum, management built a $460 million brewery so the company could increase production as market share continued to climb. But before the new plant was up and running, the company's archrival, Anheuser-Busch, made some aggressive marketing moves and stopped Miller in its tracks. Miller's market share did not increase as hoped for, the plant opening was delayed several years, and cash generation went negative. Cash flowed out of the company to build the plant, but no additional cash flowed in because sales did not increase as planned.

Even mailroom clerks have a role to play in cash generation. They sort and deliver the mail—letters, bills, check. Checks! ■

From Ram Charan, *What the CEO Wants You to Know: Using Business Acumen to Understand How Your Company Really Works* (Crown Business, 2001).

- Major stockholders such as pension funds and mutual funds
- Independent auditors
- Professional associations such as the American Institute
  of CPAs

Every one of these gatekeepers has failed to perform its duty in one corporate fraud after another. But no failure has been as abject as that of the audit watchdogs that have turned out to be lapdogs. They have seriously eroded the credibility of audited financial statements and thrown a monkey wrench into the efficient functioning of the securities markets. They have been derelict in their duty to investors, employees, creditors, and the public. How is the lost trust in auditors going to be restored?

The Remedies

In 2002 the U.S. Congress passed the Sarbanes-Oxley Act in response to the flood of corporate frauds. The main provisions of Sarbanes-Oxley are as follows:[6]

- The previous self-regulation of independent auditors has been replaced by the creation of the Public Company Accounting Oversight Board, which is under the jurisdiction of the SEC.
- GAAP and GAAS will be under the oversight of the SEC.
- Independent auditing firms are no longer permitted to provide certain management consulting services to their audit clients.
- The CEO and CFO of each U.S. public company must certify that the company's financial statements fairly present and disclose its operations and financial condition.
- Directors and officers of U.S. public companies are prohibited

from fraudulently influencing, coercing, or manipulating the independent auditors.

- If financial statements are restated due to material noncompliance with financial reporting requirements, the CEO and CFO must disgorge any bonus or other incentive-based or equity-based compensation received during the twelve months following the issue of the noncompliant financial statements.

- It is a felony to knowingly destroy or create documents to impede any federal investigation, and auditors are required to maintain all audit or review work papers for five years.

How effective will these provisions be in preventing future Enrons and WorldComs? No doubt potential perpetrators of large-scale corporate fraud (including rogue accountants) will be chastened for the next few years by the punishments meted out to present offenders. But memories can quickly recede, and the chastening effect will probably fade all too soon.

Will the Remedies Work?

It is difficult to object to any or all of the Sarbanes-Oxley provisions. All seem to be benign and helpful. The real question is whether they are likely to deter future corporate frauds and delinquent auditors. This is far from certain, for reasons such as the following:

- Some of the recent audit failures were not due to the inadequacy of preexisting rules. They resulted because existing rules were clearly violated. Therefore just to add extra rules, as Sarbanes-Oxley does, is no guarantee that the new rules will be followed any more observantly than the old rules were.

■ It is not clear that prohibiting independent auditors from performing certain business consulting services for their audit clients will be effective. On one hand, it is true that consulting fees often exceed audit fees from the same client and consulting is far more profitable than the highly competitive auditing business.[7] This leads to the opinion that consulting erodes the independence of auditors and should be cut back severely in order to bolster auditor independence. But it could also be true that depriving auditors of lucrative consulting work may increase their hunger for fees from auditing and make them more reluctant to stand up to audit clients wishing to bend the rules of financial reporting. This may reduce auditor independence. It may not be a coincidence that the recent flood of accounting scandals occurred at about the same time that the large CPA firms were parting company from their business consulting divisions.[8]

■ Sarbanes-Oxley confers greater power and responsibility upon the SEC to combat fraud and to improve audit quality. The SEC has come under criticism for the weakness of its enforcement activities, and it has been called a paper tiger. True, the SEC has not received sufficient resources in the past to fully perform its duties, but its critics also note that it has not used its limited resources as effectively as it should have. In consequence, it must be questioned how well the SEC will fulfill its enhanced mission to enforce the Sarbanes-Oxley Act.

■ Sarbanes-Oxley was enacted in haste by the U.S. Congress under pressure from the torrent of corporate scandals and lacking direct knowledge of what auditors actually do and what pressures auditors are under. All the gatekeepers responsible for safeguarding the integrity of large corporations have been ineffective. The passivity of boards of directors, audit committees, regulators such as the SEC, major stockholders such as pension funds and mutual funds, and professional accounting associations such as the American Institute of CPAs has allowed some unethical corporate officers to run rampant and loot without restraint. To whom would honest auditors turn to report fraud by corporate officers? When directors, regulators, and major stockholders close their eyes, auditors have no support against unethical corporate officers, who can easily fire an honest audit firm and without difficulty replace it with a more accommodating audit firm. A flaw in Sarbanes-Oxley is its failure to provide protection for the honest auditor who wants to blow the whistle but finds no one willing to hear it. It would be ethical for the honest audit firm to fall on its sword and lose the audit engagement. But the record shows too many cases where audit firms have not sacrificed the audit engagement and have taken the easy way out, just like the other compliant gatekeepers. One possible remedy would be to prohibit the dismissal of an auditor unless approved by a supermajority of shareholders, and perhaps also to require the express permission of the SEC. If there is inertia on the part of directors, regulators, and major stockholders, why not force crooked executives to overcome that very inertia if they wish to get rid of an honest auditor? Then gatekeeper inertia would work in favor of corporate integrity, instead of against it, as is presently the case.

■ If the auditor receives a carrot in the form of protection for being honest, should there not also be a stick to stiffen the spine of an auditor reluctant to confront a powerful management that wants to bend the rules? One suggestion is to require audit firms to be bonded for very substantial dollar amounts. If audit firms were required to be bonded against malpractice, there could be several desirable outcomes:

1. The insurance company providing the bond would have a strong incentive to police the audit firm in order to prevent

any malpractice that would result in claims against the insurer by victims of the malpractice.

2. Audit firms would have every incentive to cooperate with their insurers because without bonding they could not continue to perform audits.

3. If malpractice happened to occur, the insurer would be a deep pocket to pay out compensation to victims of the malpractice. This would avoid situations like that of Arthur Andersen, which had inadequate insurance and ended up with insufficient funds to pay substantial damages when sued.

4. Current malpractice insurance for audit firms covers only negligence, but not fraud by the auditor. It is perverse for victims of fraud to have no redress. Those who sue will try to prove negligence short of fraud in order to sustain claims against insurance. The result is that fraudulent auditors escape responsibility for fraud and only face the milder allegations and lesser penalties of negligence.

Conclusions

In summary, Sarbanes-Oxley relies too much on prescribing more rules even though old rules have been violated again and again. It relies on enforcement of rules by bureaucrats who have an ineffective past record. Sarbanes-Oxley has not taken the opportunity to turn the inertia of regulators and stockholders into a plus rather than a minus for corporate integrity. It has not established a source of funds to compensate victims of fraud. Nor has it used available carrots and sticks as powerful incentives to encourage auditors to have more backbone and to help the accounting industry again to become the accounting profession.

REQUIEM FOR THE EARNINGS GAME

Robert Eccles

Business just isn't as much fun as it used to be. The stock market used to go only up. Now, more often than not, it seems to be heading in the opposite direction. Remember when the New Economy was being created? The Internet was going to change our lives for the good and eliminate those unpleasant business cycles. Now all those wonderful twenty-somethings who were creating this exciting future through their dot-com start-ups with eye-popping stock prices are out of work or, even worse, going to back to school (probably not business school). Heroic CEOs are now being lambasted in the press for excessive greed, moral laxity, and titillating private lives that rival those of Hollywood stars.

Bad press is the mildest part of the universal rebuke being delivered to the business community. Just for starters, take the Sarbanes-Oxley Act. It is like putting the strictest teacher in charge of the whole school just to make completely sure that nobody is having any fun. Executives, directors, investment banks, and accounting firms all face stiffer scrutiny and the threat of more litigation and stiffer penalties—even hard time. All will have to work harder, probably for less money and certainly less adulation and acclaim.

None of this is the worst part of the story. It is my unsought but solemn responsibility to impart the worst news of all: we are now coming to the end of the Earnings Game. Please pause with me for a moment of silence to mark its tragic passing. (Sighs and sobs, with a few gentle tears rolling down some cheeks.)

Let us honor the Earnings Game in our memory. What fun it was! Every quarter a big party was held by all. In anticipation of this party executives coyly guided analysts to a "consensus estimate" for the quarter's earnings with a little wink-wink suggesting that the company would do just a bit better than this. While a demure peck on the cheek was promised, hope was held out for a full kiss on the lips.

Those high-powered analysts, paid to advise both the chickens and the fox and told about the party before everybody else (although Regulation FD did kind of spoil some of the fun), got to tell investors and the media how much fun it was going to be through their earnings estimates. Even the drab accountants weren't left out. They got to be the referee to make sure the rules of Pin the Tail on the Donkey were being followed—sort of. What's the point of having rules if you can't bend them a little bit?

Then there was the actual party itself—earnings announcements! Just thinking about this puts a little lump in my throat. So many people got to appear on TV as earnings were announced to explain, with great excitement, that the consensus estimate had been bested by one, two, three cents, or even more. Sometimes the party was so good, the actual earnings exceeded even the whisper number and the *über*-whisper number. I remember those days with the same fondness with which I recall three-martini lunches and unfiltered cigarettes that didn't come in packages with warning labels.

While not yet completely gone, the Earnings Game, beloved by all, is clearly heading toward its demise. Executives are supposed to focus on creating long-term value for shareholders and be paid only if they do so. No more party presents of options getting vested when the stock went up because (surprise!) earnings were better than expected. Even worse, executives are now supposed to accurately report their performance and not stretch accounting rules when they do so. Bah, humbug. Why, some people are even saying the presents should be returned if just a few little liberties were taken when playing the game and shareholders actually turn out to be losers rather than winners when the final score is tallied.

It's just as bad for independent directors. Rather than having lots of fun with their CEO pals before and after board meetings on the golf course and in the bar, they are supposed to fulfill a fiduciary responsibility to, ugh, shareholders. Even worse, they have to approve the numbers reported by management. Talk about risk of injury. But the real killjoy here is that directors are going to have to spend a lot more time making sure that management really isn't playing that oh-so-fun Earnings Game anymore. Might as well stay home and watch golf on TV. Certainly less chance of injury.

It's not more fun for accountants either, but then again, they aren't supposed to have fun. Back to making sure those pesky numbers are right, even if that means an unpleasant conversation with the host of the party and taking a principled stand on accounting standards. And all these new rules to learn now that the game is being changed: audit rotations, oversight boards, service restrictions for audit clients, limitations in career paths to clients . . . Maybe actuarial work doesn't look so bad after all.

The situation for analysts is so bad that they may even start to envy the accountants—the football star longing to be a nerd. All the accountants have to do is make sure past numbers are correct. Can you believe that people are saying that analysts should actually be judged on the recommendations they make? I mean, who can see the future? It sure was a lot more fun, and certainly easier, to just issue a buy recommendation and spend time in the makeup room getting ready to appear on TV: "And now, ladies and gentlemen, it's time for *[drumroll]* the Earnings Game!"

The media will suffer less from the end of this wonderful game. It certainly was a good run and they will be sad to see it go, but there's always a new story deserving breathless and immediate commentary (the facts and full story be damned—we've got advertising to sell here!). Even better, the press gets to be both a player and a referee. "We get to talk and write about everybody, but why would we be so stupid as to do this to ourselves?" Okay, maybe that's too harsh, because the media do bear some responsibility for ending the Earnings Game with their reporting on Enron, WorldCom, and such. I'm sure they feel just as bad about this as everybody else does.

So where does that leave us? Executives, board directors, accounting firms, analysts, and the media all practicing a spirit of transparency in their actions and the information they provide. All holding themselves accountable to shareholders and to each other. All putting personal integrity above beating that alluring little consensus estimate. It certainly seems rather drab compared to the great fun we had for so long!

So let us have one more moment of silence for the Earnings Game. You were great while you lasted, kid, and it was a pretty good run. Too bad everybody decided to grow up and quit playing it.

TRANSPARENCY: SEEING THROUGH THE SEERS OF WALL STREET

Harrison Hong

One of the hallmarks of the U.S. stock market is its transparency. Unlike their counterparts in some other countries, companies here are supposed to accurately report public balance sheets and a wide array of other information that investors can then use to assess the rewards and risks of their investments. This transparency is generally credited with helping to attract international investors, which boosts stock prices and lowers the cost of capital for U.S. companies. But with the recent revelations of accounting fraud at major companies such as Enron and WorldCom, investor confidence in the U.S. stock market has been deeply shaken. As evidence of this crisis of confidence, there are myriad congressional inquiries under way to investigate the corporate malfeasance and related Wall Street excesses that occurred during the stock market bubble of the late nineties.

An important part of this scrutiny is aimed at sell-side security analysts, the personable prognosticators on CNBC and other networks that offered predictions and recommendations on stocks. Just as companies are supposed to truthfully disclose information, many, particularly individual investors, thought that the earnings forecasts and stock recommendations made by these analysts would be somewhat objective. However, when well-known analysts such as Mary Meeker, Henry Blodget, and Jack Grubman continued to be cheerleaders for dot-com and telecom stocks even as their once sky-high valuations collapsed, the objectivity of sell-side analysts was called into question. The congressional hearings under way are seeking reforms to protect naive individual investors who lost money as a result of these overly optimistic recommendations.

A fundamental question that these hearings are attempting to address is why analysts issued such wildly biased forecasts. There are three possible answers to this question. The first is career concerns or conflicts of interest—analysts are rewarded for biased forecasts by their employers (brokerage houses) who want them to hype stocks so that the brokerage house can garner trading commissions and win underwriting deals. The second is selection bias—analysts follow only stocks that they recommend and do not issue forecasts on those that they do not like. The third is cognitive and behavioral bias—analysts become too attached to the companies that they cover, and lose objectivity.

Not surprisingly, lawmakers are predisposed toward the first explanation, while brokerage houses and their analysts favor the latter two. More broadly, these hearings bring to the foreground the issue of whether sell-side analysts are paid to be objective, as brokerage houses claim, or to hype stocks. Understanding security analysts' career concerns or incentives and their role in the financial system is necessary before lawmakers can enact any effective reforms.

Once relegated to producing boring reports on stocks in the back rooms of brokerages, security analysts became an integral part of Wall Street profit centers over the last decade. Through media outlets such as CNBC, they reach millions of individual investors. At the same time, investment bankers rely on them to help land investment banking deals. As a testament to the growing importance of analysts, CEOs report in surveys that the reputation of a brokerage house's analyst covering the company's industry is an important factor in their choice of underwriter for their initial public and seasoned equity offerings. Analysts who are influential among institutional buyers such as mutual fund managers can also generate hefty trading commissions for their brokerages.

Unfortunately, the growing importance of analysts in a brokerage house's investment banking and trading businesses appears to have deeply compromised their objectivity. A number of studies have found that analyst forecasts, earnings projections, and stock recommendations are optimistically biased and became even more so during the stock market bubble of the late nineties.[1] Importantly, studies also find that an analyst from a brokerage house that has an underwriting relationship with a stock tends to issue more positive predictions than analysts from unaffiliated houses.[2] These findings suggest but do not definitively prove that analysts' biased forecasts are due to their career concerns or conflicts of interest, as opposed to the other explanations such as selection or cognitive biases.

However, anecdotal evidence indicates that such allegations have merit. Congressional inquiries reveal that internal memos at Merrill Lynch, the largest brokerage house in the country, quoted sell-side analysts as saying that they were peddling stocks that they knew to be losers. Moreover, analysts who do not go along with optimistic projections (often made by the management of companies) are reportedly passed over by their brokerage houses in favor of analysts who do.[3] An oft-cited example during the nineties is the departure of Jonathan Cohen and the subsequent hiring of Henry Blodget by Merrill Lynch. Cohen, more old-school in his forecasts of technology stocks, used valuation models and was unable to go along with the numbers given by management. In contrast, Blodget, a history major without any background in business other than experience as a reporter for CNN's business news division, was happy to follow management's optimistic projections. Indeed, even after the collapse of the dot-com stocks that Blodget championed, Merrill Lynch assigned him to cover Microsoft, a highly coveted assignment.

Recent research by myself and Jeffrey Kubik of Syracuse University finds that analysts are systematically rewarded for being optimistic.[4] As the example of the hiring of Blodget and firing of Cohen by Merrill Lynch makes clear, not all analysts are able to be cheerleaders for stocks, depending on their moral concerns or aptitude. So an interesting question is whether those who are optimistic are rewarded with better jobs or assignments. To answer this question, we studied the brokerage house employment and earnings forecast histories of roughly twelve thousand analysts working for six hundred brokerage houses between 1983 and 2000. We found evidence that analysts are indeed systematically rewarded for being optimistic as long as the optimism is within a range of accuracy that maintains their credibility. Analysts who are relatively more optimistic compared to their peers are much less likely to be fired by or to leave a top brokerage house and much more likely to be hired by a better house. They are also given better assignments such as covering large and well-known stocks.

For analysts who cover stocks that are underwritten by their brokerage houses, we find that the dependence of their career prospects on forecast accuracy is significantly attenuated. In other words, analysts are judged less on accuracy when it comes to stocks underwritten by their houses. This finding is a novel piece of evidence supporting the conflict-of-interest allegation. Interestingly, the dependence of career prospects on forecast optimism is also significantly larger for these analysts.

Importantly, we also found that accuracy mattered much less for career concerns in the 1996–2000 period than in earlier years, while forecast optimism mattered much more. So it appears that brokerage houses threw whatever concern they had for objectivity in their research out the window in the midst of the stock market mania of the late 1990s, and the job description for being an analyst became more tied than ever to promoting stocks.

In sum, brokerage houses apparently value analysts who are optimistic, presumably because they help promote stocks and hence generate investment banking business and trading commissions. Moreover, the weight of the evidence strongly indicates that analysts' career concerns and conflicts of interests are the most likely reason behind their wildly optimistic forecasts during the stock market bubble.

Our findings also offer some guidance for policy, as current congressional hearings are debating whether and what types of regulations to impose on brokerage houses. Since analysts are rewarded for promoting stocks generally and not just for stocks underwritten by brokerage houses, the current attention on underwriting relationships as the sole conflict of interest may be too narrow. Also, the post-Enron outcry to regulate explicit incentives, such as having security analysts disclose which stocks they are buying for their personal portfolios, is too narrow. Our findings indicate that implicit incentives such as analyst's reputation, hiring and firing patterns, and allocation of assignments are equally important, if not more so, in affecting analyst behavior. Unfortunately, it is much more difficult to regulate such implicit incentives. Rather, some form of public education or warning to investors to be alert to the recommendations of certain analysts may be more helpful. But at the end of the day investors ultimately need to see through the seers of Wall Street.

ON STOCK OPTIONS

Bob Metcalfe

I founded 3Com, but in June of 1982 the board of directors of the company told me they thought I'd make a better vice president in charge of sales than a chief executive officer. This was a blow. I considered flouncing out the door, slamming it shut, and shouting "You bastards!" as I left.

The thing was, I owned more stock in 3Com than anyone else. They weren't firing me; they just thought I'd be better in marketing. My stake in the company was a strong incentive to stay and try to work out our differences. I stood to profit because my interests coincided with those of the company.

So I've felt in my own experience the way stock ownership can motivate workers to give their best and be team players. If you don't get along with someone and you have no stake in the group, you can just take your basketball and go home, but if you do have a stake, you're more likely to plow ahead and try to work things out.

There are certain rules you should follow, though. Options should be something extra, a bonus on top of a competitive compensation package. A company should never ask employees to buy stock out of their paychecks—especially low-level workers for whom the purchase of stock would represent a high proportion of their net worth. No one should ever be asked to make a financial sacrifice to buy shares in an employer.

A corporation must pay competitive wages. A 401k retirement plan is part of that compensation. A 401k plan should not put too much money in any single company, especially not the one you work for. That's your nest egg, and if things go sour and you lose your job, that's when you most need that nest egg. You don't want everything going wrong at once.

Used well, though, stock options—the chance to purchase corporate stock at a fixed price—can be a great retention tool. (If the company's share price rises, the holder of the option could buy stock at a below-market price and resell at the higher value, pocketing the difference. When stock prices fall below the exercise price of an option, the option is said to be "below water" and is worthless.)

One of the greatest things about stock options is you usually have to wait until they vest (that is, until they can be used). People tend to stay with a company longer under that scenario, so it's a fantastic retention tool.

Options are good at all levels in the company. There's no better way to go than to align the interests of the employees and the corporation. This is especially true for start-ups, but then there's that unfortunate event called "going public" (when a company sells shares over an exchange). After that, the upside is more limited and it's harder to motivate people in the same way.

I'm a Silicon Valley veteran. I've drunk the grape juice of stock options, and I know they work. You'll see people working longer hours and cooperating more with each other. It's ironic to me that socialists—those who think the people should own everything—will do whatever they can to prevent workers from owning stock in the companies they work in.

Of course, some people will be dumb. They'll mortgage their houses based on their unvested options, and so on. It's hard to prevent occasional stupidities. But you have to treat people like adults who entered into certain agreements with their eyes open.

Stock options are a great motivator on the selfish side, but they can also work on the altruistic side. I remember the first huge company picnic at 3Com. It was a shocker to me to see thousands of people there, including spouses and children. I thought, "Holy smoke! Look at all those college tuitions I'm responsible for!" Knowing that some employees were counting on their stock options to pay those bills made me want to work even harder for 3Com. That was a heavy burden of responsibility, a responsibility to succeed, to make good decisions.

Don't get me wrong. Stock ownership is not the same thing as employee-owned companies. One is an incentive; the other is chaos. In employee-owned companies it's hard to figure out who makes the decisions. (In employee-owned groups stock is often evenly split among workers.) Who's the boss? That can be a real mess.

These day, with the Enron stuff (which includes controversy over the energy trading group forcing workers to buy its stock through 401k plans), people are losing sight of the fact that stock options can make people wealthy. I remember a few years ago, Howie Schultz—CEO of the coffee chain Starbucks—was sanctified for offering stock options to low-level workers. If the stock goes up, you're a hero; if not, people will make you out to be a villain.

Anyway, stock options are a good thing, and anyone who says otherwise is talking bullshit.

4. Strategy

Make Sure You Take the Right Fork in the Road—On the Importance of Strategic Direction

WHEN THE SOVIET UNION WAS COLLAPSING ECONOMI-cally, people used to joke that communism was simply the shortest distance between capitalism and capitalism. Communism was a failed strategy for making the average Russian rich.

Similarly, for companies strategy is about direction. What does a company have to do in order to create wealth and stay wealthy? Strategy is about defense as well as offense.

There are many views and schools of strategy. Some people think about strategy opportunistically. They want their companies to be nimble and quick enough to seize an opportunity whenever it is presented and to match their competitors in the market. This makes sense if you are small or in a business that does not require massive capital spending, or if only a portion of your business is under attack, or if a competitor does something really smart that you can duplicate or outdo. If, for example, Wendy's suddenly and successfully begins selling Caesar salads in its fast-food restaurants, McDonald's and Burger King can move to match Wendy's success.

But what do you do if you are Microsoft, whose success is based upon selling its Windows operating system, and Linux—which is available free—makes an appearance on the scene? Or GM, with $100 billion or more invested in sophisticated manufacturing plants, and Toyota invades your turf? Or the now defunct Digital Equipment Company, which made billions of dollars in profits from building state-of-the-art minicomputers that were soon eclipsed by the PC? Or what used to be called Big Steel—U.S. Steel and Bethlehem Steel? These massive companies once dominated the economy. They took raw ore from the ground, smelted it in massive open-hearth blast furnaces, and sold it to companies that made bridges, buildings, cars, and ships. But Big Steel was made extinct by steel from Brazil, Poland, and China, and by the advent of so-called minimills—companies in the United States that recycled cheap scrap steel rather than making steel from ore.

There are as many approaches to strategy as there are strategic problems to solve. In this section, Adrian Slywotzky, who pioneered the concept of "profit zones," and other contributors, such as Michael Porter, who developed the Five Forces concept of strategy, tackle these problems and more. They offer insight not only into which strategy to employ but also about how to think strategically.

J.K.

THE FALL AND RISE OF
STRATEGIC PLANNING

Henry Mintzberg

When strategic planning arrived on the scene in the mid-1960s, corporate leaders embraced it as "the one best way" to devise and implement strategies that would enhance the competitiveness of each business unit. True to the scientific management pioneered by Frederick Taylor, this one best way involved separating thinking from doing and creating a new function staffed by specialists: strategic planners. Planning systems were expected to produce the best strategies as well as step-by-step instructions for carrying out those strategies so that the doers, the managers of businesses, could not get them wrong. As we now know, planning has not exactly worked out that way.

While certainly not dead, strategic planning has long since fallen from its pedestal. But even now, few people fully understand the reason: *strategic planning* is not *strategic thinking*. Indeed, strategic planning often spoils strategic thinking, causing managers to confuse real vision with the manipulation of numbers. And this confusion lies at the heart of the issue: the most successful strategies are visions, not plans.

Strategic planning, as it has been practiced, has really been *strate-*

gic programming, the articulation and elaboration of strategies, or visions, that already exist. When companies understand the difference between planning and strategic thinking, they can get back to what the strategy-making process should be: capturing what the manager learns from all sources (both the soft insights from his or her personal experiences and the experiences of others throughout the organization and the hard data from market research and the like) and then synthesizing that learning into a vision of the direction that the business should pursue.

Organizations disenchanted with strategic planning should not get rid of their planners or conclude that there is no need for programming. Rather, organizations should transform the conventional planning job. Planners should make their contribution *around* the strategy-making process rather than *inside* it. They should supply the formal analyses or hard data that strategic thinking requires, as long as they do it to broaden the consideration of issues rather than to discover the one right answer. They should act as catalysts who support strategy making by aiding and encouraging managers to think strategically. And, finally, they can be programmers of a strategy, helping to specify the series of concrete steps needed to carry out the vision.

By redefining the planner's job, companies will acknowledge the difference between planning and strategic thinking. Planning has always been about *analysis*—about breaking down a goal or set of intentions into steps, formalizing those steps so that they can be implemented almost automatically, and articulating the anticipated consequences or results of each step "I favour a set of analytical techniques for developing strategy," Michael Porter, probably the most widely read writer on strategy, wrote in the *Economist.*[1]

The label "strategic planning" has been applied to all kinds of activities, such as going off to an informal retreat in the mountains to talk about strategy. But call that activity "planning," let conventional planners organize it, and watch how quickly the event becomes formalized (mission statements in the morning, assessment of corporate strengths and weaknesses in the afternoon, strategies carefully articulated by 5 P.M.).

Strategic thinking, in contrast, is about *synthesis*. It involves intuition and creativity. The outcome of strategic thinking is an integrated perspective of the enterprise, a not-too-precisely articulated vision of direction, such as the vision of Jim Clark, the founder of Silicon Graphics, that three-dimensional visual computing is the way to make computers easier to use.

Such strategies often cannot be developed on schedule and immaculately conceived. They must be free to appear at any time and at any place in the organization, typically through messy processes of informal learning that must necessarily be carried out by people at various levels who are deeply involved with the specific issues at hand.

Formal planning, by its very analytical nature, has been and always will be dependent on the preservation and rearrangement of established categories—the existing levels of strategy (corporate, business, functional), the established types of products (defined as "strategic business units"), overlaid on the current units of structure (divisions, departments, etc.). But real strategic change requires not merely rearranging the established categories, but inventing new ones.

Search all those strategic planning diagrams, all those interconnected boxes that supposedly give you strategies, and nowhere will you find a single one that explains the creative act of synthesizing experiences into a novel strategy. Take the example of the Polaroid camera. One day in 1943, Edwin Land's three-year-old daughter asked why she could not immediately see the picture he had just taken of her. Within an hour, this scientist conceived the camera that would transform his company. In other words, Land's vision was the synthesis of the insight evoked by his daughter's question and his vast technical knowledge.

Strategy making needs to function beyond the boxes, to encourage the informal learning that produces new perspectives and new combinations. As the saying goes, life is larger than our categories. Planning's failure to transcend the categories explains why it has discouraged serious organizational change. This failure is why formal planning has promoted strategies that are extrapolated from the past or copied from others. Strategic planning has not only never amounted to strategic thinking but has, in fact, often impeded it. Once managers understand this, they can avoid other costly misadventures caused by applying formal technique, without judgment and intuition, to problem solving.

The Pitfalls of Planning

If you ask conventional planners what went wrong, they will inevitably point to a series of pitfalls for which they, of course, are not responsible. Planners would have people believe that planning fails when it does not receive the support it deserves from top management or when it encounters resistance to change in the organization. But surely no technique ever received more top management support than strategic planning did in its heyday. Strategic planning itself has discouraged the commitment of top managers and has tended to create the very climates its proponents have found so uncongenial to its practice.

The problem is that planning represents a *calculating* style of management, not a *committing* style. Managers with a committing style engage people in a journey. They lead in such a way that everyone on the journey helps shape its course. As a result, enthusiasm inevitably builds along the way. Those with a calculating style fix on a destination and calculate what the group must do to get there, with no concern for the members' preferences. But calculated strategies have no value in and of themselves; to paraphrase the words of sociologist Philip Selznick, strategies take on value only as committed people infuse them with energy.[2]

No matter how much lip service has been paid to the contrary, the very purpose of those who promote conventional strategic planning is to reduce the power of management over strategy making. George Steiner declared, "If an organization is managed by intuitive geniuses there is no need for formal strategic planning. But how many organizations are so blessed? And, if they are, how many times are intuitives correct in their judgments?"[3] Peter Lorange, who is equally prominent in the field, stated, "The CEO should typically not be . . . deeply involved" in the process, but rather be "the designer of [it] in a general sense."[4] How can we expect top managers to be committed to a process that depicts them in this way, especially when its failures to deliver on its promises have become so evident?

At lower levels in the hierarchy, the problem becomes more severe because planning has often been used to exercise blatant control over business managers. No wonder so many middle managers have welcomed the overthrow of strategic planning. All they wanted was a commitment to their own business strategies without having to fight the planners to get it!

The Fallacies of Strategic Planning

An expert has been defined as someone who avoids the many pitfalls on his or her way to the grand fallacy. For strategic planning, the grand fallacy is this: because analysis encompasses synthesis, strategic planning is strategy making. This fallacy itself rests on three fallacious assumptions: that prediction is possible, that strategists can be detached from the subjects of their strategies, and, above all, that the strategy-making process can be formalized.

The Fallacy of Prediction

According to the premises of strategic planning, the world is supposed to hold still while a plan is being developed and then stay on the predicted course while that plan is being implemented. How else to explain those lockstep schedules that have strategies appearing on the first of June, to be approved by the board of directors on the fifteenth? One can just picture competitors waiting for the board's approval, especially if they are Japanese and don't believe in such planning to begin with.

In 1965, Igor Ansoff wrote in his influential book *Corporate Strat-*

egy, "We shall refer to the period for which the firm is able to construct forecasts with an accuracy of, say, plus or minus 20 percent as the *planning horizon* of the firm."[5] What an extraordinary statement! How in the world can any company know the period for which it can forecast with a given accuracy?

The evidence, in fact, points to the contrary. While certain repetitive patterns, such as seasons, may be predictable, the forecasting of discontinuities, such as a technological innovation or a price increase, is virtually impossible. Of course, some people sometimes "see" such things coming. That is why we call them "visionaries." But they create their strategies in much more personalized and intuitive ways.

The Fallacy of Detachment

In her book *Institutionalizing Innovation,* Mariann Jelinek developed the interesting point that strategic planning is to the executive suite what Taylor's work-study methods were to the factory floor—a way to circumvent human idiosyncrasies in order to systematize behavior. "It is through administrative systems that planning and policy are made possible, because the systems capture knowledge *about* the task." Thus "true management by exception, and true policy direction are now possible, solely because management is no longer wholly immersed in the details of the task itself."[6]

According to this viewpoint, if the system does the thinking, then strategies must be detached from operations (or "tactics"), formulation from implementation, thinkers from doers, and so strategists from the objects of their strategies.

The trick, of course, is to get the relevant information up there, so that senior managers on high can be informed about the details down below without having to immerse themselves in them. Planners' favored solution has been "hard data," quantitative aggregates of the detailed "facts" about the organization and its context, neatly packaged and regularly delivered. With such information, senior managers need never leave their executive suites or planners their staff offices. Together they can formulate—work with their heads—so that the hands can get on with implementation.

All of this is dangerously fallacious. Innovation has never been institutionalized. Systems have never been able to reproduce the synthesis created by the genius entrepreneur or even the ordinary competent strategist, and they likely never will.

Ironically, strategic planning has missed one of Taylor's most important messages: work processes must be fully understood before they can be formally programmed. But where in the planning literature is there a shred of evidence that anyone has ever bothered to find out how it is that managers really do make strategies? Instead many practitioners and theorists have wrongly assumed that strategic planning, strategic thinking, and strategy making are all synonymous, at least in best practice.

The problem with the hard data that are supposed to inform the senior manager is they can have a decidedly soft underbelly. Such data take time to harden, which often makes them late. They tend to lack richness; for example, they often exclude the qualitative. And they tend to be overly aggregated, missing important nuances. These are the reasons managers who rely on formalized information, such as market-research reports or accounting statements in business and opinion polls in government, tend to be detached in more ways than one. Study after study has shown that the most effective managers rely on some of the softest forms of information, including gossip, hearsay, and various other intangible scraps of information.

My research and that of many others demonstrates that strategy making is an immensely complex process, which involves the most sophisticated, subtle, and, at times, subconscious elements of human thinking.

A strategy can be deliberate. It can realize the specific intentions of senior management, for example, to attack and conquer a new market. But a strategy can also be emergent, meaning that a convergent pattern has formed among the different actions taken by the organization one at a time.

In other words, strategies can develop inadvertently, without the conscious intention of senior management, often through a process of learning. A salesperson convinces a different kind of customer to try a product. Other salespeople follow up with their customers, and the next thing management knows, its products have penetrated a new market. When it takes the form of fits and starts, discoveries based on serendipitous events, and the recognition of unexpected patterns, learning inevitably plays *a*, if not *the*, crucial role in the development of novel strategies.

Contrary to what traditional planning would have us believe, deliberate strategies are not necessarily good, nor are emergent strategies necessarily bad. I believe that all viable strategies have emergent and deliberate qualities, since all must combine some degree of flexible learning with some degree of cerebral control.

Vision is unavailable to those who cannot "see" with their own eyes. Real strategists get their hands dirty digging for ideas, and real strategies are built from the occasional nuggets they uncover. These are not people who abstract themselves from the daily details; they are the ones who immerse themselves in them while being able to abstract the strategic messages from them. The big picture is painted with little strokes.

The Fallacy of Formalization

The failure of strategic planning is the failure of systems to do better than, or even nearly as well as, human beings. Formal systems, mechanical or otherwise, have offered no improved means of dealing with the information overload of human brains; indeed, they have often made matters worse. All the promises about artificial intelligence, expert systems, and the like improving if not replacing human intuition never materialized at the strategy level. Formal systems could certainly process more information, at least hard information. But they could never *internalize* it, *comprehend* it, *synthesize* it. In a literal sense, planning could not learn.

Formalization implies a rational sequence, from analysis through administrative procedure to eventual action. But strategy making as a learning process can proceed in the other direction too. We think in order to act, to be sure, but we also act in order to think. We try things, and those experiments that work converge gradually into viable patterns that become strategies. This is the very essence of strategy making as a learning process.

Formal procedures will never be able to forecast discontinuities, inform detached managers, or create novel strategies. Far from providing strategies, planning could not proceed without their prior existence. All this time, therefore, strategic planning has been misnamed. It should have been called strategic programming, distinguished from other useful things that planners can do, and promoted as a process to formalize, when necessary, the consequences of strategies that have already been developed. In short, we should drop the label "strategic planning" altogether.

Planning, Plans, and Planners

Two important messages have been conveyed through all the difficulties encountered by strategic planning. But only one of them has been widely accepted in the planning community: business-unit managers must take full and effective charge of the strategy-making process. The lesson that has still not been accepted is that managers will never be able to take charge through a formalized process. What then can be the roles for planning, for plans, and for planners in organizations?

Planners and managers have different advantages. Planners lack managers' authority to make commitments, and, more important, managers' access to soft information critical to strategy making. But because of their time pressures, managers tend to favor action over reflection and the oral over the written, which can cause them to overlook important analytical information. Strategies cannot be created by analysis, but their development can be helped by it.

Planners, on the other hand, have the time and, most important, the inclination to analyze. They have critical roles to play alongside line managers, but not as conventionally conceived. They should work in the spirit of what I like to call a "soft analyst," whose intent is to pose the right questions rather than to find the right answers. That way, complex issues get opened up to thoughtful consideration instead of being closed down prematurely by snap decisions.

Planning as Strategic Programming

Planning cannot generate strategies. But given viable strategies, it can program them; it can make them operational. For one supermarket chain that a colleague and I studied, planning was the articulation, justification, and elaboration of the strategic vision that the company's leader already had. Planning was not deciding to expand into shopping centers, but explicating to what extent and when, with how many stores, and on what schedule.

An appropriate image for the planner might be that person left behind in a meeting, together with the chief executive, after everyone else has departed. All of the strategic decisions that were made are symbolically strewn about the table. The CEO turns to the planner and says, "There they all are; clean them up. Package them neatly so that we can tell everyone about them and get things going." In more formal language, strategic programming involves three steps: codifications, elaboration, and conversion of strategies.

Codification means clarifying and expressing the strategies in terms sufficiently clear to render them formally operational, so that their consequences can be worked out in detail. This requires a good deal of interpretation and careful attention to what might be lost in articulation: nuance, subtlety, qualification. A broad vision, like capturing the market for a new technology, is one thing, but a specific plan—35 percent market share, focusing on the high end—is quite another.

Elaboration means breaking down the codified strategies into substrategies and ad hoc programs as well as overall action plans specifying what must be done to realize each strategy: build four new factories and hire two hundred new workers, for example.

And conversion means considering the effects of the changes on the organization's operations—effects on budgets and performance controls, for example. Here a kind of great divide must be crossed from the nonroutine world of strategies and programs to the routine world of budgets and objectives. Objectives have to be restated and budgets reworked, and policies and standard operating procedures reconsidered, to take into account the consequences of the specific changes.

One point must be emphasized. Strategic programming is not "the one best way" or even necessarily a good way. Managers don't always need to program their strategies formally. Sometimes they must leave their strategies flexible, as broad visions, to adapt to a changing environment. Only when an organization is sure of the relative stability of its environment and is in need of the tight coordination of a myriad of intricate operations (as is typically the case of airlines with their needs for complicated scheduling), does such strategic programming make sense.

Plans as Tools to Communicate and Control

Why program strategy? The most obvious reason is for coordination, to ensure that everyone in the organization pulls in the same direction. Plans in the form of programs—schedules, budgets, and so on—can be prime media to communicate strategic intentions and to control the individual pursuit of them, in so far, of course, as common direction is considered to be more important than individual discretion.

Plans can also be used to gain the tangible as well as moral support of influential outsiders. Written plans inform financiers, suppliers, government agencies, and others about the intentions of the organization so that these groups can help it achieve its plans.

Planners as Strategy Finders

As noted, some of the most important strategies in organizations emerge without the intention or sometimes even the awareness of top managers. Fully exploiting these strategies, though, often requires that they be recognized and then broadened in their impact, like taking a new use for a product accidentally discovered by a salesperson and turning it into a major new business. It is obviously the responsibility of managers to discover and anoint these strategies. But planners can assist managers in finding these fledgling strategies in their organizations' activities or in those of competing organizations.

Planners can snoop around places they might not normally visit to find patterns amid the noise of failed experiments, seemingly random activities, and messy learning. They can discover new ways of doing or perceiving things, for example, spotting newly uncovered markets and understanding their implied new products.

Planners as Analysts

In-depth examinations of what planners actually do suggest that the effective ones spend a good deal of time not so much doing or even encouraging planning as carrying out analyses of specific issues. Planners are obvious candidates for the job of studying the hard data and ensuring that managers consider the results in the strategy-making process.

Much of this analysis will necessarily be quick and dirty, that is, in the time frame and on the ad hoc basis required by managers. It may include industry or competitive analyses as well as internal studies, including the use of computer models to analyze trends in the organization.

But some of the best models that planners can offer managers are simply alternative conceptual interpretations of their world, such as a new way to view the organization's distribution system. As Arie de Geus, the one-time head of planning at Royal Dutch/Shell, wrote in his *HBR* article "Planning as Learning" (March-April 1988), "The real purpose of effective planning is not to make plans but to change the . . . mental models that . . . decision makers carry in their heads."

Planners as Catalysts

The planning literature has long promoted the role of catalyst for the planner, but not as I will describe it here. It is not planning that planners should be urging on their organizations so much as any form of behavior that can lead to effective performance in a given situation. Sometimes that may even mean criticizing formal planning itself.

When they act as catalysts, planners do not enter the black box of strategy making; they ensure that the box is occupied with active line managers. In other words, they encourage managers to think about the future in creative ways.

Such planners see their job as getting others to question conventional wisdom and especially helping people out of conceptual ruts (which managers with long experience in stable strategies are apt to dig themselves into). To do their jobs, they may have to use provocation or shock tactics like raising difficult questions and challenging conventional assumptions.

Left- and Right-Handed Planners

Two very different kinds of people populate the planning function. One is an analytic thinker, who is closer to the conventional image of the planner. He or she is dedicated to bringing order to the organization. Above all, this person programs intended strategies and sees to it that they are communicated clearly. He or she also carries out analytic studies to ensure consideration of the necessary hard data and carefully scrutinizes strategies intended for implementation. We might label him or her the *right-handed planner*.

The second is less conventional but present nonetheless in many organizations. This planner is a creative thinker who seeks to open up the strategy-making process. As a "soft analyst," this planner is prepared to conduct more quick and dirty studies. He or she likes to find strategies in strange places and to encourage others to think strategically. This person is somewhat more inclined toward the intuitive processes identified with the brain's right hemisphere. We might call him or her the *left-handed planner*.

Many organizations need both types, and it is top management's job to ensure that it has them in appropriate proportions. Organizations need people to bring order to the messy world of management as well as challenge the conventions that managers and especially their organizations develop. Some organizations (those big, machine-like bureaucracies concerned with mass production) may favor the right-handed planners, while others (the loose, flexible "adhocracies," or project organizations) may favor the left-handed ones. But both kinds of organization need both types of planners, if only to offset their natural tendencies. And, of course, some organizations, like those highly professionalized hospitals and educational systems that have been forced to waste so much time doing ill-conceived strategic planning, may prefer to have very few of either!

The Formalization Edge

We human beings seem predisposed to formalize our behavior. But we must be careful not to go over the formalization edge. No doubt we must formalize to do many of the things we wish to in modern society. That is why we have organizations. But the experiences of what has been labeled strategic planning teach us that there are limits. These limits must be understood, especially for complex and creative activities like strategy making.

Strategy making is not an isolated process. It does not happen just because a meeting is held with that label. To the contrary, strategy making is a process interwoven with all that it takes to manage an organization. Systems do not think, and when they are used for more than the facilitation of human thinking, they can prevent thinking.

Three decades of experience with strategic planning have taught us about the need to loosen up the process of strategy making rather than trying to seal it off by arbitrary formalization. Through all the false starts and excessive rhetoric, we have learned what planning is not and what it cannot do. But we have also learned what planning is and what it can do, and perhaps of greater use, what planners themselves can do beyond planning. We have also learned how the literature of management can get carried away and, more important, about the appropriate place for analysis in organizations.

The story of strategic planning, in other words, has taught us not only about formal technique itself but also about how organizations function and how managers do and don't cope with that functioning. Most significant, it has told us something about how we think as human beings, and that we sometimes stop thinking.

"LOCATION, LOCATION, LOCATION": CLUSTERS AND COMPETITION

Michael Porter

Thinking about competition and strategy at the company level has been dominated by what goes on inside companies. Thinking about the competitiveness of nations and states has focused on the economy as a whole, with national economic policy seen as the dominant influence. In both competition and competitiveness the role of location is all but absent. If anything, the tendency has been to see location as diminishing in importance. Globalization allows companies to source capital, goods, and technology from anywhere and to locate operations wherever it is most cost-effective. Governments are widely seen as losing their influence over competition to global forces.

This perspective, although widespread, does not accord with competitive reality. In *The Competitive Advantage of Nations* (1990) I put forward a theory of national, state, and local competitiveness within the context of a global economy. This theory gives clusters a prominent role. Clusters are geographic concentrations of interconnected companies, specialized suppliers, service providers, firms in related industries, and associated institutions (for example, universities, standards agencies, and trade associations) that compete but also cooperate in particular fields. Critical masses of unusual competitive success in particular business areas, clusters are a striking feature of virtually every national, regional, state, and even metropolitan economy, especially in more economically advanced nations.

While the phenomenon of clusters in one form or another has been recognized and explored in a range of literatures, clusters cannot be understood independent of a broader theory of competition and the influence of location in the global economy. The prevalence of clusters in economies, rather than isolated firms and industries, reveals important insights into the nature of competition and the role of location in competitive advantage. Even though old reasons for clustering have diminished in importance with globalization, new roles of clusters in competition have taken on growing importance in an increasingly complex, knowledge-based, and dynamic economy.

The cluster concept represents a new way of thinking about national, state, and city economies, and points to new roles for companies, governments, and other institutions striving to enhance competitiveness. The presence of clusters suggests that much of competitive advantage lies outside a given company or even outside its industry, residing instead in the locations of its business units. The odds of building a world-class mutual fund company are much higher in Boston than in most any other location; a similar statement applies to textile-related companies in North Carolina and South Carolina, high-performance auto companies in Germany, or fashion shoe companies in Italy.

The importance of clusters creates new management agendas that are rarely recognized. Companies have a tangible stake in the business environments in which they are located, and it goes far beyond taxes, electricity costs, and wage rates. The health of the cluster is important to the health of the company. A company may actually benefit from the presence of local competitors. Trade associations can be competitive assets as well as lobbying and social organizations.

Clusters also create new roles for government. The proper macro-economic policies for fostering competitiveness are increasingly well understood, but they are necessary and not sufficient. Government's more decisive influences are often at the microeconomic level. Removing obstacles to the growth and upgrading of existing and emerging clusters should be a priority. Clusters are a driving force in increasing exports, and they serve as magnets for attracting foreign investment. They constitute a forum in which new types of dialogue can, and must, take place among firms, government agencies, and institutions (such as schools, universities, and public utilities).

What Is a Cluster?

A cluster is a geographically proximate group of interconnected companies and associated institutions in a particular field, linked by commonalities and complementarities. The geographic scope of a cluster can range from a single city or state to a country or even a network of neighboring countries. Clusters take varying forms depending on their depth and sophistication, but most include end-product or service companies; suppliers of specialized inputs, components, machinery, and services; financial institutions; and firms in related industries. Clusters also often include firms in downstream industries (that is, channels of customers); producers of complementary products; specialized infrastructure providers; government and other institutions providing specialized training, education, information, research, and technical support (such as universities, think tanks, and vocational training providers); and standardsetting agencies. Government agencies that significantly influence a cluster can be considered part of it. Finally, many clusters include trade associations and other collective private-sector bodies that support cluster members.

Location and Competition

In recent decades, thinking about the influence of location on competition has taken a relatively simple view of how companies compete. Competition has been seen as largely static and as resting on cost minimization in relatively closed economies. Here what is decisive, is comparative advantage in factors of production (labor and capital)—or, in the most recent analyses, economies of scale.

Yet this picture fails to represent real competition. Competition is dynamic and rests on innovation and the search for strategic differences. Three conditions contribute to rendering factor inputs per se less valuable: the expanded input supply as more countries open to the global economy, the greater efficiency of national and international factor markets, and the diminishing factor intensity of competition. Instead, close linkages with buyers, suppliers, and other institutions contribute importantly not only to efficiency but also to the rate of improvement and innovation. While extensive vertical integration (for example, in-house production of parts, services, or training) may have once been the norm, a more dynamic environment can render vertical integration inefficient, ineffective, and inflexible.

In this broader and more dynamic view of competition, location affects competitive advantage through its influence on productivity and especially on productivity growth. Productivity is the value created per day of work and unit of capital or physical resources employed. Generic factor inputs themselves are usually abundant and readily accessed. Prosperity depends on the productivity with which factors are used and upgraded in a particular location.

The productivity and prosperity of a location rest not on the industries in which its firms compete but on how they compete. Firms can be more productive in any industry—shoes, agriculture, or semiconductors—if they employ sophisticated methods, use advanced technology, and offer unique products and services. All industries can employ high technology; all industries can be knowledge-intensive. The term *high-tech*, normally used to refer to fields such as information technology and biotechnology, thus has questionable relevance. A more descriptive term might be *enabling technology*, signifying tools that enhance technology in many industries.

Conversely, the mere presence of high-tech in an industry does not by itself guarantee prosperity if the firms are unproductive. Traditional distinctions between industries, such as *high-tech* or low-tech, manufacturing or services, resource-based or knowledge-based, have in themselves little relevance. The proper goal is to improve the productivity of all industries, enhancing prosperity both directly and indirectly, as the improved productivity of one industry increases the productivity of others.

The prosperity of a location depends, then, on the productivity of what firms located there choose to do. This sets the wages that can be sustained and the profits that can be earned. Both domestic and foreign firms contribute to the prosperity of a location, based on the productivity of their activities there. The presence of sophisticated foreign firms often enhances the productivity of domestic firms and vice versa.

The sophistication and productivity with which companies compete in a location are strongly influenced by the quality of the business environment. Firms cannot employ advanced logistical techniques, for example, unless a high-quality transportation infrastructure is available. Firms cannot compete using high-service strategies unless they can access well-educated people. Firms cannot operate efficiently under onerous amounts of regulatory red tape, requiring endless dialogue with government, or under a court system that fails to resolve disputes quickly and fairly. All of these situations consume resources and management time without contributing to customer value. The effects of some aspects of the business environment, such as the road system, corporate tax rates, and the legal system, cut across all industries. These economywide (or horizontal) areas can represent binding constraints on competitiveness in developing economies. For more advanced economies, however—and, increasingly, everywhere—the more decisive aspects of the business environment are often cluster-specific (for example, the presence of particular types of suppliers or university departments). Cluster thinking thus assumes an important role in both company strategy and economic policy.

Clusters and New Business Formation

Many, if not most, new businesses (that is, headquarters, not branch offices or ancillary facilities) form within existing clusters rather than at isolated locations. This occurs for a variety of reasons. First, clusters provide inducement to entry through better information about opportunities. The existence of a cluster in itself signals an opportunity. Individuals working somewhere in or near the cluster more easily perceive gaps to fill in products, services, or suppliers. Having had this insight, these individuals more readily leave established firms to start new ones aimed at filling the perceived gaps.

Opportunities perceived at cluster locations are pursued there because barriers to entry are lower than elsewhere. Needed assets, skills, inputs, and staff, often readily available at the cluster location, can be assembled more easily for a new enterprise. Local financial institutions and investors, already possessing familiarity with the cluster, may require a lower risk premium on capital. In addition, the cluster often presents a significant local market. The entrepreneur seeking to benefit from established relationships often prefers to stay in the same community. All of these factors—lower entry barriers, multiple potential local customers, established relationships, and the presence of other local firms that have "made it"—reduce the perceived risks of entry. The barriers to exit at a cluster can also be lower due to reduced need for specialized investment, deeper markets for specialized assets, and other factors.

While local entrepreneurs are likely entrants to a cluster, entrepreneurs based outside a cluster frequently relocate, sooner or later, to a cluster location. The same lower entry barriers attract them, as does the potential to create more economic value from their ideas and skills at the cluster location or the ability to operate more productively.

Established companies based in noncluster locations (foreign and domestic) often establish subsidiaries at clusters, seeking the productivity benefits and innovation advantages discussed above. The presence of an established cluster not only lowers the barriers to entry for outside firms but also reduces, as noted above, the perceived risk (this is particularly the case where other "foreign" firms have already moved into the cluster). Many firms have relocated entire business units to a cluster location or have designated their cluster-based subsidiary as their regional or world headquarters for that particular line of business.

The advantages of a cluster in new business formation can play a major role in speeding up the process of cluster innovation. Large companies often face constraints or impediments of various sorts to innovating. Spin-off companies often pick up the slack, sometimes with the blessing of the original company. (A large company, for example, may support a smaller firm serving a niche it cannot address economically.) Larger companies in a cluster develop close relationships with innovative smaller ones, helping in their establishment, and acquiring them if they become successful.

The Socioeconomy of Clusters

The mere presence of firms, suppliers, and institutions in a location creates the potential for economic value, but it does not necessarily ensure the realization of this potential. Social glue binds clusters together, contributing to the value creation process. Many of the competitive advantages of clusters depend on the free flow of information, the discovery of value-adding exchanges or transactions, the willingness to align agendas and to work across organizations, and strong motivation for improvement. Relationships, networks, and a sense of common interest undergird these circumstances. The social structure of clusters thus takes on central importance.

A growing economic and organizational literature examines the importance of network relationships found in effective companies and communities. Economic activities are seen as embedded in ongoing social relationships. Much research undertakes to map these networks, to understand the number of nodes feasible, and to verify the importance of repeated interaction and of time in making networks effective. Examinations of the structure of networks has revealed that the social relationships among individuals (their "social capital") greatly facilitates access to important resources and information.

Cluster theory focuses on how juxtaposition of economically linked firms and institutions in a specific geographic location affects competitiveness. While some cluster advantages are largely independent of social relationships (for example, available pools of capital or employees), most, if not all, have at least a relationship component. A firm's identification with and sense of community, derived from membership in a cluster, and its civic engagement beyond its own narrow confines as a single entity translate directly, according to cluster theory, into economic glue. Cluster theory further extends notions of social capital by exploring the mechanisms through which a structure of network relationships within a geographic location produces benefits for particular firms. The benefits of trust and organizational permeability, fostered through repeated interactions and a sense of mutual dependence within a region or city, clearly grease the interactions within clusters that enhance productivity, spur innovation, and result in the creation of new businesses.

Cluster theory bridges network theory and competition. A cluster is a form of a network that occurs within a geographic location, in which the proximity of firms and institutions ensures certain forms of commonality and increases the frequency and impact of interactions. Well-functioning clusters move beyond hierarchical networks to become lattices of numerous overlapping and fluid connections among individuals, firms, and institutions. These connections are repeated, constantly shift, and often expand to related industries. Strong ties and weak ties occur together. Modest changes in the pattern of relationships within a cluster may have significant consequences for productivity and the direction of innovation.

Network theory can greatly inform understanding of the way clusters work and of how clusters can become more productive. As will be discussed further, successful cluster upgrading depends on paying explicit attention to relationship building, an important characteristic of cluster development initiatives. Trade associations play important roles in facilitating the formation of networks.

For its part, cluster theory also provides a way to connect theories of networks, social capital, and civic engagement more tightly to business competition and economic prosperity—and to extend them. Cluster theory identifies who needs to be in the network for what relationships and why. Clusters offer a new way of exploring the mechanisms by which networks, social capital, and civic engagement affect competition and market outcomes. Cluster theory helps isolate the most beneficial forms of networks. Relationship and trust resulting in cartels, for example, undermine economic value, while those facilitating open information exchange between customers and suppliers enhance it. The workings of clusters also suggest the efficiency and flexibility possible in network structures built on proximity and informal local links compared to those defined by formal or hierarchical relationships between companies or between institutions and companies. Cluster theory may also reveal how network relationships form and how social capital is acquired, helping to unscramble questions of cause and effect; for example, do strong relationships and trust arise because a cluster exists, or are clusters more likely to develop from existing networks? Cluster theory, then, helps illuminate the causes of network structure, the substance of network activity, and the link between network characteristics and outcomes.

PROFITS DON'T JUST HAPPEN: THE SEARCH FOR THE EVER-SHIFTING PROFIT ZONE

Adrian J. Slywotzky

There was a time when market share was the best predictor and the best guarantor of profitability. But in the last decade the classic rules of strategy have broken down in a fundamental way. Consider the experiences of IBM, DEC, Kodak, United Airlines, U.S. Steel, GM, Ford, and a host of other companies that succeeded fantastically in winning the market share game but didn't enjoy the profitability that was supposed to follow. Several of these companies in recent years have reversed their strategic thinking about market share and profitability and have initiated radical changes in their business designs, achieving in the process some of the success that had been eluding them.

Such success in today's marketplace begins with several questions:

- How does profit really happen in our industry?
- Where is the "profit zone"—the area within a specific industry in which profit is allowed?

■ How do I design my business model in order to reach and operate in the profit zone?

Where Will Profit Be Allowed?

Value migration plays itself out in discrete patterns. In the computer industry, for example, the pattern has been linear over time, as the opportunity for greatest profit growth shifted from mainframes to mini-computers to PCs to some of the subsets of the PC business. Symptomatic of this process is what happened to Microsoft. The very year it won ultimate leadership of the desktop the ground started to change again as the Internet began to gain viability. Microsoft executives were faced with deciding whether to pledge allegiance to their traditional success model or move to the next one to stay ahead of customer shifts and the competition. They chose the latter.

Perhaps one of the toughest and most difficult patterns we discovered in our research on value migration was the shift to a no-profit industry. For example, net profit generation in the airline industry—that is, plain profit, not profit in excess of the cost of capital—has been zero for the last ten or twenty years. Unfortunately, in the next several years examples like this will not be the exception; they are becoming a familiar part of our economy.

As no-profit zones grow, managers must be able to anticipate where structural unprofitability will occur and then, if they are to significantly improve both the health of their organization and shareholder return, move away from it by changing their business design.

Understanding Profits on Your Own Terms

Profitability must be understood for each company on its own terms. For example, Intel, as well as other consumer electronics companies and PC makers, creates profit from a simple time-based profit model. After a new product is introduced, cost comes down, but price comes down more rapidly. Large profit margins for these companies happen within the first four to five months of a new product launch. In this industry a company may work very hard, have very talented engineers, and spend a lot of capital on factories. But unless it builds a business design that creates and maintains a two-year lead over the competition, it will reach only the break-even point.

Different still is the way profitability is created at a company such as SMH, the parent company of Swatch. SMH has built a product pyramid in which the layers perform different functions within the overall system. The Swatch layer at the base of the pyramid serves as a firewall brand, making it difficult or impossible for competitors to develop the economics that would allow them to move up the pyramid. But 70 to 80 percent of the company's profitability is derived from the three or four high-priced, high-margin, luxury watch brands at the top. This profit model was first invented by GM in the 1920s, and today it is practiced by Mattel, Nokia, and companies in other industries where the price points in the product line allow this kind of stratification.

General Electric has probably answered better than anyone else the question of how manufacturers can make money. In the early part of the decade GE's business model was based on the principle of either being number one or number two or getting out of the business. At that time, being the market-share leader was the pathway to highest profitability. By the mid-1980s, however, that was no longer true because GE's customers—everyone from Wal-Mart to Ford to GM to Boeing—began to focus on getting the lowest price.

The business model dictated by this shift was based not only on being number one in market share but also on securing the number one position in productivity. High market share without the best productivity would no longer ensure profitability. That model worked for several years, but by the early '90s, being number one in market share and being

My Years with General Motors

ALFRED P. SLOAN JR.

■ It is not easy to say why one management is successful and another is not. The causes of success or failure are deep and complex, and chance plays a part. Experience has convinced me, however, that for those who are responsible for a business, two important factors are motivation and opportunity. The former is supplied in good part by incentive compensation, the latter by decentralization.

But the matter does not end there. It has been a thesis of this book that good management rests on a reconciliation of centralization and decentralization, or "decentralization with co-ordinated control."

Each of the conflicting elements brought together in this concept has its unique results in the operation of a business. From decentralization we get initiative, responsibility, development of personnel, decisions close to the facts, flexibility—in short, all the qualities necessary for an organization to adapt to new conditions. From co-ordination we get efficiencies and economies. It must be apparent that co-ordinated decentralization is not an easy concept to apply. There is no hard and fast rule for sorting out the various responsibilities and the best way to assign them. The balance which is struck between corporate and divisional responsibilities varies according to what is being decided, the circumstances of the time, past experience, and the temperaments and skills of the executives involved. ■

From Alfred P. Sloan Jr., *My Years with General Motors,* edited by John McDonald with Catherine Stevens (Doubleday, 1963).

the most productive in hardware was not enough to create sustained profit growth—at least not from selling the product, the "box," alone. The profit was in selling the full package, so GE began to develop services, solutions, and other ancillary activities to ensure profit growth.

Unfortunately, business is not as straightforward as it used to be. While at least two dozen profit models exist today, another dozen will likely be discovered in the next twelve to eighteen months. However, the models we know about today can lead managers to powerful new ways of thinking that can be used immediately.

Every company needs to create its own customized list of no-profit zones and then determine how profit happens in the business. Ask yourself:

- What is the profit model by which my company makes money?
- Is the company constructed and aligned to support the profit model, or is it set up to contradict the model?
- Will today's profit model endure into tomorrow, or must a different way of creating profitability be invented to ensure success in the next five-year cycle?

Reinventors Think Differently About Profitability

An extraordinary subset of companies that we refer to as "reinventors" (e.g., ABB, GE, Microsoft) have become almost habitually customer-centric and profit-centric. They change their business design every five years, and they expect that process to continue.

One of the common characteristics of all reinventors is that they think differently about profitability and the customer. They challenge the assumption of who is the most important customer in the system. They focus on finding out which subsets of the customer base will have the greatest impact on future profitability and future success in the industry. And they work hard to build their next-generation business design around the customers that will matter most in driving the success of the system in the future.

Core Competencies

VICTORIA GRIFFITH

■ Companies should follow their "core competencies," wrote Gary Hamel and C. K. Prahalad in their 1994 book *Competing for the Future.*

The notion is deceptively simple: that corporation should do what they are best at doing. It's so appealing that even art schools and self-improvement courses these days talk about following personal core competencies.

Yet if managers understood the concept only on this level, they would soon be in trouble. Should typewriter manufacturers stick with typewriters, even when the machines are becoming extinct? Of course not. That's why a rigorous application of the core competencies model is necessary.

Core competency is not the same as a product line. Nike's core competency is not making tennis shoes, but design and merchandising. McDonald's core competency is not making hamburgers, but providing convenience at mealtime. Sony's core competence is not producing electronics, but miniaturization.

To fit Hamel and Prahalad's definition, a core competency must create customer value. It should allow the company to access a number of markets. A core competency should be difficult for competitors to imitate, so it should be derived from a complex harmonization of organizational procedures and know-how, not simply a one-off technical skill or product.

Successful companies constantly reassess their core competencies to survive. Consider the battle between Apple Computer and IBM in the 1970s. IBM made the mistake of judging its core competency to be production of mainframe computers. That narrow definition allowed Apple to come in and steal the personal computer market. "At worst, laggards follow the path of greatest familiarity," wrote Hamel and Prahalad. "Challengers, on the other hand, follow the path of greatest opportunity, wherever it leads." ■

This concentration on the customer is an almost total reversal of the traditional value chain, which starts with assets and core competencies and then moves toward the customer. Reinventor companies first ask what the top priorities of the customer are and how those priorities are changing. Then they check to see if these priorities flow through the rest of the system. They focus on the channels through which the customer buys and the offerings that must be put together. Finally, they determine what assets and core competencies will be required to meet their customers' needs.

Perhaps the most remarkable focus and achievement of the reinventor companies is their understanding of a new need to protect profitability, not only against competitors but also against growing customer power. A business design with no source of strategic control is like a vessel with a hole in the bottom—it will sink sooner than it needs to. Reinventors build multiple sources of strategic control into their business models. As a result, they experience greater longevity for their current business designs, lower volatility in their earnings, and remarkably stable (and even increasing) margins. Strategic control allows them not only to protect their profitability but to enhance it over time.

By examining these reinventors and the new way of thinking they represent, it's possible for a group of managers to work through a different thought process in developing a strategy—a next-generation business design.

Placing the Customer First

The rules have changed in a fundamental way and are continuing to be modified. Many of our traditional axioms have been reversed, calling for a reversal in our thinking. This new style of thought leads to a new type of hard work—not only in understanding the organization, but also in understanding the customer and in understanding exactly how profit happens. By placing the customer at the front of the process and ensuring that all other actions follow from that point, however, the company can reap incredible rewards—rewards in profitability and in the advantage of living a step ahead of the change curve within the industry.

In the next five to seven years company leaders will place increasing importance on strategic imagination and creativity. Each of the businesses built by reinventors was unique in its category. When its uniqueness was threatened by imitation, every reinventor company moved to create a next-generation model to retain its uniqueness—a model that enabled it to be the first choice of its most important customers, to be the most profitable organization in its industry, and to have the most protected profit stream.

By taking advantage of the learnings these companies have created, adapting some of their techniques, and using some of their processes and styles of thought, every company can invent a next-generation business design to exploit its own profit zone.

THE SYSTEM: MEASURING AND MANAGING YOUR WAY TO SUCCESS USING THE BALANCED SCORECARD

Arthur M. Schneiderman

The Balanced Scorecard (BSC) is a management system that evolved from the recognition that management based solely on financial performance was tantamount to steering a ship by its wake. Its origins lie in Total Quality Management, where measurement focuses on nonfinancial measures such as quality, cycle time, and yield. But as with any evolving concept, remnants of its earlier manifestations persist today, along with deviations from its main track. Consequently, defining the BSC is impossible, since in today's environment it exists in many different, albeit valuable, forms.[1]

The major uses of these BSCs are as:

1. A project management tool for ensuring *accountability* for initiative progress against plan
2. A training tool to *educate* employees on the use of nonfinancial measures

3. A *communications* tool to translate strategy into terms that employees can more easily understand
4. A tool to monitor key *process control* measures
5. A tool to *manage* unwanted *trade-offs*
6. A *goals deployment* approach for cascading and aligning execution tactics down through the organization
7. A management system for focusing scarce resources on the most strategically leveraged improvements needed for successful *strategy execution*

The elements of this list are not mutually exclusive in that any given scorecard can be used for multiple purposes. However, the list is roughly in order of degree of difficulty. Whatever the scorecard's chosen purpose, it is characterized by the process followed for its creation, use, and refinement as well as the actual output document itself. This article will focus on the last and latest of these various BSCs.

The Balanced Scorecard is currently being promoted for the seventh use: as a new management approach for linking strategy to action. Although both its consultant proponents and internal champions declare its success in achieving that objective, there is little evidence that their assertions are anything more than the expected exuberance of zealots.

Yet the logic of the BSC remains compelling: determine what has to happen in order to achieve the strategic objectives, and deploy those guidelines to the action agents who then make it all happen. Now go one step further: develop a set of measures and goals that will provide evidence that those actions are being taken and that they have the desired effect.

The problem of linking strategy to actions is not new. But executives have been reluctant to admit this disconnect in the absence of any credible solution. The BSC, by providing a solution in principle, allows them to finally acknowledge this critical failure in their past strategic planning efforts.

Reality and theory, however, do not always converge when the details of actual implementations are viewed through independent eyes. Thus it might make sense to just write the Balanced Scorecard off as the fad of the '90s. Yet there remains that underlying and still unsatisfied need for a process that will assist in the noble effort to guide the organization down its path of greatest reward.

That process must include a step-by-step recipe that is capable of producing the desired result. But that's not enough. Providing the missing link between strategy and action represents a major cultural change. As such, it is subject to the same set of requirements common to any such change initiative. Without them, the organization's immune system, which is as important to its health as it is to any individual's, will be triggered and the desired change rejected. Satisfying the cultural requirements provides the needed environment for nurturing the organization's long-term acceptance of this desirable new process. So for the successful implementation and eventual internalization of the BSC, there exist both cultural and structural prerequisites, the former common to any change initiative and the latter unique to the BSC process itself.

Cultural Requirements

In the early 1980s I had the opportunity to study world-class implementations of Total Quality Management (TQM). I visited companies throughout the world as well as the current gurus of that movement— leaders such as Deming, Juran, Imai, Ohno, and Ishikawa, for example. It became clear that successful implementations of TQM shared six characteristics, all of which were necessary:

1. Top management commitment
2. A sense of urgency
3. A systematic approach

4. A deployment strategy based on pilot projects
5. Eventual organization-wide involvement
6. Integration into all existing management systems

Over the years I have witnessed other similar change initiatives, most recently the BSC. I came to realize that these six requirements are shared in common by any significant organizational change, be it TQM, material requirements planning (MRP) activity-based costing (ABC), or more recently the BSC.

One way of defining organizational culture is as the unwritten guidelines that individuals rely on to make their day-to-day decisions. In other words, organizations have written policies and procedures that specify the appropriate action to take in a specific circumstance. But it is impossible for them to cover every conceivable situation. In the absence of a prescribed answer, individuals facing a decision fall back on the organization's culture to guide them. It captures, in an often intangible format, "the way we do things around here." Consequently, I've chosen to call these six the cultural requirements.

Since my development of that list of six, it has become clear that I need to add a seventh one:

7. Avoidance of organizational overload

This seventh requirement acknowledges the fact that organizations have a finite change capacity, and that exceeding it yields certain paralysis. Let's look at each of these in more detail.

1. Top Management Commitment

It is well recognized that positive organizational change must be driven from the top. But what does that really mean, and why is it really important? Two factors contribute to this essential requirement: the natural resistance of an organization to change and the presence of what are perceived as higher priorities. Under the excuse, often well substantiated in the past, that "this too will pass," individuals take a de facto position to do nothing, or at most do something but in form only. Also, why admit that their plates are not already filled with other, more pressing activities? Seldom does a new initiative come with instructions on what to stop doing so that time is made available for working on it.

Top management must break this cycle by offering clear proof to the organization that the change is really important. And the best way of demonstrating their commitment to it is by the amount of time they spend in its promotion. That is the most convincing sign to the organization that they should really take this one seriously.

Deming referred to this as "constancy of purpose." Any suggestion that management's interest has moved elsewhere or any conflicting signals send a message that will quickly erase all progress and make it difficult or impossible to regain forward momentum. Many a TQM effort faltered irreversibly when employees were laid off as a reward for their own productivity gains. Any executive who is in a position to issue a conflicting signal must be visibly and persistently committed to that change.

2. Sense of Urgency

Unless a sense of urgency is created, work on any change initiative will be relegated to the back burner while the company deals with daily crises. Leadership must raise the change to a high enough level to counter this force. Usually this involves the existence of actual or potential threats to things that are deemed important by the organization. In some cases it is the organization's very survival. In others it is the survival of things highly valued by the organization, such as growth, financial reward, and career advancement. Whatever the particular motivator, it must be important enough to the people involved in the change to make it worth their added effort.

3. Systematic Approach

The time, if there ever was one, when an organization took it on faith that their leadership knew how to get them to their destination appears to be long gone. Today members will follow only when they see both a need and a logical path to satisfying that need. It has been said that if you don't know where you're going, any road will get you there. Implicit in that statement is that if you do know where you're going, you need a specific map to reach your destination—what I call a systematic approach. That map constitutes a step-by-step plan of what needs to be done and why, as well as who is going to do it and when.

Although there is no single approach that all organizations should follow, all must nonetheless identify up front the key steps that they plan to follow. Like many such journeys, the first time through may require many modifications along the way as unanticipated obstacles are encountered and overcome. But each repeated trip should represent a refinement of the previous one as the terrain becomes more familiar. The value of a desired change can be continuously increased by improvements in both the efficiency of execution of this systematic approach and the effectiveness of its results in advancing the organization's objective.

4. Pilot Projects

We all recognize the term *NIH*, "not invented here." Some of us even feel that we've worked for or with the organization that coined it. NIH represents the organization's immune response to any new idea introduced from the outside: "Yes, it might work for them, but we're different and it will not work here." It is amazing how that reaction seems to be independent of educational level. The only sure countermeasure is to provide examples of it working within that very organization. These examples require carefully chosen pilot projects. The projects should be important, led by widely respected role models, and have a high probability of timely success. Management must take every possible action to ensure their success, since failures will simply reinforce organizational skepticism.

Pilot projects provide the needed fodder for both promotional activities and training, key elements of any successful deployment strategy. It is not unusual for members of pilot project teams to subsequently lead new projects as the approach catches on within the organization.

The alternative to this pilot project deployment strategy is a mass organization-wide rollout in an attempt to push the new approach onto the organization. Time has proven that that approach will likely fail, primarily because of the many disappointing outcomes that will inevitably occur when support resources are spread too thin. The pull strategy implied in the use of pilot projects works because individuals are drawn to the real success stories that they represent.

5. Organization-wide Involvement

While the key to success is to start small, with carefully selected pilot projects and their resulting success stories, eventually everyone must embrace the new approach. Any pockets of the old way will flourish in times of organizational stress and fuel recidivism.

It may be necessary to switch from a pull system of deployment to a push system to complete the transformation. Completion occurs when the organization change is so embedded throughout the organization that it is viewed as the only way to operate. Now resistance to change is on the side of the desired state.

6. Integration with Other Management Systems

If a change is to be internalized by the organization, then it must be in harmony with all of the organization's other activities. For example, asking for a new behavior while continuing to reward the old one will all but guarantee failure. All of the existing processes—planning, resource allocation, recruiting, rewarding, recognition, and so on—must be carefully examined and if necessary modified in order to make them supportive of the desired change.

Perhaps the single most important process to be revisited is the compensation system. The BSC, for example, gives an organization an incentive to focus its efforts on the nonfinancial measures that are the leading indicators of future financial performance. Yet most compensation systems still reward individuals on the basis of past financial performance. Furthermore, individual incentives often discourage the cross-functional teamwork that is generally required to achieve BSC performance goals. Obviously, this is likely to undermine the objectives of the BSC.

7. Organizational Change Capacity

Organizations have a limited capacity for addressing change. This results from the obvious observation that change consumes people's time. They need time to learn and fully understand what is expected of them and more time to translate that change into their day-by-day activities. But they also have that daily job: those ongoing activities that create the value that fuels the organization itself. The more time they spend on change, the less that's available for those daily job activities.

Yet it is rare to find an organization that includes as part of its change plan the identification of what will not get done by the participants while the change is occurring. Leading-edge practitioners of Hoshin Kanri, a Japanese goals/means deployment process and early predecessor of the BSC, explicitly address this issue by having all participants document their current daily activities and identify which ones will be transferred to others or omitted while they dedicate time to achieving the Hoshin Kanri goals.

Management must explicitly address the question "What is our available organizational capacity, and are we attempting too many initiatives to fit within this capacity?" When manufacturing organizations attempt to operate their factories near capacity, they inevitably discover that throughput declines. Many operations managers believe that throughput peaks at a utilization rate of 75–85 percent. The same is likely the case for the optimal rate of utilization of an organization's available change capacity. Exceed that optimum and the rate of change will slow dramatically. It takes a truly enlightened executive to dole out change initiatives in manageable bites.

Satisfying these seven cultural requirements is a necessary but not sufficient condition to ensure BSC success. They provide an environment in which the changes in how an organization implements strategy can occur. But, as with any change initiative, there also exists a unique set of specific structural requirements. It is the satisfaction of the combination of these cultural and structural requirements that is the prerequisite to success.

Structural Requirements for a BSC

In 1999, at the request of its editors, I wrote an article for the *Journal of Strategic Performance Measurement* entitled "Why Balanced Scorecards Fail."[2] That article addressed the most important structural reasons that I had found for ineffective BSCs. Let's look at my current version of that list:

1. Too many measures
2. The wrong measures (not the vital few that are critical to success)
3. Poorly defined measures
4. Missing or inappropriate milestone goals
5. Not deployed to action agents (individuals and teams)
6. Obsolete improvement process used
7. Impatience (due to unrealistic expectations of linkage to financials)

As you can see, this list is specific to the Balanced Scorecard, whereas the previous list applies to any change initiative, including the BSC. This distinction was not recognized by some of the subsequent critics of these identified failure modes.

Let's briefly review these structural requirements.

1. Too Many Measures

Since 1999 I have had the opportunity to serve as the subject matter expert on two American Productivity and Quality Center (APQC) consortium studies of the BSC. We had the opportunity to visit ten organizations identified as representing best practice and to survey many more. These included:

Site Visit and Survey

- 3M
- Boeing Commercial Airplane Group, Customer Support Organization
- Caterpillar Wheel Loader and Excavator Division
- GTE Human Resources
- Nortel Networks Canadian Customer Service
- Naval Undersea Warfare Center, Division Newport
- Principal Financial Group
- Scripps Health
- Nova Scotia Power
- NCR

Thirty-five other organizations completed surveys on the BSC. On each site visit we asked about their biggest problem with their BSC. Every one of them had the same answer: "We still have too many measures on our scorecards." This ubiquitous weakness prompted me to add it as a seventh failure mode to my earlier published list of six. It is related to the issues around organizational capacity addressed earlier.

Symptoms of too many measures include little or no improvement on any of them and a lack of focus on the vital few. Limited resources are simply spread too thin on each of the measures. The organization becomes paralyzed when people must switch their attention among a plethora of measures.

By rank-ordering metrics in terms of their impact on the BSC's objective function, its reason for being, focus can be easily achieved and a cut line drawn at the optimal point for overall impact, subject to the constraint imposed by limited organizational capacity. I still recommend a maximum of five to seven measures on any given scorecard. These measures change from level to level as the scorecard is deployed to the individuals and teams that will make the desired change happen.

2. The Wrong Measures

There is much merit to the old slogan "You get what you measure"—that is, of course, if you get anything at all. Measure the wrong things and the result is both obvious and a dangerous waste of organizational capacity. Any BSC process must ensure that the scorecard measures and goals it yields, once achieved, will significantly advance the organization toward its desired objective.

3. Poorly Defined Measures

All too often scorecard measures are defined so loosely that different individuals looking at the same underlying data will calculate significantly different values for the measure. Should visual defects that don't affect performance be included? Should queue time be included in cycle time? What about opportunity cost? The questions will go on and on unless thoughtfully written operational definitions are provided for each and every measure. I recommend but rarely see a metrics manual that defines how each scorecard measure is calculated. Without this, it is impossible to provide essential credibility to the metric.

4. Missing or Inappropriate Milestone Goals

A good scorecard metric without a time-based goal is like a one-sided coin or a single-pole magnet: it just doesn't exist. Every scorecard goal should have associated with it a goal for that metric along with a target date for its achievement. Flat-line goals are useless since they imply that you can wait an infinite amount of time for their achievement. I believe that with rare exceptions all scorecard measures must be for the purpose of improvement, not control. A control measure has as its goal its acceptable historical value. In other words, it is a measure that has the status quo as its objective. Since there are countless critical control measures in any organization, their inclusion on a scorecard will merely contribute to metrics overload.

5. Not Deployed to Action Agents

Unless individuals know specifically how they personally can contribute to the achievement of the organization's scorecard objectives, they will more than likely conclude that its achievement is someone else's job. Rarely are people in an organization just sitting around looking for something to do. Their roles need to be made explicit, and scorecard deployment is the best way to make that happen.

Each scorecard measure is broken down into its independent drivers. These are the changes that are required in order to make that metric advance toward the goal. Individuals and teams are assigned responsibility for improving these drivers. In some cases further disaggregation is required until the point is reached where the group assigned to the subordinate metric can actually make the needed changes. Only in this way can there be an unambiguous linkage between strategy and action.

6. Obsolete Improvement Process Used

It is sad to see a well-designed and executed scorecard with metrics that are not significantly improving over time. Organizations often spend lots of time planning but fail in the timely execution of those plans. Why? Because there appears to be a widespread misconception by senior management that planning is the hard part, while the doing is easy.

During the 1980s and early '90s Total Quality Management was the business rage. Virtually all organizations had companywide initiatives in training and promoting the use of a systematic approach to process improvement. Many long-term TQM projects demonstrated an order-of-magnitude increase in the rate of improvement of key process measures over pre-TQM improvement rate levels. Unfortunately, in the vast majority of cases TQM was not absorbed into the organization's culture, and slowly but surely these organizations have reverted to their pre-TQM approach of trial and error. To a great extent, Six Sigma represents a reintroduction of TQM methods in a new suit. Whether one chooses TQM, Six Sigma, or some other proven approach to rapid improvement, it is essential that at least equal effort be directed at achieving rapid improvement once the appropriate scorecard metrics are identified.

7. Impatience

Impatience can doom any BSC. Patience is required because of the long lag times normally involved in changing stakeholder behavior, the ultimate target of a BSC. Whether it's owners looking for increased stock price or customers whose relative satisfaction guides their buying choices, behavior follows perception, which in turn follows actual performance. And each of these sequential stages takes time—lots of time. It may be several years before real improvement in the key nonfinancial measures yields the expected financial rewards. And there may be exogenous changes that mask potential financial results. An organization may be doing all of the right things, but a dominating economic or industry downturn can still drive its stock price down. And the opposite can also be the case: a company can do the wrong things, but its stock price or earnings may improve as a result of unrelated factors.

In fact, it is not unusual to find that the lag time exceeds the term expectancy of the CEO and the executive group. A change of leadership before the other shoe drops is the rule, not the exception, in today's environment. Unfortunately, long-term change processes such as the BSC seldom survive these frequent transitions.

Impatience, however, is appropriate in terms of the leading indicators on a BSC. These indicators are the precursors of future success, and without their rapid improvement the overall objectives of the BSC cannot be achieved. So while patient impatience may seem to be an oxymoron, it is part of the art of successful leadership.

Is It Worth All That Effort?

Seven cultural requirements and seven more structural requirements—fourteen in all, and none of them very easy. Is it really worth it? Organizations have been successful in the past without the BSC and will be in the future. So why bother? With all of the recent exposure of the emperor's-new-clothes nature of strategy, no one has tried to explain these successes.

Each organization must explicitly address the question of whether the cost/benefit ratio for implementing a BSC is high enough for it to make the very substantial investment needed to meet these fourteen requirements. Each must ask, "How will a BSC improve our chances of achieving our strategic objectives?" For some, the consensus will be that without a system for aligning organizational efforts around the vital few keys to strategic success, they will likely fail unless fortune is on their side. For others, survival itself is the key issue, and continuing to do as they have in the past will clearly lead to their eventual demise. Whatever the reason, there must be a nucleus of leaders who truly believe that the BSC is worth the effort.

It is important to remember that the BSC is nothing more than a tool. Any true craftsperson knows how to choose the appropriate tool to get the particular job done. The BSC should be treated in the same way. Given the organization's limited resources, leaders must consider this same kind of choice as they execute their important craft.

As with any list of requirements, some elements are more important than others. Certain ones need to be done first, while others can be addressed later. Each organization that chooses to implement a BSC must establish a battle plan that is consistent with available resources. That plan must be continuously adjusted as the organization identifies its current obstacles. To do that, every BSC implementation plan should include a formal diagnostic step in which it identifies the obstacles and appropriate countermeasures for further progress. Learning is an essential element for the BSC process.

When the journey is successfully completed, though, the organization can look back and see that it has met all of the cultural and structural requirements along the way.

5. Managing

Is Getting Paid for Other People's Home Runs

FOR SEVERAL YEARS I RAN A CONSULTING FIRM. THE firm was made up of a core staff and an outside network of specialist contributors. To work with clients we formed teams that often included both groups.

One day I realized that it was much easier to manage and motivate the outside group than the inside group, even though both groups were competent and bright.

If I called outsiders and asked if they wanted to work on a project, I would get either a yes or a no. If a project was right for them and they had the time, they would do it, and because I paid them well they were usually eager and motivated to work.

The outsiders had hustle, to use an old baseball term, but the insiders frequently seemed to be a problem. If we won a new piece of work and I sent around an e-mail asking my colleagues to volunteer to join the client team, too often—far too often—they would tell me about the mountain of work they had to do or about some other obstacle that precluded them from joining the team.

I racked my brain trying to figure out how to change things. Why were these two groups different? Why weren't the insiders as eager and willing as the outsiders?

To try to fix things, first I did what I do best—act without thinking. I began by offering incentives, everything from bonuses and options to free dinners and even cash. This worked, but not for long.

Then I tried thinking. I read a lot of management books. I went on Web sites and looked at articles. As a result, we began to implement a series of longer, deeper, and more thorough evaluations—which also worked, but not for long.

In desperation at the continued disparity between the inside and outside groups, I even tried taking a more authoritarian approach. For a day or so I barked out orders, demanded compliance, and scowled in the corridors. The problem was that no one on the inside team took me seriously. They knew me too well.

Then it dawned on me. The outsiders—some of whom devoted 100 percent of their working time to projects for me—had better motivation because they felt like entrepreneurs. They owned a skill or a competence, and they peddled it in the market. They thought of themselves as businesspeople, not employees.

Though their enterprises were small, these independent men and women had swagger and a big sense of personal responsibility and pride. They realized that their work reflected on *them*, and they took it personally. Work was not something they did to put bread on the table. It was their lifestyle.

While the outsiders sought swagger, the insiders were looking for security. They were an extraordinarily competent group of people who climbed rocks and bungee-jumped on the weekends but were helpless to get from New York to Boston if the shuttles were grounded because of weather. They were always nervous when there was a glitch in the software that direct-deposited their checks.

To put some strut into the insiders, I did what every manager does—held meetings. We talked about it and covered the walls with paper from the flip chart.

To amp up their behavior, I told the inside team they were—please excuse the term—empowered to do whatever they needed to do to boost their performance. I also told them that since we were a small firm, they did not have to ask me in advance for permission.

Oddly enough, by walking away from the problem, rather than trying to fix it, I solved it. They huddled among themselves, talked, grumbled, and caroused while I closed my office door and pretended to work. I heard laughter and arguments. My exit was their cue to perform.

What this experience taught me was that it is just as easy to over-manage people as it is to undermanage them, and that many people—especially those without much experience—are likely to do one or the other.

Leaders can't mold a group as though it were a slab of clay. Rather, a group and its leaders are one. And unless coercion or fear is involved, because they are a unit they must work in concert. Leaders must take their cues from the group and vice versa.

Nothing prepared me for the fact that my inside team worked better when I got out of their way. But once I learned this rather distressing fact, I did get out of their way and—for the most part—let them find their own path.

Leadership and managing both take courage. Neither is easy to do. Both require a high degree of faith that once a direction is charted, people usually can get there by themselves. For control freaks, novices, and nervous people of all stripes, this is not comforting news. After all, if a team wins a big victory on its own, it's the manager's self-esteem that is suddenly put in doubt.

J.K.

WHY EXECUTION IS THE SOURCE OF COMPETITIVENESS

James Champy

E conomists always seem surprised when the productivity of U.S.-based companies jumps by a percentage point. Maybe that's because the improved efficiency of fewer very well-run companies must be averaged over a much larger number of slow movers. Or maybe it's that broad productivity improvements brought about by advances in technology just happen slowly. But for the last ten years I have not been surprised by improvements in productivity. In fact, I have been disappointed that most companies haven't become even more efficient. Advances in information technologies, combined with fundamental process change, can produce dramatic performance improvements. It's now up to managers to determine how quickly companies will realize those improvements.

In 1992 Michael Hammer and I argued that companies must change the way they operate. We said that bureaucracy and fragmentation were adversely affecting performance. Companies needed to rethink how they organized and performed work, not from a departmental or task perspective, but with a process view. By looking at processes—such as new product development, order fulfillment, and procurement—

companies could improve their efficiency, quality, and customer service. We called it *reengineering*.

The idea took off, and so did a book by the same name. Many companies significantly improved their operations. Others just downsized in order to cut costs and called their actions reengineering. Often the effect of such short-term actions was that half the people were left to do twice the amount of work. Workforces were demoralized, and customer service got worse. But well-run companies recognized that they had to make real changes in order to compete and to take advantage of technology that enabled new ways of doing work. Lots of genuine reengineering was done, but I estimate that most companies have accomplished only 10 percent of the process change that they will eventually be required to make.

That first part of the evolution of corporate change went on principally within the walls of a company. Customers and suppliers were affected, but generally no one asked them to change their processes. The next round of process change can and must cross organizational boundaries in order to reduce the extraordinary inefficiencies still present in many industries. For example, in most health care systems, 35 to 40 percent of every dollar is spent on administrative activities, such as claims processing and the creation of redundant medical files. What if that money could be spent on the delivery of real health care?

In the $2-trillion-a-year logistics industry, a similar 40 percent of each dollar is spent on administrative processes—mostly paperwork. For some transocean shipments, twenty-six different documents are still produced. The only value in all this work may be for paper companies.

But a single company cannot fix these processes, or the many other processes that are likewise inefficient and redundant. Taking performance improvement to the next level will require the collaborative efforts of many companies, their customers, and their suppliers. I call this work *X-engineering*. The *X* stands for crossing organizational boundaries. It is made more possible today by information technologies such as the Internet.

Managers, however, will be challenged to achieve the degree of collaboration that X-engineering demands. X-engineering requires all of the process design and change management skills that reengineering demanded. This collaboration will also take managers into some uncomfortable territory. In particular, it will require a greater degree of openness between companies and between companies and their customers; call it a new level of transparency. Additionally, whole industries will have to standardize processes and information technologies.

But the real challenge of accomplishing operational change, in this first decade of the new millennium, may be in moving managers themselves. Today many managers and their companies lack an appetite for change. They have slowed in their adoption of new ideas, some of which could move them to a new level of productivity. Possibly managers have been frightened by the collapse of the technology bubble or distracted by the threat of new government regulations. Whatever the cause, it's time to get moving again. Growth doesn't come from adopting a fortress mentality.

Corporate change, however, always takes more time than we anticipate. It doesn't matter what brand of change you practice—reengineering, X-engineering, Six Sigma, transformation, or reinvention—corporate change can also wear managers down. Here are some ideas for starting up again and maintaining a healthy momentum.

Refocus on Operations and Execution

The last five years have been a period of company growth spurred by mergers and acquisitions. Public companies used their stock—often inflated in value by heady capital markets—to buy capability, territory, and products. The prevailing wisdom was that it was easier to buy than to build. Nothing was new in this idea except the extreme to which it was taken.

I watched many companies buy capability through mergers or acquisitions. The objective was usually to integrate the capabilities of the companies to develop an improved value proposition for customers. Hewlett-Packard merges with Compaq Computer. IBM buys PWC Consulting. These efforts have generally failed to deliver the expected value, often because of cultural differences between the merged or acquired companies or because managers were naive about the real work required to merge the processes of different companies.

I'm not arguing that companies cannot grow thorough intelligent mergers or acquisitions, but I am concerned that we may have educated a generation of managers who believe that business success lies in the art of the deal rather than in intimately knowing and understanding the operations of their company and their industry. For several years capital markets rewarded companies for their success in deal making, and companies rewarded managers for short-term performance improvements that turned out to be mostly on paper rather than producing sound business operations.

No sustainable business performance improvement happens unless there is an improvement in operations. You may have the short-term benefit of an increased demand for your product, but even an increased demand requires an improved response from operations. If this logic doesn't convince you of the criticalness of operational excellence, consider the following three propositions.

■ Today a company must be a low-cost producer in its industry. Markets are becoming increasingly commoditized, and customers just expect price competitiveness. Operational efficiency is a prerequisite to competitiveness.

■ You cannot connect with other companies and your customers—that is, X-engineer—unless you have reengineered. Your processes must be of high quality to work with the processes of other companies. Customers expect flawless execution.

■ As markets commoditize and companies become increasingly transparent in terms of both their costs and their operations, a company's ultimate source of competitiveness may be in its ability to execute. Bright ideas alone will not deliver an improved business performance.

All this argues for managers to reinvest themselves in the operations of their companies and, now, also in the operations of their suppliers and customers. Doing deals without carefully managing corporate change will only result in chaos. Just look to the telecommunications industry for proof.

Expect Change to Take Even Longer Than You Think

Peter Drucker is my hero, as he is for many managers. His clear and pragmatic thinking is always authentic. But I recall one lecture in which Drucker argued that a company's culture is like a country's culture and that it is just as foolish to try to change the culture of a company as it would be to try to change the food tastes of the French. People and their behaviors just don't change that easily, and companies—like countries—are made up of people. I was discouraged by Drucker's assertion. I have always believed that it is possible to change corporate culture, and still do. It's just that it will take a long—possibly very long—time.

In the early days of reengineering it was possible to confuse radicalness with speed. "Get big things done fast" was the motto and expectation. It was sometimes possible to change part of a company within months. But most big corporate changes take years. Individual behaviors in corporate culture are usually the drag. There is plenty of new technology out there and no shortage of new ideas. But corporate change comes slowly. This will be especially true in going forward, changing processes across organizational boundaries and for whole industries. You may be able to tell your suppliers what you want them to do, but you certainly will not be able to order around your customers or your competitors.

It is important today to be realistic about the pace of culture, technology, and business change and to set realistic objectives as to when you will deliver improved business performance. The mantra "Change or die" doesn't work anymore to frighten people into action. They were fooled too many times during the technology bubble.

Rather, think of creating a plan for corporate change that lays out what business change will be accomplished and when. Then map out how your company's various constituencies (e.g., customers, suppliers, workers, and shareholders) will experience those changes.

This will allow you to plan realistically for required resources and how those resources will be spread over time. Many change programs fail because they run out of money or resources before the new ideas and processes that they offer are adopted. People also get worn out, discouraged, and distracted. Understanding real rates of change will also allow you to pace your energy—although don't expect the business world to slow down.

Learn to Breathe Differently

If there is one condition that managers share today, it's breathlessness and a sense of overwork. The urgent seems to force out the important. Personal time must be guarded or it is lost. The speed of communications and the pace of decision making have accelerated. Companies and work will take all that you give. If a sense of overburden exists within a company, it will be hard to get people energized for what will certainly be several years of technology and process change.

Understanding the source of this breathlessness and overburden

ON BEANCOUNTERS

Iacocca: An Autobiography

■ By their very nature, financial analysts tend to be defensive, conservative, and pessimistic. On the other side of the fence are the guys in sales and marketing—aggressive, speculative, and optimistic. They're always saying, "Let's do it," while the bean counters are always cautioning you on why you shouldn't do it. In any company, you need both sides of the equation, because the natural tension between the two groups creates its own system of checks and balances.

If the bean counters are too weak, the company will spend itself into bankruptcy. But if they're too strong, the company won't meet the market or stay competitive. That's what happened at Ford during the 1970s. The financial managers came to see themselves as the only prudent people in the company. Their attitude was: "If we don't stop them, these clowns are going to break us." They saw their mandate as saving the company from the wild-eyed dreamers and radicals who would spend Ford into oblivion. What they forgot was how quickly things can change in the car business. While their company was dying in the marketplace, they didn't want to make a move until next year's budget meeting. ■

From Lee Iacocca with William Novak, *Iacocca: An Autobiography* (Bantam Books, 1984).

helps. First, companies bring this condition on themselves. When companies downsize without changing how work gets done, the people who are left on the job just have to work harder. Usually customers suffer too, as service degrades. Only shareholders seem to benefit from quick cost reductions. But even these benefits are not long-lasting. Unless the operations of a company are changed in some way, its business will eventually falter.

The second factor that contributes to breathlessness and overburden is more subtle. It results when information technology is poorly or incompletely applied and when process redesign doesn't go far enough. Recently I attended the senior management meeting of a large hospital system. The nursing executives were complaining bitterly about the burden of maintaining medical records under a new set of government regulations. No one was arguing that patients wouldn't eventually be better served. But new systems and processes were just being overlaid on top of old systems and processes. There were now twice as many forms to complete—some on paper, others electronic—and lots of redundant information. New work had been added, but no old work had been removed. This is not an unusual condition. Smart process redesign is simply lacking in many enterprises.

In addition to the mistakes that companies make, a major environmental condition is also contributing to breathlessness. The combination of the Internet and process redesign will create acceleration in almost all work process, and nothing is likely to slow down. Information moves faster, money moves faster, and services and products move faster. Consumers and customers expect almost instantaneous response because it is now possible.

There is much that managers will have to do in order to adapt to accelerated processes, and taking early retirement isn't part of it. Breathing differently requires two actions: go far enough in the redesign of processes and the application of information technology to create a truly efficient operation, and don't leave around old processes that either are redundant or create no value. Get rid of old work. Resist starting something new until you have determined what you will stop doing.

Think Big and Go Broad

Managers are often inclined to focus a change program on a limited part of a company. "If we are going to experiment with something new, let's try it in part of the company, like sales"—so the argument goes. "Once we have learned how to do work differently, we can apply what we learned to other parts of the company."

This approach never succeeds. During the time of the technology bubble, many companies assumed that they would not be able to transition quickly enough to doing business over the Internet. So they formed separate business units, the e-businesses and dot-coms. If these businesses succeeded—and most of them failed—the parent company never learned a thing and certainly didn't change.

The challenge today is for companies to adapt their processes to new technologies, and the requirement is that they become dramatically more efficient. The only way that will happen is to affect the core business and to look broadly at the opportunities for change across a company's whole value chain—and the value chains of a company's customers and suppliers. Just operating on a local part of a company will not deliver enough change or enough value. Besides, it's easier for corporate antibodies to kill a smaller change program than to kill something big. And it takes managers as much time and effort to chase a small ambition as it does to do something great.

Regaining and maintaining momentum for corporate change will call on all of a manager's capabilities: sensing, pacing, balancing, executing, and having the right ambition. Corporate change programs must be broadly participatory. But they never start from the bottom up. They must be initiated and led from the top. Employees, customers, and investors are waiting. It's time for managers to start moving again.

"IT'S THE PROCESS, STUPID!": THE PLODDING SEARCH FOR BETTER BUSINESS MODELS

James Womack

Business is becoming more efficient. There's no doubt about it when we look at the statistics. According to *Consumer Reports*, cars produced in 2000 had 80 percent fewer defects than cars produced in 1980.

But it's a two-steps-forward, one-step-back thing. Sometimes when we think we're making progress we're not. Just look at Amazon. They took advantage of the Internet to create a new business, but the process improvement was not as impressive as it first seemed. When I look at those huge warehouses they've built—part of the whole bricks-and-mortar thing—I want to fall down laughing.

In the warehouses things are done no differently than they were fifty years ago. People move around in there, picking out the books needed to fulfill orders. The only change is that instead of carrying around a list, they use those wrist computers. Big deal!

These new management software programs for corporations are another example. Many people are working under the illusion that if a

Six Sigma

VICTORIA GRIFFITH

■ In 1987 Motorola's chairman, Bob Galvin, launched a quality initiative under the banner Six Sigma. The goal was to improve manufacturing so much that no more than 3.4 parts per million would be defective. Under the program, managers were rated by their "sigmas"—the number of defects their division generated. Six Sigma was the pinnacle of success, the best managers could do.

Managers at the company became so enamored with the approach that they became Six Sigma missionaries, preaching their theories to others. Jack Welch, CEO of GE, was an early convert. He included knowledge of the theories in performance reviews and at one point bragged that the practice had saved the company $2.6 billion in just one year. Managers had to undergo extensive Six Sigma training to be considered for promotion.

The philosophy was an outgrowth of the Total Quality Management movement but used its own jargon. While the Six Sigma philosophy proved extremely popular in the late 1980s and 1990s, it probably contributed to a backlash against confusing management terms.

Six Sigma advocates often spoke in a language few could understand. Project leaders, for instance, were referred to as "black belts" and reported to "master black belts," who coordinated improvement efforts around the corporation. "Green belts" had black belt training but stayed in their present position, while "champions" were high-up executives who understood Six Sigma methodology.

Most workers didn't understand the Six Sigma program, and the movement quickly fell out of favor. ■

lot of information is good, tons of information must be even better. So they create these increasingly complicated software programs that promise to tell you everything about the business you're working in.

These programs are great for old-fashioned top-down managers who think it will somehow help them to know what the people way down on the bottom are doing. They are control freaks. But the whole thing can be counterproductive.

I went to a manufacturing plant the other day and saw one of these software programs in action. What I saw was this incredibly costly system being sabotaged by the workers. The computer would tell them what they should be doing, based on its calculations and forecasts. But a woman was running around with little slips of paper that dictated what people actually did.

Now, you could clamp down hard on those employees and insist they follow the program's instructions. Or you could ask yourself why they are not doing so. The answer is probably that they've realized forecasts are good for nothing. They're relying on traditional upstream/downstream communication and it's working well for them. So maybe they don't need that expensive new system.

The trouble is that too often people think new technology spells progress, when it's actually advances in the process that make a difference. This has always been true. Take Sam Colt's factory for firearms in the nineteenth century. The revolver was great, but the system he invented—to use interchangeable parts to create a variety of firearms at a low cost—is what was truly revolutionary.

Henry Ford's continuous-flow process changed the automobile market. Cars were a nice invention, but Ford's rapid throughput meant he could make the product cheaply. That's what made the difference. Michael Dell of Dell Computer revolutionized that industry, again by changing the process. Like Colt 150 years earlier, he figured out that personal computers had gotten to the point that you could make them quickly from interchangeable parts.

Total Quality Management

VICTORIA GRIFFITH

■ Japanese companies searching for ways to compete effectively after World War II were anxious to find an American advisor. Yet the lectures of most American consultants left them cold. In W. Edwards Deming they found someone they could listen to, and who would listen to them.

Deming was an unusual American, by the Japanese way of thinking. He lived in a musty old house. They were impressed by his lack of materialism and identified with his spiritualism. He asked them questions and paid attention to what they had to say.

From these cross-cultural conversations emerged one of the most important management movements of the twentieth century—Total Quality Management, or TQM. Deming told his receptive Japanese audience that managers, not workers, are responsible for the quality of a company's products. That's because 85 percent of an employee's effectiveness, according to Deming, is determined by the corporation's system and just 15 percent by the worker's own skills.

To produce top-quality goods, managers must scrutinize the manufacturing process from beginning to end. Japanese industry was transformed under Deming's stewardship. Deming talked of driving out fear in organizations, of co-opting workers into the process of quality management, and of constantly searching for improvement. He believed TQM could work only if everyone in the company was involved and committed to the strategy. Deming argued that by spending more to improve quality, corporations' earnings would grow.

While Deming was becoming a guru in Japan, he went largely unnoticed in the United States. This changed when Japanese corporations became the envy of the world in the 1980s. Suddenly Americans wanted to imitate the Japanese. To do so they had to follow the teachings of Deming. Ford, Procter & Gamble, GE, Boeing, and Xerox adopted the TQM approach.

Others expanded on Deming's

teachings. Joseph Juran, for instance, argued for the human contribution to quality management. In his view, workers would respond to improvement efforts as long as they were properly trained. His theories led to the creation of quality circles, groups of employees who studied and made recommendations about quality management in an organization.

In the early 1980s Armad Feigenbaum helped popularize TQM in the United States, arguing the entire company should embrace quality control.

In the 1990s American corporations realized that TQM would not save them from the devastating effects of global competition and domestic recession. They began to turn to new management theories, including reengineering. Reengineering adherents focused on cost cutting, anathema to TQM followers. As Japan entered into recession itself and some of its biggest corporations stumbled, U.S. managers lost interest in the movement.

Many of the values of TQM have endured in the U.S. workplace, however. Worker empowerment, teamwork, and on-the-job training are a few of the tenets of Deming's original work.

Deming never lost his place in the heart of Japanese businesspeople, however. "There is not a day I don't think about what Dr. Deming meant to us," said Shoichiro Toyoda, president of Toyota Motor Corporation, at a ceremony honoring the guru in 1991. "Deming is the core of our management." ∎

Taking a page from Ford, Dell also figured out how to create a business using almost no investment. He made the computers so quickly that customers paid Dell before he had to pay his suppliers.

Even the best processes can't ensure success forever. Competitors copy them, for one thing. For another, the market changes. Ford did great until the automobile business matured enough that people wanted variety. His system proved unable to adapt. Everyone knows the saying—you can get a Model T in any color you want so long as it's black. But it was actually much more than that. Those cars were 100 percent identical, from one end to the other. It took the Japanese company Toyota to figure out how to provide variety cheaply in the automobile industry.

As markets mature, people do go off the deep end. At some point companies offer so much variety that it misses the mark. That happened with sound systems. The selection of products was so wide that people didn't have time to evaluate it. Or take the computers that custom-fit jeans to your body. We may not want to take the time to go through a fitting. And my body shape changes so rapidly that I wonder if the jeans would still be custom by the time I went to pick them up.

It's easy to lose track of how process thinking really works. The concept has to do with making goods that customers want, fast, cheap, and well. There's no trade-off between quality and speed. The best processes take care of both. If you rely on inspecting your products after they're made, for instance, there's something wrong with your process. You shouldn't have to inspect. Consumers want good products, not inspected products. And inspecting is expensive.

A lot of companies think they can become more efficient by hiring consultants to show them how to run their businesses. That's baloney. Managers, not consultants, fix businesses.

So much of this stuff is faddish. Look at the whole teamwork thing. If you went by what you read in the media, you'd think every company in America was organized around teams. They are not. When a company says it has a team structure, either no one is in charge or the team structures are probably very weak, consisting of a mailbox in which people from different areas of the company deposit comments. Corporations are organized around divisions—functions, not teams. So far no one's found a good replacement for that structure.

In some areas we've made a lot of progress. Yet it's uneven. Carmakers and electric goods manufacturers have come far, but the aerospace industry is still in the dark ages. Assembly plants have moved ahead, but suppliers have barely budged in improving efficiency.

PRODUCTIVE AND NONPRODUCTIVE LABOR

An Inquiry into the Nature and Causes of the Wealth of Nations

ADAM SMITH

■ There is one sort of labour which adds to the value of the subject upon which it is bestowed: there is another which has no such effect. The former, as it produces a value, may be called productive; the latter, unproductive labour. Thus the labour of a manufacturer adds, generally to the value of the materials which he works upon, that of his own maintenance, and of his master's profits. The labour of a menial servant, on the contrary, adds to the value of nothing. Though the manufacturer has his wages advanced to him by his master, he, in reality, costs him no expence, the value of those wages being generally restored, together with a profit. But the maintenance of a menial servant never is restored. A man grows rich by employing a multitude of manufacturers: he grows poor, by maintaining a multitude of menial servants. The labour of the latter, however, has its value, and deserves its rewards as well as that of the former. But the labour of the manufacturer fixes and realizes itself in some particular subject or vendible commodity, which last for some time at least after that labour is past. It is, as it were, a certain quantity stocked and stored up to be employed, if necessary, upon some other occasion. That subject, or what is the same thing, the price of that subject, can afterwards, if necessary, put into motion a quantity of labour equal to that which had originally produced it. The labour of the menial servant, on the contrary, does not fix or realize itself in any particular subject or vendible commodity. His services generally perish in the very instant of their performance, and seldom leave any trace or value behind them, for which an equal quantity of service could afterwards be procured. ■

It's the process, stupid. If you want big success, you have to come up with something new. You've got to have the only functioning road through a mountain pass that everyone needs or wants to get through.

The path to a better process is a plodding one. No one has come up with the perfect, bulletproof way of doing business. But slowly we are moving toward leaner, more efficient business methods.

THE WELL-OILED MACHINE:
ORGANIZATIONAL MODELS THAT WORK

Stuart Crainer

Humans have been asking themselves the question of what an efficient organization looks like since the formation of the very first families and tribes. The dilemmas are age-old. How much hierarchy is necessary? How authoritarian do those at the top need to be? How much responsibility should each individual take? How should members of the organization interact? How is information effectively passed on?

These questions are complex: after all, they are at the very root of human relationships. Yet—perhaps for fear of getting bogged down in the swamp of human interactions—early management theorists preferred not to consider emotions and motivations at all.

The alternative, they believed, was to view a business not as a human stew but as a machine. The champion of this approach was, perhaps not coincidentally, an inventor of machines: Frederick Taylor, a brilliant mind from the late nineteenth century.

Taylor sought to transfer his knowledge of efficiency in the realms of agriculture and sports to the world of business. He held over forty patents on inventions that included, in his own description, an "apparatus for moving growing trees and the like" to a "combined hothouse

ON PRODUCTIVITY:

My Life and Work

HENRY FORD

■ If a device would save in time just 10 percent, or increase results by 10 percent, then its absence is always a 10 percent tax. If the time of a person is worth fifty cents an hour, a 10 percent saving is worth five cents an hour. If the owner of a skyscraper could increase his income 10 percent, he would willingly pay half the increase just to know how. The reason why he owns a skyscraper is that science has proved that certain materials, used in a given way, can save space and increase rental incomes. A building thirty stories high needs no more ground space than one five stories high. Getting along with old-style architecture costs the five-story man the income of twenty-five floors. Save ten steps a day for each of twelve thousand employees and you will have saved fifty miles of wasted motion and misspent energy. ■

From Henry Ford with Samuel Crowther, *My Life and Work* (Doubleday, 1922).

grapery and greenhouse." He also won the doubles at the U.S. tennis championships. Having studied efficiency in these spheres, Taylor decided to tackle the challenge of organization at work.

One of the very first management theorists, the inventor analyzed business practices with an eye to distinguishing between those that worked and those that didn't. With his scientific background, Taylor was unable to brook uncertainty. He preferred to see employees as robots carrying out well-defined tasks.

"Each employee should receive every day clear-cut, definite instructions as to just what he is to do and how he is to do it, and these instructions should be exactly carried out, whether they are right or wrong," Taylor advised. A disciple of Taylor's, Harrington Emerson, later coined the term "efficiency engineering."

In an efficient organization, Taylor believed, there is no room for debate. People should perform their jobs as if they were cogs in a well-oiled machine.

Taylor's theories were widely embraced throughout much of the twentieth century as companies worked to become mechanically efficient. Henry Ford was a prominent adherent of Taylor's theories. At his company, supervisors were obsessed with numbers and measurements. The idea of the assembly line broke workers into functions as if they were bits of machinery.

To a certain extent Taylor's ideas worked. They were especially successful in enabling mass production—maximizing output and minimizing time. But the concepts came unstuck when quality became as important as price, and service became as highly valued as a physical product.

As the twentieth century rolled on, companies came to recognize that employees are humans, not merely machine parts. Yet this realization did not mean managers were still willing to loosen the organizational reins.

Workers, as humans, needed to be controlled, the thinking went. And so the organizational model of the business machine gave way to the paradigm of the business as military.

Military organizations are easy to understand. They operate under ornate hierarchies in which everyone's job is clearly defined. In the 1970s the management structure of British Steel was so complex that in pictorial form it easily filled an entire wall. Organizations were viewed as armies led by mighty generals marching to war against the competition.

Executives consumed books such as Sun Tzu's *The Art of War*, Karl von Clausewitz's *On War*, and Basil Liddell Hart's *Strategy* in the hope that the next day they would be able to convert unmotivated workers into the business equivalent of a winning army.

Yet military models sit uneasily in the contemporary world of business. Eventually managers came to realize that it was difficult to motivate workers under rigid hierarchies. And some of them even began

The Peter Principle

LAURENCE J. PETER AND RAYMOND HULL

■ So my analysis of hundreds of cases of occupational incompetence led me on to formulate The Peter Principle: In a Hierarchy Every Employee Tends to Rise to His Level of Incompetence.

A New Science!

Having formulated the Principle, I discovered that I had inadvertently founded a new science, hierarchiology, the study of hierarchies.

The term "hierarchy" was originally used to describe the system of church government by priests graded into ranks. The contemporary meaning includes any organization whose members or employees are arranged in order of rank, grade or class.

Hierarchiology, although a relatively recent discipline, appears to have great applicability to the fields of public and private administration.

This Means You!

My Principle is the key to an understanding of all hierarchical systems, and therefore to an understanding of the whole structure of civilization. A few eccentrics try to avoid getting involved with hierarchies, but everyone in business, industry, trade-unionism, politics, government, the armed forces, religion and education is so involved. All of them are controlled by the Peter Principle. ■

From Laurence J. Peter and Raymond Hull, *The Peter Principle* (William Morrow & Company, 1969).

to believe that employees on the low end of the totem pole might be capable of delivering valuable information to those at the top.

So the models shifted once more. Hierarchical organizations gave way to flat organizations. Managers at the top encouraged workers to challenge orders. Employees on car assembly lines actually curried favor by pointing out problems. Talk centered on worker "empowerment."

By the end of the twentieth century theorists were questioning

Management's New Paradigms

PETER F. DRUCKER

■ One hears a great deal today about "the end of hierarchy." This is blatant nonsense. In any institution there has to be final authority, that is, a "boss"—someone who can make the final decisions and who can expect them to be obeyed. In a situation of common peril—and every institution is likely to encounter it sooner or later—survival of all depends on clear command. If the ship goes down, the captain does not call a meeting, the captain gives an order. And if the ship is to be saved, everyone must obey the order, must know exactly where to go and what to do, and do it without "participation" or argument. "Hierarchy," and the unquestioning acceptance of it by everyone in the organization, is the only hope in a crisis. ■

From Peter F. Drucker, *The Essential Drucker* (Harper Business, 2001).

whether a formal organization was necessary at all. Couldn't businesses—and their employees—be "virtual"? A business might be defined as a venture between two divisions of rival companies; workers might flit between one group and the next.

The rise of outsourcing in the business world has grown out of this concept. By outsourcing various parts of their operations, companies fudge the lines that define where their organization starts and where it ends. Workers stationed in customers' offices are often perceived as employees of the customer. At the height of the 1990s boom some theorists reasoned that it would be better to organize work around "projects" rather than official businesses.

Of course, this kind of thinking can be taken too far. For all the talk of virtual organizations, it's difficult to define such entities. While rigidity may sap employees of motivation and creativity, a free rein can turn them into an undisciplined mob.

The most effective organizations must take into account both the strengths and the weaknesses of human interaction. That brings us back to the challenge of complexity—something the earliest management theorists were understandably loath to face.

WORKING IN A TEAM AND OTHER UNNATURAL BUSINESS ACTIVITIES

Warren Bennis

The reason teams exist is that two or more people can often accomplish more if they work together than if they work on their own. Period. It's so straightforward.

Translating this to the corporate world isn't always the easiest thing. Working in a team can seem an unnatural act. But it's a necessity to achieve better results.

Of course, forming a team in and of itself won't solve anything. There are good teams and bad teams. Teams work in different ways. But they can help deal with the increasing interdependence of tasks in an organization, especially as the complexity and speed of those tasks grow. Organizations that don't know how to create the social architecture necessary to align workers' efforts will not live up to their potential.

We don't hear about teams as much as we did a few years ago. This is partly because we choose to focus on different topics at different times. A few years ago we were fascinated by heroic leaders such as Jack Welch of GE. Now, everyone's gone anti-Welch, and quiet leaders are in vogue.

But I think we're also talking less about teams because we're taking them more for granted. Projects have become a way of life at most corporations. Teamwork is taken as a given. Look at the world we live in now. In high-tech companies, consumer groups, or car manufacturers, people are organized into teams to come up with a new product or make some other change in the organization.

The reason organizations exist in the first place—and that includes corporations—is that you sometimes need more than one person working on his or her own to achieve a certain goal. So corporations are by definition already teams.

It's hard for one person to effect change alone. What's needed is a group effort. But to make the team function, people need to be clear about what they are trying to do. We've all been in meetings that seem pointless. Eyes glaze over; people get these exasperated expressions. They ask themselves what they are doing there and if the whole thing isn't a waste of time.

That's when you know the team isn't performing well. But if you have an exciting objective, those meetings take on a very different tone. You have to believe you're going to change the world, at least the small part of the world you occupy. You have to believe you can make a difference. You have to think, "Hey, we're going after the Holy Grail, and we're going to make it." It must be sincere; fake enthusiasm is too easy to spot.

If you've got the right group working together, you've got it made. I once interviewed Robert Oppenheimer, head of the Manhattan Project, the group that created the nuclear bomb. Regardless of what you think about atomic weapons, that was an example of a great team. They had a goal and worked together to get there.

Oppenheimer said something very telling about the Manhattan Project: "Whatever we didn't know, we explained to each other." That's what teamwork is—abandoning egos to learn from each other.

There's no recipe for good teamwork, but there is a prerequisite: a leader who acts as more of a facilitator, someone who doesn't dominate but guides the conversation, along the lines of the facilitator in a therapy session.

The democratic nature of teams—that no one dominates, but everyone participates—is probably what makes them difficult at times to manage. Sometimes people feel more comfortable with an old-fashioned hierarchical setting.

I recently published a book called *Geeks and Geezers*, about people under thirty and over seventy, and a striking difference between those two age groups is that the young group—let's call them the Grand-kids—is so much more comfortable with the notion of working on teams than the older group, which we'll call the Grandparents.

Why? I have a few theories. There are some obvious answers, such as the fact that universities—and especially business schools—have all oriented their instruction around teams. So the Grandkids are forced at a young age to learn what teamwork is all about.

But I think there's something else. The Grandkids are the sons and daughters of the 1960s generation. They grew up with the idea that together we can accomplish a lot. The 1960s was the time of big move-ments, co-ops, working with others. That philosophy really shows up in the way their children face their work and life. The Grandparents care more about the organization, the corporation as a whole. The Grandkids are more concerned with the personal relationships they have with their immediate peers.

There are a number of tasks that are probably more easily ac-complished alone—writing poetry, for example, or playing a violin. There was a British author in the nineteenth century, Ford Madox Ford, who befriended Joseph Conrad and wanted to write a novel with him. It didn't work. Mathematical geniuses too are probably best left on their own.

But teams are the best way to tackle most challenges in the corpo-rate world. That's because corporations are human communities. And in human communities, people need to cooperate.

EMPOWERMENT

Rosabeth Moss Kanter

The idea that workers should be empowered to exercise choices and make decisions, rather than be closely supervised and expected to conform to predetermined templates, was always a subtext in modern management.

But organizational practice in the modern manufacturing era was dominated by belief in the importance of rules, procedures, and systems to ensure predictability. Mechanical images prevailed. The human element was a wild card that could throw plans off track, and innovators were mavericks who could interfere with the smooth operation of the organizational machine.

This was not just how factories were run; it also influenced white-collar and managerial ranks. The 1950s in the United States, the decade of the "organization man," probably represented the apogee of bureaucratic conformity, desire for uniformity, and belief in mass everything: mass manufacturing, mass markets, and even mass housing developments creating undifferentiated boxlike dwellings in new suburbs. While the high performance of companies such as Lincoln Electric (which gave incentives to teams of workers to make decisions to improve productivity) was noted, it was not emulated.

The rationale for shifting to philosophies of empowerment gained importance with developments in the 1960s and 1970s. Youth movements of the hippie era expressed rebellion against big bureaucracies of all kinds and helped usher in a new set of standards for what workers sought from work. Economic concerns led the U.S. government to explore alternative management approaches through a national productivity office.

European models gave workers a bigger voice in decisions. Some of those models stemmed from the aftermath of World War II; fear that another authoritarian regime could arise in Germany led the occupying governments to require German industry to establish works councils as a representative governance mechanism. Scandinavian industry was known for its more democratic workplaces that delegated responsibility to worker teams; auto companies in Detroit sent managers and workers to Sweden to learn Volvo's best practices.

A movement for participatory management grew in the United States, led by companies such as Motorola and Procter & Gamble. At Motorola, then-CEO Robert Galvin's belief in empowerment was one factor in a dramatic transformation of a radio company to a high-tech powerhouse. At Procter & Gamble, numerous experiments in worker self-management in soap factories in Ohio and paper factories in Georgia gradually became the norm—and a source of high productivity that contributed greatly to P&G's prosperity.

Empowerment took off in the 1980s, when businesspeople began to look to Japanese companies that achieved high productivity and high quality through empowerment. In Japan, workers could influence if not control their work conditions, form teams to solve problems, and even decide to stop the production line.

The rapid growth of new information technology companies in the United States also accelerated the movement to empowerment. Groups in the sector followed a fresh work philosophy. They were more open and more inclusive. They were growing too fast to have many rules in place. Instead, they trusted employees at many levels to "do the right thing." In my 1983 book *The Change Masters,* I helped popularize the term *empowerment* to describe the organizational culture of new, high-innovation technology companies, which stood in strong contrast to traditional companies that stifled innovation by failing to empower the potential corporate entrepreneurs and initiative-taking leaders in their midst.

The importance of empowerment showed up in many management movements seeking excellence both inside and outside of the company. Empowerment made it possible to get problems solved quickly in the search for zero defects, as the movement for total quality management (TQM) desired; workers could take action on the spot rather than sending exceptions or problems up a chain of command or throwing them over the wall into another department of inspectors or quality controllers.

Empowerment enabled creative people to envision and champion ideas to improve products, services, and processes, or even to invent new ones, and to do this at a faster rate—something that was increasingly necessary as markets became more competitive in the global information era. Empowerment also improved customer service, as the power and primacy of customers were noted in all industries, and as service industries began to employ an ever-larger share of the workforce as manufacturing shrank.

For example, Marriott, the hotel chain, used the word *empowerment* in advertisements asserting that its front-line workers could help a guest with any problem, anytime. That meant giving workers control over some monetary decisions. Wal-Mart, now the world's largest private-sector employer, popularized the designation *associates* for its employees to show that they are a vital part of the family, empowered with customer service responsibility.

Empowerment played an important role in the economic boom of the 1990s, as large companies reduced vestiges of rules-minded bureaucracy and entrepreneurial companies with empowering cultures grew quickly; it is now a fundamental principle of twentieth-century management.

That it is often invoked as a principle does not make it always a reality in practice, however. There are still corporations entangled in procedures, bosses who cling to control, and parts of the world where empowerment feels like a foreign concept. In Brazil, for example, there is a well-known manufacturing company, Semco, led by an entrepreneur who empowers his people to make every conceivable decision, including when to set up a new subsidiary. Yet for all of Semco's financial success, its model has not spread in Latin American countries, where patriarchal bosses tend to outnumber empowered workers.

To make empowerment possible requires a great deal of trust that people will handle their enlarged scope of authority in a responsible way. Some of this stems from leaders' confidence in people and their ideas. It is thus not surprising that there is generally more empowerment where there is a carefully selected workforce of highly educated people, especially so-called knowledge workers, whose contributions stem from their ability to use their minds. But there are also circumstances that make it easier to empower people—and that add some of the controls that are still required to help organizations function effectively. When responsibility is delegated, it is especially important to ensure that individuals won't wander off in all directions, that they will act to support a coherent strategy. Empowerment works best when the following conditions are in place:

- Shared values—a desire to accomplish a common mission and an understanding of priorities
- Clear goals—well-articulated tasks as a starting point to guide action
- Education and training—ample training for workers who are not to be supervised closely, to ensure that they have the skills and knowledge to make the right choices

- Feedback—an information system to provide data to those carrying out tasks, so they can monitor progress, catch problems as they arise, and guide their own work
- Coaching and support—leaders who lend support and peers who can help each other improve performance or act jointly
- Metrics—a way to measure results and a basis for rewards

Since empowerment involves handing over some of the power to the people, it is not surprising that some bosses resist giving it up. But the best leaders understand that when they empower others, their own power grows, because more is accomplished and the pie is enlarged.

LIKE TRYING TO HERD CATS:
THE DUBIOUS STRATEGY OF
INTRAORGANIZATIONAL COMPETITION

Paul Taylor

When a rash of upstart dot-com companies promised to change the world in the mid-1990s, a shiver ran through the boardrooms of many traditional companies.

Many fretted that their new fleet-footed Internet rivals would lure away their best and most tech-savvy customers. Others, particularly financial services firms and retailers, worried that they would be "disintermediated"—bypassed by customers buying products over the Internet directly from manufacturers.

These concerns caused managers to turn, en masse, to the management strategy known as intraorganizational competition. The idea is that divisions within a company can become more dynamic and more efficient if they are pitted against each other in a battle for profit share.

Intraorganizational competition is a newer term for *intrapreneurship*—an expression coined in the mid-1970s by Norman Macrae. Conventional wisdom has long held that at some point every entrepreneurial venture becomes an established business.

The idea is that a group's very success puts it at risk of losing the inventive flair and cutting-edge culture that defined its early growth phase. Fostering intrapreneurship—encouraging entrepreneurship within established organizations—is crucial if a company is to avoid atrophy and to keep reinventing itself.

In 1986 John Naisbett cited intrapreneurship in his book *Re-Inventing the Corporation* as a way for established companies to discover new markets and new products. The concept gained ground in 1990 when Rosabeth Moss Kanter of Harvard Business School discussed the need for intrapreneurial development as a key factor in ensuring the survival of the company in her book *When Giants Learn to Dance*.

Some notable business successes have been attributed to the practice. Steve Jobs described the development of the Macintosh computer as an intrapreneurial venture within Apple, the company he founded.

3M reaped the rewards of intrapreneurism as well. The company has long encouraged employees to work on developing their own business ideas. In fact, corporate doctrine tells employees they should spend at least 15 percent of their workday on such projects. One of the big breakthroughs attributed to this scheme was the concept of Post-it notes, pioneered by an employee eager to mark pages in his hymnbook at church.

In the hysteria provoked by the Internet, however, the idea of intrapreneurism took on a life-or-death quality. The alternative to "separate and flourish" was "stay together and die." In the 1990s the writings of Clayton Christensen, a professor at the Harvard Business School, popularized the notion of company life cycles. Christensen advised companies to set up separate competitive businesses or risk being put out of existence by "disruptive" technologies from upstarts.

To counter the perceived threat from companies such as Yahoo!, Amazon.com, and E-Trade in the 1990s, traditional bricks-and-mortar companies set up separate Internet businesses or spun off their own dot-com units. The new groups would be free to act more creatively, far from the restrictions of their older, stodgier parents.

Established IT groups such as 3Com, Hewlett-Packard, and Lucent spun off totally independent companies. (3Com floated off Palm, HP created Agilent Technologies, and Lucent spun off Agere Systems.)

At a time when the share prices of Internet-related initial public offerings frequently ended the first day of trading at a substantial premium over the offer price, this strategy made a great deal of sense, particularly if the parent company retained an equity stake in its progeny.

In other cases, the spin-off took the form of a partial management buyout—an option that was particularly attractive at the height of the dot-com boom, when many companies faced the prospect of losing senior executives and key IT staff to Internet rivals.

In Britain the standout example of this strategy was Freeserve, the Internet service provider and portal set up and eventually spun off by Dixons, the High Street retail group. At one stage in 2000—albeit briefly—Freeserve was worth more than the whole of the Dixons group. Others took a different tack, preferring instead to set up internal dot-com units with the freedom to compete not only with external Internet rivals but also with their own traditional bricks-and-mortar operations. Barnes & Noble, the bookseller, which was fiercely criticized for being "behind the curve" and slow to respond when Amazon.com first set up shop on the Internet, was one of the companies to adopt this approach.

Wal-Mart, Kmart (which is now operating under Chapter 11 bankruptcy protection), and Nordstrom were among the most prominent retailers that established semi-independent entities to run their online businesses. Wal-Mart joined forces with Accel Partners, the California venture capital firm, to establish Wal-Mart.com as an independent operation based in Silicon Valley. At the time Wal-Mart argued that the partnership with Accel, which took a minority stake, would allow Wal-Mart.com to develop "at Internet speed." Kmart joined Softbank Venture Capital to found BlueLight.com, opening up in San Francisco rather than at the group's Michigan headquarters. Culturally, the business was far from that of a traditional retailer: "Employees whizz down hallways on scooters, keeping the atmosphere light and casual," the Web site boasted.

Another Internet strategy variation, adopted by Reuters, the global news organization, and British Telecom (BT), was to set up internal incubator units. Reuters' Greenhouse Fund sought out external investment opportunities. BT's Brightstar unit, on the other hand, took promising ideas from staffers within BT that were not core to the company's operations and turned those ideas into spin-off candidates.

Many responses to the dot-com threat were failures. Wal-Mart and Kmart eventually sought greater control of their Internet operations by buying out external partners and reintegrating the divisions into their main business.

Some, like Rupert Murdoch's News International group, abandoned most of their Internet projects, including those involving intracompany competition. Indeed, throughout the media industry, companies scaled back Internet operations and slashed jobs.

Staples, the U.S. office supplies retailer, set a pattern for several other "bricks-and-clicks" retailers when it took back full control over its dot-com operation.

Staples decided to combine Staples.com with its catalog business, buying out other shareholders in the online unit, including executives and venture capitalists. At the time Staples said that buying out venture capitalists, including General Atlantic Partners and Highland Capital Partners, would allow it to run its Internet operations more efficiently. "By combining [Staples' catalog business] and Staples.com, we'll be able to operate more efficiently with a unified merchandising team, marketing team and customer support team," said Thomas Stemberg, former CEO. "The integration also will allow us to eliminate the administrative costs that come from operating separate business units."

But the reintegration of autonomous or semiautonomous Internet units has not been confined to the retail market. Among other sectors, media and financial services have seen similar trends. For example, Viacom, the media group, shelved its plan to float MTVi, its online music network, reflecting the market's continued disenchantment with Internet offerings.

"There's no reason we would spin off something if the market isn't going to appreciate the value of it," said Mel Karmazin, chief operating officer of Viacom at the time, arguing that MTVi would better contribute to overall results if the subsidiary remained inside the group.

The decision of many companies to bring their Internet operations back in-house reflects the fact that the IPO market has dried up, all but eliminating the chance for a traditional company to cash in on the spin-off of its Internet operations. But there's more to it than that. The Internet experience shows that institutionalized intracompany competition is very difficult to pull off. Retailers have discovered that it is often more efficient to centralize online operations. This allows management to exploit the opportunities for cross promotions between sites and physical stores.

Other spin-offs were brought down by personal rivalries. As many companies discovered when they spun off their Internet units, those left behind were often deeply resentful. Not only did they view the start-up venture with suspicion, but they also resented the pay and other perks that were lavished on dot-com colleagues. As a result, employees in Internet units often complained about a lack of cooperation and claimed that crucial resources were withheld from them.

Some spin-offs flourished. Palm managed to hold on to its position as the leading maker of handheld computers despite fierce competition from rivals including Handspring and others.

Agere and Agilent also prospered despite the tough market conditions for technology companies over the past two years. But as Britain's Freeserve demonstrates, spin-offs are not always a recipe for success. After being floated by the Dixons Group, Freeserve was acquired in 2001 by Wanadoo, the Internet unit of France Telecom, for £1.6 billion.

Intrapreneurship still has some value as a management strategy. But the dot-com era shows that if intraorganizational competition is to be successful, it requires considerable planning and management skill. Slight separation from the parent—say, another facility—is probably more workable than an all-out spin-off. And the strategy is likely to fail completely if it is rushed. Creating your own competition is not always the best way to thrive.

INFORMATION TECHNOLOGY FOR
PEOPLE IN SUITS

Thornton May

Business historians will label C-level executives operating in the late 1990s as the last executives to preside, Nero- and Marie Antoinette—like, over a world of ever-increasing corporate spending on computer technology. The popular culture of our recent past mandated constantly expanding additions to the market basket of individual technology assets (e.g., PCs, PDAs, Walkmans, cell phones, Game Boys, and MP3 players).

Every month, in conjunction with a longitudinal research study examining the link between information technology spending and business value creation, I speak candidly with at least one large group of chief information officers, vendor executives, and venture capitalists. I ask each group to divide the thirty-year period between 1987 and 2017 into computational eras (no more than ten years, no fewer than two). The years before 2000 tended to be demarcated by what devices were being bought (e.g., mainframes, PCs, client servers). The years after 2000 were demarcated by whether technology was being purchased at all, by what portions of the installed technology base were being rationalized and consolidated, and by what value was being created.

We have moved from being technology-focused to being value-obsessed. We are moving from managing disparate pieces of functionally applied technology to managing enterprise information technology portfolios. The millennium did not just mark the end of a calendar group of years; it ushered in a whole new era of computational behaviors. Many in the technology industry are only now waking up to the new realities of a reduced-expenditure environment.

Living in a World on a Technology Diet

Historians from a later age will no doubt tell us that we overconsumed and underassimilated technology. This is because we focused on the wrong side of the technology equation—the technology itself, not what the technology could do for us. Technology invention is one thing. Technology application and value creation are quite another.

The gestalt of the current period (2002–2005) posits that there is more money to be made making technologies disappear (e.g., rationalizing platforms and turning off low-value systems and devices) than in making new technologies appear on the organizational landscape (e.g., doing innovative things with new technology). The technology gorging of the past came about because line-of-business managers were not directly involved in technology decision making. Accountability and responsibility were outsourced to the separate and not quite equal IT organization.

Technology Curriculum for Suits

Dennis Flanagan, longtime editor of *Scientific American*, tells of once meeting the famous *New Yorker* movie critic, Pauline Kael. After they introduced themselves, Kael admitted to Flanagan that she knew "absolutely nothing" about science. Flanagan responded: "Whatever became

How to Win Friends and Influence People

DALE CARNEGIE

■ When Theodore Roosevelt was in the White House, he confessed that if he could be right 75 percent of the time, he would reach the highest measure of his expectation.

If that was the highest rating that one of the most distinguished men of the twentieth century could hope to obtain, what about you and me?

If you can be sure of being right only 55 percent of the time, you can go down to Wall Street and make a million dollars a day. If you can't be sure of being right even 55 percent of the time, why should you tell other people they are wrong?

You can tell people they are wrong by a look or an intonation or a gesture just as eloquently as you can in words—and if you tell them they are wrong, do you make them want to agree with you? Never! For you have struck a direct blow at their intelligence, judgment, pride,

and self-respect. That will make them want to strike back. But it will never make them want to change their minds. You may then hurl at them all the logic of a Plato or Immanuel Kant, but you will not alter their opinions, for you have hurt their feelings.

Never begin by announcing "I am going to prove so-and-so to you." That's bad. That's tantamount to saying: "I'm smarter than you are. I'm going to tell you a thing or two and make you change your mind."

That is a challenge. It arouses opposition and makes the listener want to battle with you before you even start.

It is difficult, under the most benign conditions, to change people's minds. So why make it harder? Why handicap yourself?

If you are going to prove anything, don't let anybody know it. Do it so subtly, so adroitly, that no one will feel that you are doing it. ■

From Dale Carnegie, *How to Win Friends and Influence People,* editorial consultant, Dorothy Carnegie, editorial assistance, Arthur R. Pell, Ph.D. (Simon & Schuster, 1936).

of the idea that an educated person is supposed to know a little something about everything?" In today's economy, all executives need to know a little something about information technology. The questions are what they know and what they should know. If we are to avoid the excesses of the past, line-of-business executives need to develop competencies in the following areas:

Information opportunity
Application IQ
Information economics
Information exchange
Sociology/ethnography of the supply side
Information management danger zones

Information Opportunity

When Franklin Roosevelt died suddenly on April 12, 1945, Eleanor Roosevelt herself broke the news to Harry Truman. "Harry," she told him, one arm across his shoulder, "the president is dead." Too stunned to speak for a moment, Truman finally asked if there was anything he could do for her. "Is there anything we can do for you?" she replied. "For you are the one in trouble now."

In this interchange Eleanor Roosevelt embodies a skill too often missing in IT shops today: the ability, in the face of massive distraction, to see the world in its entirety, to lift oneself out of one's own space and see the total problem. IT decision making chronically suffers from an inability to see the big picture. Ariel Sharon, Israel's warrior-politician, puts great stock in holding the high ground, controlling lines of sight and measuring distances in terms of artillery range. IT is too often blinded by the glare of the day-to-day to reach the strategic mind-set that would let it contextualize the problem at hand. Rarely will one see created a spectrum of innovative alternatives to address the problem. Time-pressured executives too often settle on the first solution that sort of fits the problem at hand.

Future value-creating executives need to be able to set a much more robust table of options for technology investment. In the past, vendors tended to monopolize the creation of technology "menus." We were told that what they were selling was what we needed.

Business schools fall embarrassingly short in their teaching of IT decision making. High-performing enterprises are being forced to create their own training and certification programs in IT value creation. In a fashion similar to Microsoft offering training and certification in what is a core competency for them, programming and system engineering, so too will companies have to create curricula that help their executives focus information technology investments on high-value targets.

The first set of basic questions we need to answer includes:

Do we all agree on which problem we are trying to solve?
Do executives agree on the facts associated with that problem?
Have we created a rich array of alternatives that might address
    the problem we are trying to solve?

Application IQ

I am frequently asked by board members to conduct postmortem examinations on failed application development projects. In a sense, I serve as a fiscal forensic examiner at technology crime scenes. The most frequent point of failure with technology in the recent past has been the "technology Vietnam" phenomenon. The Vietnam War was lost in part because of a lack of popular support. Applications fail because of a lack of popular support. Does the application solve a problem that the user community actually wants solved? Does the user community agree on how the application should work in practice?

Future executives will need to be able to determine whether the linkage between the business problem being addressed and the technology solution being implemented is rock solid. The future will see proposed solutions prototyped and simulated in actual operating conditions.

Carl von Clausewitz told us in his book *On War* that no rational person should start a war without having a clear objective. And no rational person should go forward with an application development project without knowing how to stop it or without some type of exit strategy.

Information Economics

Future executives need to be able to determine whether the chosen solution set is being pursued in the most cost-effective manner and what, if any, economic benefit was actually delivered. The total cost associated with technology solutions was rarely examined on an ex ante basis in the past.

Long before computers came along, other societies, including the Chinese and Islamic empires, displayed great technical virtuosity. What has really differentiated American capitalism has been our ability to apply technology in an economically useful fashion.

Information technology is like boxing in many respects. Like boxing, it is (but should not be) terribly adversarial. Like boxing, the hype consumes more energy than the actual action. Like boxing, the exercise tends to end with one party defeated. Most important, like boxing, information technology is very subjective. Unless there is a knockout, the scorecards of the judges determine the winner. Information economics needs to replace the voyeuristic judgments of sideline yahoos with unambiguous performance and success metrics.

Information Exchange

At several steps in the life cycle of a given technology (e.g., design, build, deploy, operate, and maintain) a broader set of players needs to be involved. The "only insiders" way of thinking is outdated, dangerous, and—in our increasingly litigious age—high-risk. "Involve all early" is the new mantra. As we pointed out earlier, the conversations being conducted in the design and build stages were quite limited and tended to include only the IT organization and the vendor. Great companies are introducing radical transparency into their cradle-to-grave technology management processes. We need to add new voices to the deliberative process. We need to make the technology management process less opaque, less mysterious, and much more accessible to investors, customers, employees, and regulators. After all, what are we hiding?

In the future, information risk and privacy executives will need to be able to attest that the right information is being exchanged with the right parties at the right time.

Many executives are increasingly coming to use a map room to chart progress and direct resource allocations associated with major IT initiatives. They link these map rooms with a small and frequently convened group of trusted experts to keep things on track.

Sociology / Ethnography of the Supply Side

Future executives will need to understand the strengths, weaknesses, biases, and behavior drivers of the various executives on the supply side of the house. For many line-of-business executives, all IT people "look alike" to them. Worse, many consider IT staffers low-level service workers—information wait staff. Eleanor Roosevelt told Truman, "If you can get on a personal basis with Mr. Churchill, you will find it easier." If line-of-business executives can get on a personal basis with IT leaders, it will be easier.

Information Management Danger Zones

The immediate tests of future executives as to whether they can create value with IT will come in the areas of:

Supply chain
Customer relationship management
Customer self-service/configurator

The perspective provided by speaking with a large number of IT leaders working in specific companies in different vertical markets paints a grand picture of a constant struggle between the realities of uniqueness (each company is truly different) and the supply side quest for uniformity (can we standardize what we are doing, and rationalize the tools we are doing it with?). We live in an economy defined by technology "markets of one" (i.e., "my company"). Unfortunately, important elements of the technology supply side—venture capitalists, software and hardware vendors, subscription research firms, and systems integrators—operate from a dated industrial age/mass market mind-set.

Chief information officers are trying to solve problems unique to their enterprise, while the versi, despite their verbal protestations to the contrary, continue to push "universal" solutions. This gave rise to the general framework defining the current computational environment— "my" versus "mass." As we make the transition to a technology "age of one," the very different orientations of the people who sell technology solutions and those of the people who buy them creates this challenge: Who can best manage a habitat in which the core competencies in greatest demand include the ability to identify and then integrate inexpensive technology "pieces parts" that work at scale and which can be integrated?

SEVEN RULES FOR SURVIVAL:
MANAGING THROUGH VOLATILE TIMES

George Conrades

Managing a start-up company is never easy. But managing a high-tech start-up through the dot-com frenzy and its bleak aftermath forced senior executives to rethink all they had learned about leading a young company.

Akamai Technologies was founded in late 1998 by a group of MIT technologists. Its innovative method of speeding content delivery on the Internet was quickly embraced by a receptive marketplace, and the new company flourished. By January 2000 Akamai had more than eleven hundred employees and a stock price that peaked at $345 a share. With a market capitalization of more than $35 billion, we were bigger than General Motors, and on paper the founders were all billionaires. In fact, three hundred of our first employees became millionaires.

Having spent more than forty years in the high-tech industry, I was the company's chief executive and elder statesman. I had played a significant executive role at IBM for more than thirty years and overseen the restructuring and eventual sale of BBN, a software company with long-established roots in the industry. Though I was extremely excited about coming to a start-up such as Akamai, I fought hard not to get swept up in the dot-com mania. The same year that our stock peaked, we had $4 million in revenues and $60 million in losses. We simply had no business being compared to behemoths like GM.

We didn't have much time to experience this surreal euphoria. As 2000 unfolded, the dot-com bubble began to burst and companies began to vanish faster than the morning mist. Though most of our early customers were dot-com companies, we did not think of ourselves as a dot-com. We were selling a capability that all companies seeking to do business online would require. Like everyone else's, our stock price plummeted throughout 2000 and 2001. But we were determined to ride it out and survive.

Our efforts to stay afloat and find a path to growth and profitability were staggered on September 11, 2001. One of our cofounders and our chief technology officer, Daniel Lewin, was on board American Airlines flight 11 from Boston to Los Angeles. Only thirty-one years old, he perished when the hijacked plane crashed into the World Trade Center.

Losing a key personality is hard enough for a start-up. Losing one in this set of circumstances was quite devastating. But Danny Lewin's magnetic personality and intense determination had become part of the fabric of Akamai, and rather than fold under the pain, we actually strengthened our resolve to succeed.

Beyond that, we returned to the tried-and-true tenets of business that I'd been immersed in throughout my career. Trying to grow a business out of nothing and do it quickly requires you to rip up the rulebook and make sure there are no impediments in the way of getting the job done. But at some point that freewheeling attitude has to shift. What I told my company was simple: "This is the real world now. Now you are seeing things that our forebears understood." We had to transition from simply operating to operating within a budget, to embrace strategic planning, to write down the best of our thinking. I call it the fierce urgency of now.

Having operated in one mode from the outset—full speed, all the time—we have watched as things slowed down, offering a chance for more deliberation and thoughtful planning. But that doesn't mean we can slow decision making. More than ever, in a downturn and a long sell cycle, we have to have the fierce urgency of now. It's a different form of intensity.

Whereas in the past we would forgo bureaucracy and make decisions on the fly, now we think and act with more deliberation. However, we don't want that to translate into less of a sense of urgency. We have to keep pressure in the system to get the job done. We have to tell the young workforce, many of whom have never been through a down cycle, that it will indeed yield results.

For example, part of keeping pressure in the system is for our sales force to be present and in the customer's face. The sell cycle is long and painful, but we have to be out there as if we were still a start-up, reminding people who Akamai is and what we do. They'll remember us when the buying time comes, and it *will* come. Even if they are not buying today, they will buy tomorrow, and if we have a strong message, they will respond. As Woody Allen once said, "Eighty percent of success is showing up." It took us twelve months to sell to Verizon, but their order is twenty times as big as our traditional orders had been.

Having leading-edge solutions, a dominant market position, and a strong management team that made a commitment to stick it out for the long term provided the stability we needed to keep going. We also evolved our product line so that we didn't stagnate as the market shifted around us. Instead of selling just content delivery, we now sell the assembly, presentation, and delivery of Internet data. This new product suite is especially appealing to enterprise customers seeking to control infrastructure costs.

But selling into the enterprise is a very different sales effort from what our team was used to. It is not only a longer process but more of a consultative one. We must meet multiple decision makers along the way inside target companies. We also have to decide how much to rely on our direct sales force and how much to share with our resellers, including systems integrators and computer makers. In other words, we must change who we are and what we do while maintaining the essence of the company we founded.

Seven Rules for Survival

Start-ups, especially high-tech start-ups struggling through weak economies, must embrace seven key factors for survival and growth.

1. Are we still working on the next big thing? Are we still relevant? Are we still exciting? Keep in mind that most start-ups rely on options to attract and retain the best and brightest employees. We have a strong pipeline to MIT and believe we've hired some of the finest young minds in the business. But when the stock is underwater and we're losing more customers than we're gaining, these same people need a reason to stay.

2. So naturally, the next key is: Do our employees enjoy coming to work? Are they working with smart and talented people they respect and admire? I've always perceived that the money, while important, is not at the top of the list of reasons why people come here. They want to feel that they are part of something special. Especially for research and development people, they want to work on exciting things, and as long as they believe there is a vision and a drive to do something exciting with their work, they won't lose their faith. We saw that as our stock fell from $345 to the single digits.

3. At the same time, we couldn't assume that employees would ignore the financial realities. We had to quickly address the compensation issue in order to keep employees in the game, and we came up with some inventive ways to restructure options using restricted shares that

would never lose their value entirely. We don't have the cash for bonuses, so we remain an options-driven company. By significantly lowering the threshold for options to be in the black, we made it clear to our workforce that they are essential to our success.

4. We also fought to retain an open, collaborative decision-making environment. The same things that made us quick and agile in boom times—the willingness to hear and implement ideas from everyone—must apply when all hell is breaking loose.

5. We also needed to avoid the burnout factor, a common malady for start-ups. We began to push people into new jobs even if it wasn't in their area of expertise. If they focus on something new and get their skill sets growing, they stay more energized and committed.

6. Senior management must get out there in the trenches. We decided that senior managers, including myself, would start making regular sales calls so that the sales reps would never look us in the eye and say, "You sent us out there in this nuclear winter and you're sitting back in the office in your suit. You don't have a clue." We were on those calls with them, so we understood the pain. And more important, we could say, "Yes, it's hard. But it will work if you persist."

7. Senior management must demonstrate their commitment and belief. The top leaders took salaries of $20,000 per year through this dismal time. I own all my shares in the company. I still buy shares in the company. I'm at a station in life where I could walk. I told the employees that. But I'm still here because I believe. That was a powerful message.

Ironically, I learned quite a bit about start-ups while working for IBM. I learned what *not* to do. I saw IBM hit its nadir before the arrival of Lou Gerstner, the turnaround specialist who revitalized the company. There was a lot of strife among senior executives and a lot of finger-pointing. We don't allow that here at Akamai. We *communicate, communicate, communicate.* We are very honest about the issues and what we have to do, and we take action as fast as we can. At IBM, senior management was divorced from the problems in the labs and in the field. There was a lot of talk about doing the right thing but no sense of urgency. I became very sensitive about that and about people not being honest with each other. A start-up requires honesty, and we've been brutally candid with everybody here.

In the long run the winners will emerge from the companies that have enough cash to stay in the game. We vowed to stay cash-positive. We try to maintain $100 million in cash in the bank at all times, and we'll take whatever actions we have to in order to keep the company alive. Around here, the balance sheet is king. We've had two workforce reductions, eliminating a quarter of our population. I hated it. We all hated it. We cut into household names, people who were important and influential. We told them we would hire them back in an instant when things get better. But we had to make a fierce commitment to the budget.

And perhaps most important, I tell employees today what I told them when we hit $345 a share: Don't look at the stock price. Forget about it. Focus on the job at hand, stay positive and excited, and the glass will always be at least half full.

6. Human Resources

Why Brains Trump Brawn

PETER DRUCKER, IN HIS USUAL FARSIGHTED WAY, coined the term "knowledge worker" decades before anyone else, just as computers were making their way from the government's Defense Department to businesses' marketing and finance departments. He understood that companies compete based on what they know and that computers would enable companies to share that knowledge. Soon after Drucker's observations were published, people began talking about "intellectual capital" and how to measure and value it.

Sadly, while we are adept at measuring the value of a factory, we are not very smart when it comes to measuring the value of the contents of our minds. When politicians think of allocating money to support programs at Berkeley, Stanford, Caltech, or the Massachusetts Institute of Technology, to name a few, they think in terms of costs. What are the budgets of these august institutions, and can we afford them? Few, if any, think in terms of the value these four institutions provide. Few, if any, really consider that much of the technological advantage gained by the United States that led to the start-up of thousands of companies (not to mention Silicon Valley or Route 128 themselves) resulted from the value-creating power of minds trained at these and other schools. And if the tech-savvy, tech-dependent U.S. military really is the world's number one fighting force, then knowledge truly is power.

Companies are no different, as Drucker noted. Corporations such as Intel, Fujitsu, IBM, and others make money from putting their best ideas to work. The current battle between Airbus and Boeing over leadership in the commercial aircraft industry has very little to do with aluminum, steel, and jet fuel. It's really about whose *concept* of an airliner is best and which comes closest to serving its customers' needs.

This is only more so in the current era of alliances and outsourcing. Boeing and Airbus build planes by weaving together complex global networks of contractors and subcontractors that shape steel, pound aluminum, weave carbon fiber, and vacuum-form plastic. These networks create complex electronics and engines. The plane is an assemblage of design ideas turned solid. Millions of tiny bits are joined to form larger bits that finally are snapped together to form the planes in which we fly.

At the center of this syncopated dance of stuff are the minds of the companies doing the design work and integration. Informing these big corporate minds are tens of thousands of little minds—glued to computers, huddled in offices, talking to customers, researching, writing, thinking, and endlessly communicating. Everything we make and do is the result of thought and chatter.

Managing the mental game of business is something new. For thousands of years it didn't take much in the way of thinking to conduct commerce. Digging canals took arithmetic, scheduling workers took algebra, building pyramids took geometry, figuring out navigation took trigonometry, launching missiles took calculus.

Competition today is fierce. It takes direct knowledge (if we are producers) and indirect knowledge (if we are customers) of materials science, computing, statistics, chemistry, physics, and a host of other subjects. In medicine we've gone from the era of herbs and poultices to designer molecules.

So how do businesses get smart and stay smart? How do they share knowledge? That's what this section is about.

J.K.

"THE THINGS WE KNOW BEST ARE THE THINGS WE HAVEN'T BEEN TAUGHT": HOW KNOWLEDGE HAPPENS IN ORGANIZATIONS

Bernard Avishai

Like a planned economy, knowledge management is one of those concepts that immediately suggests hubris, but also the promise no sane boss can resist. Big businesses—software, pharmaceuticals, electronics, oil and gas, financial services, you name it—have become engines of invention, with an increasing proportion of profit coming from product or process refinements introduced during the previous twelve months. Survival depends on the ability of various company teams to "sense and respond" to markets (to use IBM's Stephen Haeckel's nice phrase) or coordinate with alliance partners.

So companies innovate with (and largely under the pressure of) Web-based technologies of all kinds: portals, messaging, groupware, XML, informatics. Instant, global exchange of facts and ideas is the solution that is also the problem. Especially in larger companies, general managers do not so much shape their organizations for specific markets as train their organizations to take advantage of opportunities as they arise. They play basketball, not football. A collaboration platform—that is, managed knowledge—is essential to such flexibility. One serious projection has global corporations spending $35 billion annually on intranet and collaboration technologies after 2004.

Portals to Nowhere?

A good part of these investments so far have been steered into "knowledge portals," corporate Web sites that bosses hope will become, in effect, libraries of best practices. Their logic goes something like this:

- Once senior managers articulate a forward strategy, employees gain a repertoire of strategically necessary skills and methods—the know-how, know-about, and know-why that constitute a major part of the company's intellectual capital.
- With or without Web technology, managers can increase productivity by assigning managers to discover, organize, qualify, and disseminate directories of proven skills, best methodological documents, and other tools that align with the business's strategy.
- With Web technology, dissemination is at the speed of light.
- All employees should therefore feel invited—or compelled—to share what they know so that others can learn. For big businesses, this is a vindication of bigness, and a change-management problem that can eventually be licked.

What's wrong with this logic? For people who believe in a planned economy, nothing. But learning in big organizations has proven thornier than this. Companies that have tried the knowledge portal approach—I myself helped lead a global initiative of this kind in a Big 4 accounting firm in the mid-1990s—have found that most "shelves" in the portal either fill up with some of last year's work or remain empty of useful current content. Where employees are expected to make "knowledge deposits," like authors to a library, they respond very much like authors, with writer's block, the fear of humiliation, the fear of betraying confidences, the sense that they have no time, the question "What's in it for me?" and a vague anxiety that they are giving away precious thought to others. Knowledge managers—soliciting, capturing, editing, and tagging content—come to seem like editorial nags.

So users approach the knowledge portal with the (hyped-up) hope of solving an immediate problem, come to despair that they will ever get what they need, contribute perfunctorily, and rarely come back. Getting a bureaucratic system like this to work by hiring change-management consultants is a little like getting state socialism to work by hiring more commissars. Advocates for knowledge management, alas, are facing a challenge much like what Total Quality Management counselors faced in the 1980s, which was to make practical a high concept whose strategic justification was self-evident, whose enabling technologies are maturing, but whose initial deployments were valuable mainly for teaching us what *not* to do.

The point is—and, given the experience of civil society, we might have expected this—we cannot "manage" knowledge. We *can* create an enabling infrastructure that allows educated people to share their thinking and deliverables within, and as a by-product of, ordinary work. The real challenge is to turn the enterprise (and its many alliances) into something like the Web in microcosm—a platform for sharing that is self-organizing, like an idea market. We can already see the outlines of a system of this kind: it would build organically from hundreds, even thousands of ad hoc team collaboration spaces, the only efficient substitute for "reply to all," through which most business is currently conducted. The key for the future is to get this collaboration infrastructure to build not only organically but also *systematically*.

Companies Are Swarms of Teams

What is ordinary work? How does knowledge get into the knowledge economy? Several years ago I spoke with Chi Sun Lai, Motorola's first country manager for China. "People speak of the problems of dealing with the Chinese bureaucracy," Lai recalled, "but ninety percent of my problem was in Motorola. My team and I started to develop a comprehensive marketing and manufacturing plan that would include a range of obvious products—cell phones and so on. I would be committing myself to Chinese officials—and then I would have to coordinate with as many as forty-five Motorola executives and functional teams, negotiating with all of *them* to get the consensus I needed to close the deal with the government."

Lai's challenge: innovation, coordination, commitment, consensus. Business knowledge is mostly improvised in settings like his, by people like him, in the course of dealing with problems like those. A company's "knowledge assets" are not, or not only, finished intellectual properties (formulas and methodologies, structured scientific findings, software designs) snapped smartly into a product development process. Managing knowledge cannot mean taking custody of "corporate memory" or "core competencies" or "what Tom knows, in case Tom gets hit by a truck" (as if a company can "know" the past any better than a country—or Tom—can).

Knowledge is, rather, an enabled process: a continuously rewoven web of contentious ideas and transactions that are contextual, dialectical, dynamic—personal. And it is governed by the values of openness that allow ideas to compete. Companies learn, in other words, because swarms of interfunctional teams learn by analogy to past work, bring to bear systematic expertise, rely on certain structured data (e.g., experimental results, inventory levels, sales projections), recognize new patterns, and improvise new deliverables.

There are teams that ascertain customer reactions, teams that design new prototypes, teams that procure new sources of supply, teams that create new marketing collateral, teams that secure financing—teams that conceive better ways to manage teams. And what holds teams together is negotiation. Employees and partners from outside firms are continuously making commitments to one another, individuals to teams and teams to one another, on projects that may last only a few months. The functional structure of companies is becoming less important than the channels they create for the exchange of information.

Knowledge "happens," therefore, when the business infrastructure enabling the work of teams—appropriate technology, a deliberate atmosphere of openness—enables the natural propensity of individual employees to trade expertise and experiences so that, as team members, they can meet commitments to deliver negotiated work products. The team is, correspondingly, more than the seat of action. It is also the context for producing valuable content. And context is everything.

Knowledge Architecture and External Content

The late physicist Richard Feynman observed that the eye is not a collector of information but a filter of it. If the eye could see all wavelengths of the spectrum (X rays, gamma rays, radio waves), we could make sense of nothing; the abundance of information and the clashing of contexts would paralyze us—which is why the eye allows us to see only what we can touch. What we need to touch is a function of what we need to *do*.

But here is the problem. How do we narrow filters on information so that they can bring help to employees in the specific contexts of specific teams? We know that our browser can access virtually all the information we need, mostly for free, but who has the time to browse? While writing this essay, I searched for "supply chain management" on

ON WORK

Parkinson's Law

■ Work expands so as to fill the time available for its completion. General recognition of this fact is shown in the proverbial line, "It is the busiest man who has time to spare." Thus, an elderly lady of leisure can spend the entire day in writing and dispatching a postcard to her niece at Bognor Regis. An hour will be spent in finding the postcard, another in hunting for spectacles, half an hour in a search for the address, an hour and a quarter in composition, and twenty minutes in deciding whether or not to take an umbrella when going to the mailbox in the next street. The total effort that would occupy a busy man for three minutes all told may in this fashion leave another person prostrate after a day of doubt, anxiety, and toil.

Granted that work (and especially paperwork) is thus elastic in its demands on time, it is manifest that there need to be little or no relationship between the work to be done and the size of the staff to which it may be assigned. A lack of real activity does not, of necessity, result in leisure. ■

From C. Northcote Parkinson, *Parkinson's Law, and Other Studies in Administration* (Houghton Mifflin, 1957).

Google and got more than 1.2 million hits. "Merck" produced 1.5 million hits (in .08 seconds, though this seemed of little consolation). How to enable exploration of such richness, especially when internal content (produced organically in the company's own messaging and collaboration spaces) is added in?

First, senior managers must forget the technology and do what institutions of higher learning have always done, namely, bind critically important knowledge domains within a system of classification that maps to anticipated communities of practice. This is art, not science, but somebody has to do it; a half-right classification is better than none at

all. Managers must provide a knowledge architecture for the organization—a unique corporate context for filtering content—that reflects the
likely ways teams would self-identify. This usually means articulating
the matrixes of the organization (for one of Mr. Lai's reports, "marketing," "cell phones," "corporate development," "China"). Given this system, presentations, white papers, discussion threads, and unstructured
scientific findings take on critically helpful tags *as they are created*, and
fly around the company preclassified for retrieval by increasingly powerful search engines.

Corporate matrixes change quickly, and getting them approved
can be a little like getting a bill passed in Congress. But even if classifi-
cations of practice areas and content types are only temporarily stable,
they become the spine of the collective workspace, physical *and* virtual.
The real challenge of groupware is the group, not the ware. And like
physical architecture when it is right, a knowledge architecture of this
kind stops us in our tracks and excites the imagination of those we seek
to teach, implying a vivid sense of what the company stands for. Management will now need to find a way to shape the freewheeling messaging environment without imposing rigid direction, much like the Web
itself does. Employees and partners will have to think outside the box, so
management will have to supply boxes.

Once stipulated, the knowledge architecture has obvious advantages for filtering what is external to the company. There is a universe
of Web-based information that teams need to stay on top of: news, analyst reports, and so on. Companies can now augment search engines
such as Google and Yahoo! with filtering algorithms, largely developed
in the intelligence services, that get fewer but more-relevant hits for
them. (For, say, "information risk management," the firm I worked
for deployed customized Boolean search strings as complex as a short
encyclopedia article, running against only those sources that are author-
itative enough to trust.) Content aggregation and filtering companies
such as Lexis-Nexis can do this work, deploying small armies of research

librarians to write and refine filters for thousands of business topics, and run the filters against qualified sources for particular topics, news organizations, investment banks, and even universities and consulting companies.

Knowledge Architecture + Collaboration = Publication

Filtering content from internal sources is a more elaborate task, but the principle is the same. If we are right that business information is best grasped in terms of the team activity that produced it, we will need to navigate to many producers' frames of reference. How do we induce those team members to "publish" their content in the context in which it is produced and with relevant tags so that others will know where to look?

The answer is, we don't. We merely ask team leaders to name the team collaboration space according to the corporate knowledge architecture, and we *automatically* tag what is shared in such spaces. Once tagged, internal content can be filtered and retrieved exactly the way external content is. (Automatic tagging means knowing how to build an application layer that applies an XML schema to each document. Trust that it can be done—we won't go into it here.) Project work flow determines the types of content; the matrix of the organization determines the context for content. A company's most important current materials actually reside in the messaging system, as e-mail attachments, or in groupware, as part of team-based databases managed as collaborative workspaces. The point is to make this content potentially available *as it is created*. After the creation of work products (memos, presentations, unstructured findings) the problem becomes one of security, not classification—the "reading privileges" that allow only qualified employees to access certain things.

Conclusion: The Boundaries of Organization

It is in collaborative work, not as individuals coming to portals or libraries, that the most important transactions of the company should be grasped. Ray Ozzie, the visionary behind Lotus Notes and Groove Networks, argues that the most innovative thinking now happens on the margins of companies, on the boundary between an enterprise and its business partners, as teams negotiate with suppliers, customers, research groups, and others. Collaboration spaces must be launched with the idea that they will become the content management system for many portals.

In any case, knowledge management is growing up in this way, and none too soon. The growth of a company means managing partnership. The system designed to manage communities of practice in the organization is the only system likely to manage the value chain outside of the organization, connecting research groups to marketing and production partners. Which is another way of saying that knowledge infrastructure is the sinew making virtual organizations real. And virtual organizations are going to be the only ones we'll have.

INTELLECTUAL CAPITAL, NOT FINANCIAL CAPITAL, DRIVES VALUE

Des Dearlove

During the tight labor markets of the 1990s many chief executive officers began to believe that one of their main roles in the organization was recruiting and retaining the best and brightest people. Talent was elevated to the pinnacle of strategic importance, and CEOs recast themselves as chief talent scouts.

Asked to sum up the reasons for his phenomenal success at GE, for example, Jack Welch told *BusinessWeek:* "My main job was developing talent. I was a gardener providing water and other nourishment to our top 750 people."

For Virgin chief Richard Branson, the key is to identify entrepreneurial talent and channel it through the Virgin empire. "What I do best is finding good people and letting them work," he has observed. "Virgin staff are not merely hired hands. They are not managerial pawns in some gigantic chess game. They are entrepreneurs in their own right."

The success of Microsoft has been built on the company's ability to attract the brightest and the best people in its industry. "I'd have to say my best business decisions have to do with picking people," CEO Bill

Gates once said. "Deciding to go into business with Paul Allen is probably at the top of the list, and subsequently hiring a friend—Steve Ballmer—who has been my primary business partner ever since."

Gates' involvement in the recruitment process extends beyond the selection of his closest aides. If a key hire requires additional persuasion to join the company, Gates will intervene with a personal telephone call. In 1981 he was instrumental in hiring Charles Simonyi—the "father of Microsoft Word"—from Xerox PARC.

Inspired by these and other role models, CEOs everywhere have embraced the role of talent scout. In recent years they have been further encouraged by an outpouring of books, articles, and corporate pronouncements claiming that companies are now engaged in nothing short of a "war for talent." This has become a major preoccupation for many large corporations, which invested millions of dollars in initiatives designed to attract the best graduates and engender loyalty among their best people.

Talent, it was widely believed, was calling the tune, and companies did the corporate equivalent of an Irish jig. Galvanized by the attention of their CEOs, human resources departments went into overdrive as companies deployed a variety of financial inducements to persuade the best and brightest to join their ranks. MBA graduates were enticed with joining bonuses; remuneration packages were beefed up with share options. Employee perks were also ramped up as corporate pampering extended to office masseurs and corporate concierges who could organize everything from full laundry service to housecleaning and car servicing.

During the recession that began in 2001, many companies began laying off staff and putting hiring on hold. The return to higher levels of unemployment in most developed economies might be taken as a sign that talent is more plentiful. (Business schools, for example, reported in early 2002 that the number of job offers to MBA graduates was way down compared to previous years.) But this couldn't be further from the truth. Talent will remain the scarce resource for the foreseeable future.

One of the first studies to draw attention to talent shortages was a 1998 report from McKinsey & Company. Entitled "The War for Talent," it concluded that many U.S. companies were suffering from a dearth of executive talent, which was likely to be intensified by broad demographic trends. A 2001 update found that the war for talent was escalating despite the economic slowdown and the end of the dot-com boom. Some 89 percent of those surveyed thought it was more difficult to attract talented people than it had been three years earlier, and 90 percent thought it was more difficult to retain them.

Talent Drivers

Driving the war for talent are a number of convergent trends. The first is the demographic time bomb. Most of the developed nations have aging populations. If current trends continue, for example, by 2012 almost 50 percent of Germany's population will be over sixty-five. In the United States it is predicted that the number of thirty-five-to-forty-four-year-olds will fall by 15 percent by 2018.

The second trend is the shift in the old psychological contract. The bonds of loyalty between employer and employee have been loosened. Many more people now hop from one company to another or aspire to work for themselves as free agents or in entrepreneurial start-ups.

The third trend (and the one most significant for CEOs) is the shift away from financial capital to intellectual capital as the main driver of economic value. This has far-reaching implications for the role of the modern CEO. Talent is now replacing financial capital as the key strategic resource. Competitive advantage and value creation increasingly come from leveraging human capital—the ideas, expertise, and relationships that exist within the organization.

People as Strategic Resources

In their 1999 book *The Individualized Corporation*, Christopher Bartlett and Sumantra Ghoshal, professors at Harvard and London Business Schools, respectively, describe a business revolution in its early stages. The corporate model, they say, is in rebirth. Companies are trying to reorganize themselves around the scarce resource of human capital.

This turns the capitalist model on its head. Economic observers have assumed throughout the last century that financial capital is all-important and that companies should be organized around its effective use. Traditional measures—such as return on investment and earnings per share—assess the control and management of financial capital. The performance of CEOs has long been judged by such measures.

The old corporate model provided a sophisticated reporting system that pulled information to the top of the organization so that the CEO could make decisions about the allocation of financial capital. That, argue Bartlett and Ghoshal, is now changing. It's not that financial capital is no longer important; it's that it is no longer *the* constraining resource.

The constraining resource—and therefore the strategic resource—is human capital. In the emergent organizational model, human capital is more important to value creation than financial capital. This explains why billions of dollars of venture capital now chase the talent.

Good CEOs have always managed talent, of course. In the early part of the century Alfred P. Sloan of General Motors religiously attended job interviews to ensure that the company attracted the right sort of talent. Today research suggests that CEOs spend between 40 and 50 percent of their time on people issues. In the past this was reflected in the notion of "bench strength." Having a rich seam of executive talent was seen as a key indicator of corporate well-being. Companies such as IBM and GE prided themselves on having talent in depth.

Maintaining a ready supply of able understudies was integral to the smooth running of the corporate machine. Succession planning was seen as part and parcel of the CEO's job. But it was not the primary focus.

The primary responsibility of the CEO was to deliver value to the people who provided that financial capital. Shareholders ruled the roost. But if value creation now depends on attracting and retaining the best people, then shareholder value becomes a by-product of managing talent rather than the other way around. This requires CEOs to reprioritize. They have to recalibrate their strategic compass. If human capital is now true north, then managing talent is the number one task.

Today managing talent is no longer about creating a supply of people who will become the next generation of senior management. It is about harnessing the talents of a much more diverse group to create value. Today the people who really count are just as likely to be software programmers or scientists as MBAs. These new knowledge workers are scattered across the organization. Creating new value is about connecting their talents in new ways.

For CEOs the challenge is twofold: to attract and retain the best people in their fields, and to find ways to leverage their talents across the organization. Neither is easy.

In the first case, most companies currently rely on the blunt instrument of financial inducements. This is starting to unravel. In good times companies are able to use financial incentives and other carrots to attract and keep talented staff. But during a downturn these practices are harder to sustain. Salaries may be frozen, share options underwater.

When hard times hit it is harder for companies to produce the necessary bribes. Neither can they fall back on old notions of loyalty. As the current round of layoffs demonstrates, no company can guarantee job security. What is needed now is a new way for companies to engage with people. Outdated notions of loyalty need to be replaced with something more sustainable. Companies need to move beyond the traditional employee-employer relationship to one based on partnership and mutual benefits.

The role of the CEO as talent scout is to reorient the organization to regard people not as hired hands but as investors (what Bartlett and Ghoshal call "volunteer investors"). People who invest their talents in the company will expect a financial return on their human capital. They will also expect that capital to grow—their expertise, knowledge, and networks will be enhanced by working with the company. Companies must provide opportunities for people to invest their human capital.

This is also the best way to address the second challenge facing CEOs, namely, how to harness talent. CEOs, then, must become organizational venture capitalists. They must cultivate networks of talent both inside and outside the organization. They must find ways to engage the talents of the best and brightest wherever they happen to be. And they must foster a culture and environment that resonate with entrepreneurial dynamism.

To do so they will have to confront the biggest issue of all: the redistribution of value away from traditional shareholders to the new shareholders—the talent. In the old world financial capital was the scarce resource and attracted the biggest rewards. Today cash is no longer king. If talent is now the value driver, then it requires a bigger slice of the pie. It's not just about money. It's about involvement, freedom of expression, and enabling workers to pursue their own agendas. Ownership per se isn't the issue; it's how you reward talented people for the fruits of their intellectual capital.

WHEN THE ASSETS LEAVE THE PARKING LOT AT NIGHT: RETAINING AND MOTIVATING KNOWLEDGE WORKERS

Stuart Crainer

There have always been knowledge workers, people who earn their living through what and who they know. The age-old professions of law, medicine, and the church were built around people with knowledge. Though knowledge workers have been plying their intellectual trade for centuries, they were never known as such. The phrase "knowledge workers" was coined by the management thinker Peter Drucker in the 1960s. It is now widely used and applies especially to people in the business world whose knowledge is central to their employability.

The emergence of the knowledge worker in the spheres of business, management, and leadership is an important development. Management emerged as a somewhat respectable and independent discipline only at the beginning of the twentieth century. Initially, managers were overseers, supervisors, and little else. They were not professionals, but lingered in stiff collars and ill-fitting suits somewhere down the economic food chain. Slowly the world of managers expanded. Their knowledge rather than their ability to hold a stopwatch and crack the motivational whip over compliant employees became ever more important. Today managers are expected to master an array of different skills. They too are professionals, and knowledge is the cornerstone of their work. It is assumed that they no longer require a stopwatch.

In parallel to the rise of management was that of the consulting profession. The earliest management consultants were engineers, creators of processes and hierarchies. But the core of their work was—and remains—the transfer of knowledge. The growth of management consulting as a substantial worldwide industry has served to emphasize the increasing role of knowledge in running businesses.

Indeed, the entire basis of the management consulting industry rests on what is now called "thought leadership." Consultants compete on the originality and usefulness of their ideas. This fact of competitive life can now also be applied to corporations. Ideas are a competitive weapon. And if a company can institutionalize the ideas as knowledge, then the commercial potential is enormous.

The implications of the rise of knowledge workers are wide-ranging. However, there are two central issues. First, the power in organizations now rests to a greater degree than ever before with knowledge workers, those who possess the knowledge vital to an organization's competitive future. Second, organizations need to develop means of managing, retaining, understanding, and maximizing the power of the knowledge that lies within them.

At a personal level, the emergence of knowledge workers represents a major shift in the power dynamics of corporations. A single software developer can wield enormous power. Bill Gates has reflected on the importance of a mere half dozen developers to Microsoft. A senior executive is no longer a faceless cog in a machine but a person whose knowledge is vital to the company's success. Some commentators, Charles Handy among them, have pointed out that what Karl Marx wrote about has actually come to pass: workers own the means of production.

Clearly, retaining and motivating such individuals is critical for organizations both large and small. There is one problem, however. Unfortunately for corporations, knowledge is extremely portable, neatly contained within the human brain. The new Marxists can depart in an organization trice with the knowledge assembled at your expense.

Organizations have, therefore, to create environments in which knowledge workers are productive and stimulated. A small number manage to do so. Their methods are assiduously charted by competitors and emulated. If a successful corporation leaves stacks of M&Ms around, observers conclude, that must be the corporation's secret, so they go out and buy some M&Ms. The trouble is that emulating a fertile environment for knowledge workers is akin to faking sincerity.

The organizational challenge is substantial. Managing and leading knowledge workers require a new set of skills. These workers are not compliant. They cannot be easily corralled where you want them. They are loyal to themselves rather than blindly loyal to the corporation.

Missing the point, many increasingly desperate organizations now offer an array of extras to ensure that knowledge workers are retained. Free underwear has been among the perks offered to staff at Salomon Smith Barney in return for their loyalty—the firm offered staff a clothes allowance, which includes undergarments, and free toothbrushes.

A collection of slightly grubby carrots is unlikely to prove alluring to knowledge workers. Retaining and motivating knowledge workers should begin with an understanding of their knowledge and how it may be developed and enhanced. The best knowledge workers are stimulated by the acquisition of knowledge and the awareness that the more knowledge they possess, the more lucrative the rewards. If knowledge is their bargaining chip, they realize—or should realize—that out-of-date knowledge rapidly decreases in value. Organizations that offer opportunities to develop knowledge should, in theory at least, be the most successful in recruiting and retaining the best knowledge workers.

At a more general level, companies have to wrestle with the nature of knowledge. This is slippery and elusive. How can corporate knowledge be enhanced, expanded, and protected across the organization? This is even more slippery. How can knowledge be brought out into the open and maximized? This is the Holy Grail. How can you take what already exists but is hidden, and make it real, accessible, and useful?

In the search for answers, corporations have pursued three main strategies. They have invested in technology to systematize the flow of knowledge, introduced knowledge management initiatives, and made attempts to quantify and understand their intellectual capital, the value of the knowledge that resides within the organization.

These are characteristic corporate responses. Investing in more technology is usually seen as a forward-looking move. Systematizing knowledge is a good idea. Many knowledge management initiatives have involved the creation of large-scale repositories of information in databases or intranet sites. To some extent this misses the point by simply collecting data without necessarily having any understanding of its significance or usefulness.

Technology only gets you so far. Knowledge is not simply an agglomeration of information; it is the ability of the individual or the company to act meaningfully on the basis of that information. Information is not knowledge until it has been processed by the human mind. The trouble is that an emphasis on technology may lead to data being mistaken for knowledge. In addition, expensive knowledge management systems can be left unused unless people are made aware of the personal benefits of using them and rewarded for doing so. Technology may be the conduit, but the rubber hits the tarmac at the point where the human brain and the technology meet.

The launch of a knowledge management initiative is also a typical corporate response. At any one time a number of fashionable initiatives are usually under way at any large corporation. The trouble with these is that most are short-lived. Their sheer profusion means that there is a degree of corporate ennui and cynicism about their usefulness and importance. Knowledge management initiatives have a patchy track record.

Productivity

VICTORIA GRIFFITH

■ Back in the Stone Age it could take people days to put together a simple spear—weeks, perhaps, to make a necklace. Most people would agree that modern-day humans are far more productive. We can produce many more goods in a much shorter period of time.

Yet when it comes to inventions of the computer age, the progress in productivity is less clear. Does e-mail help us do our jobs faster? Wouldn't a telephone call work just as well? And how do we factor in the time we waste on e-mail, getting in touch with old friends or simply sifting through the spam that lands on our desktop every day?

Economists have long been puzzled by the glacierlike progress of productivity through the latter part of the twentieth century. After moving along at a rapid clip—3.3 percent per year—in the 1950s and 1960s, productivity gain slowed to just 1 percent annually, on average, between 1973 and 1995. Productivity gains are important because in the long run they are the only way people can afford to buy more stuff.

Some economists have theorized that in a service-based economy— one in which professionals such as teachers, lawyers, and consultants contribute more to GDP than manu-

The final automatic corporate response is to seek out ways of measuring and quantifying knowledge in the organization. The hope— rather than the expectation—is that what gets measured may well get done. This is the world of intellectual capital. Intellectual capital basically seeks to combine human capital (the skills, perspectives, brainpower, and potential of those in an organization) with structural capital (the capital wrapped up in customers, processes, databases, brands, and systems) to produce some kind of measure of its value.

The entire notion of intellectual capital is intriguing and, in many

facturers—productivity gains are harder to come by. Technology may speed up production lines, they argue, but workers who rely on their own know-how are helped only marginally by new inventions.

A rival camp of economists disagrees. This group says that the benefits from information technology are just taking time to trickle through. The electric motor was invented in the 1880s, they point out, but improvements from the innovation did not show up in productivity figures for another forty years.

These economists seemed to be vindicated when productivity began to tick up in 1996. For the final five years of the millennium productivity rose at about 2 percent per year, twice the average for the previous two decades. It rose again in the early 2000s. Even the head of the Federal Reserve, Alan Greenspan, bought into this argument and began to talk of a new economic era, in which gains in productivity would allow GDP to grow at a higher rate without risking inflation.

The jury is still out. The naysayers of the new economy believe the upturn of the late 1990s and early 2000s was a mere by-product of a boom in the demand for goods. With workers and factories churning out products at full capacity, productivity is bound to go up. Now that demand has eased and there is more slack in the system, we could very well see a decline in productivity growth. ■

aspects, commonsensical. If knowledge is valuable, then finding a reliable and consistent means of measurement would appear to make sense. The trouble is, of course, that a large amount of the knowledge in any organization is tacit rather than explicit, elusive rather than firm. Little wonder that agreeing what constitutes intellectual capital and finding a reliable means of valuing it is an ongoing and lively debate.

The growing interest in intellectual capital provides a challenge to traditional accounting. Champions of intellectual capital, such as Baruch Lev of New York University's Stern School of Business, point

out that an array of intangible assets are ignored by conventional accounting methods. The value of individual knowledge workers, for
example, is not quantified. Indeed, the departure of the most valuable
individual in a company can go unacknowledged in the accounts and
annual report.

Intellectual capital is making some headway, especially in Scandinavia, and may continue to do so as some degree of consistency across
measuring tools is established. In Sweden the financial services company Scandia has led the way in publishing annual reports of the state
of its intellectual capital. Elsewhere, companies such as Buckman Laboratories, headquartered in Memphis, Tennessee, have put intellectual
capital at the center of their agenda. Buckman has been a pioneer in
knowledge management with K'Netix, producing the Buckman Knowledge Network.

For knowledge workers this raises the intriguing possibility—
albeit in years to come—of individuals having a value placed on them.
In the same way as sports stars are valued and transferred from club to
club, knowledge workers may have prices on their heads. The good news
for them is that they, rather than their organization, are likely to receive the transfer fee. If this seems far-fetched, consider that the market
already exists to some extent in the senior executives who are poached
and take on jobs offering substantial signing-on packages.

While the array of projects, initiatives, and suchlike in the field of
knowledge management is increasing awareness, the area remains a
minefield of misunderstanding. Core elements of knowledge work are
overlooked or remain deeply mired in intellectual vagueness. Most
notable among these is the social element of knowledge work.

In many organizations the biggest stumbling block to the dissemination of knowledge is the unwillingness of knowledge workers to pass
their knowledge on to their colleagues. If knowledge is power, people
would still prefer to have it for themselves. This is human nature and
also, perhaps, indicative of a greater awareness that knowledge really
does mean power in the employment marketplace.

Companies that have succeeded in nurturing cadres of knowledge workers—and there are precious few—have usually built a corporate environment that fosters a desire for knowledge among their employees and that ensures its continual application, distribution, and creation. They reward employees for seeking, sharing, and creating knowledge. At the other end of the spectrum, one of the greatest barriers to effective knowledge management lies in the basic insecurity and fear that prevail in many companies.

This kind of "social ecology" is the central paradox that lies behind the rise of knowledge workers. While knowledge imbues individuals with great power, the dynamics of knowledge mean that its inception and spread rely on social interaction, the context created by organizations. Knowledge is a social thing, as easily accumulated over coffee as in a formal meeting.

Creative media companies, such as the design firm IDEO, with their emphasis on teamworking and dynamic creative interaction, are often cited as exemplars of knowledge management. For them, maximizing knowledge is as much a social issue as a technological one. They have table football *and* wall-to-wall iMacs. It is about relationships, environments, and emotions rather than software. The real issue for companies is how they persuade individuals to hand over their know-how when it is the source of their power—and the only guarantee of their continuing employment.

This is not to say that creative businesses have a monopoly over knowledge management. Nucor, the world's fastest-growing and most innovative steel company for the past three decades, has used effective knowledge management to build its main strategic competencies: plant construction and start-up, manufacturing processes, and the rapid adoption of new technologies ahead of the competition.

Of course, knowledge is not simply an internal issue. Generating new knowledge cannot simply come from within the organization. No organization, however smart, has a monopoly on bright ideas. Companies and individuals must seek access to new knowledge from outside their normal boundaries as a means of updating and renewing their knowledge bases. Restlessness and curiosity are necessities for knowledge workers. This is why the famously innovative American company Rubbermaid dispatches its managers to museums in search of inspiration.

If traditional corporations fail to keep knowledge workers within the fold, the implications may go beyond workers decamping to the competition. Increasingly, we are likely to see the rise of markets in knowledge. Markets used to trade in things. There were markets in tin, cocoa, silver, and the like. There was security in thinking that somewhere there was a product, something you could touch and see. You got something for your money. Now there are markets in abstractions, trade in ideas and knowledge.

This knowledge economy may unleash workers from corporate restraints, so they will no longer trade their knowledge with employers or clients but market it through online auctions. Knowledge and experience can already be bought and sold online. If this trend continues, it could mark the coming of age of e-commerce and could allow huge reservoirs of specialist knowledge to be tapped commercially for the first time. Knowledge and knowledge workers will be free at last. But their knowledge will carry a premium price.

IF YOU DON'T CREATE VALUE, YOU'RE NOT A REAL ENTREPRENEUR

Timothy J. McMahon

What is an entrepreneur? What makes a company entrepreneurial? What makes an entrepreneurial company excellent?

There probably is no other word in the vocabulary of American business that is so familiar and yet filled with such mystique. The challenge is to define this term that has come to mean so much and, I'm afraid, so little in the past few years.

As someone who makes his livelihood evaluating the management savvy and financial prospects of growing companies, I tend to define entrepreneurism as a process of value creation. We talk every day to companies that believe they have a better idea. It's our responsibility to them and to the investors putting millions of dollars into these companies to determine whether these ideas translate into business value. Entrepreneurism is the value created as good ideas become good companies; this is the purest form of entrepreneurism I can imagine. If no business value is created, you cease to have entrepreneurism. It's that simple, and that difficult.

There are countless examples of successful entrepreneurism, from

Coca-Cola to Microsoft—enterprises that have created business value over sustained periods while adapting to changing business cycles.

The meaning and value of entrepreneurism, however, became diluted and weakened in the late 1990s by the trendy notion that entrepreneurism is simply the act of inventing something or making some daring business move for the sake of being impressive. For proof, look no further than the vast landfill of dot-com failures. Remember how many of these ventures said they would revolutionize the world as we know it and profit from first-mover advantage?

One example of this sort of flash-in-the-pan entrepreneurism is Cozone.com, a Web business started by CompUSA stores to sell computer gear online. The fact that you probably haven't heard of Cozone.com illustrates the lesson of what happens when risk taking combines with jump-on-the-bandwagon incentives to create a kind of pseudoentrepreneurism that lacks any real chance of longevity.

Arguably, the most memorable achievement of Cozone.com was its TV commercials (featuring Donald Trump trying to make pottery), which—$20 million later—were still airing even as the decision was being made to pull the plug on the business. In essence, the ads outlived the company; "Cozone in the Ozone" was the headline used by a business magazine when it wrote about the company's failure. While Cozone.com and countless other e-business failures all earn credit for bravado, they are not what future business leaders should look upon as true entrepreneurism.

To be fair, it's not just the much-maligned Internet start-ups that distorted the core idea of entrepreneurism. Over the decades, gadgets and gold diggers of every imaginable description have hit the market, a few perhaps making a momentary splash. It's culturally irresistible not to be entertained and maybe even impressed by some of these phenomena.

But when we most need it—like now, with the stock market in turmoil and consumer confidence at dramatic lows—we should not lower our standards and say "entrepreneur" the minute someone gets an idea or finds some cash to start a business. This is important, not just because it helps us discuss entrepreneurism intelligently but because it will prevent us from becoming unduly pessimistic about the state of entrepreneurism in America. There is certainly cause for cynicism, but only if you believe in the kind of short-term entrepreneurism that has become the antihero of the U.S. economy.

But We're So Much Smarter Now

By popular definition, entrepreneurism works something like this: an inventor gets an idea that creates a new technology, extends an existing one, or disturbs an entrenched market pattern with a brilliant new way of doing things. Investors and customers then move quickly to capitalize on this flash of brilliance.

And surely, in the age of hydrogen fuel cells, human cloning, and intelligent networks, you would think entrepreneurism in the twenty-first century is a whole new ball game. The truth is, in most respects it's the same as it was in the nineteenth century.

If Plato and Adam Smith were to have a discussion in our twelfth-floor conference room, they might well decide that entrepreneurism is not just a fascinating but esoteric topic of discussion. Entrepreneurism, with its dynamic blend of courage, creativity, and discipline, is the perfect platonic form or template for all business endeavors—the ideal point of reference for what business should be, no matter what size the company is or in what social climate it operates.

There is something very American about the view of the emerging company's triumph in the marketplace, and it reflects the globally accepted affinity between U.S. markets and entrepreneurs. This view of entrepreneurism is inseparable from the way in which our country developed. You might even say that America itself is the greatest entrepreneurial idea the world has ever known. Ingenuity and risk taking are a way of life. It is no surprise, then, that we so heavily reward these characteristics in business.

Unfortunately, our penchant for tinkerers, inventors, and risk takers has created a false notion of what entrepreneurism means in the modern age.

Dreamers and geniuses aren't necessarily entrepreneurs, even though most great (and lasting) businesses stem from someone's dream and prosper through various kinds of genius—from the kind of technical genius we associate with Steve Wozniak, cofounder of Apple, or the strategic genius of someone like Bill Gates.

The key to all of this is *adaptability*. The initial spark of an idea typically comes as a person or group reacts to the circumstances around them. While it might start as a mere brainstorm, in some way it represents a push against the current norm, a first act of adaptation. But from this state of raw creativity comes the challenge of doing something with that idea and shepherding the process through the various obstacles facing every change to the status quo. Having the idea is "inventional"; stewarding that idea to business success—adapting countless times—is entrepreneurial.

To illustrate, there are two telling examples that addressed a similar problem with vastly different solutions. Each was entrepreneurial in the truest sense, even though they followed strikingly different paths and offer different lessons.

Decades ago, when electric typewriters were the predominant office machines and stockrooms were piled high with ink ribbons and carbon paper, two individuals created innovative new products, and each founded a business around the product. Both were entrepreneurial, but in entirely different ways. What they had in common was entrepreneurial excellence, at least at the outset.

In the 1950s Bette Nesmith, a bad typist but a trained artist, created a solution to the drudgery of retyping. Using her knowledge of paints, she developed a quick-drying, highly opaque correction fluid that became the ubiquitous Liquid Paper. The prodigiously intelligent An

Wang looked beyond individual corrections in the 1970s and saw the potential of microprocessors to eliminate conventional retyping altogether, creating the first widely distributed word processors.

Their inventions earned Nesmith and Wang millions. Today, Liquid Paper is somewhat marginalized, though still useful for photocopying and touch-up work. On the other hand, Wang Laboratories, the company Wang founded to build his machines, is obsolete. After flaring brightly but briefly, its dedicated hardware for typing was buried by the PC revolution.

Wang is widely credited with inventing word processing and introducing the term to business. But when word processing migrated from hardware to software, Wang Laboratories was unready and failed to enter the business, much less lead it.

So were Nesmith's and Wang's enterprises entrepreneurial? In my opinion, yes. They certainly met the better-mousetrap test in their initial stage of adaptation and went on to generate wealth over a period of time. But in terms of entrepreneurial excellence, I would argue that Nesmith was actually a better entrepreneur. While you can walk into any Staples or Office Depot and buy Liquid Paper, Wang word processors are nowhere to be found, relegated to computer museums as historical artifacts.

More than anything, Liquid Paper represented the triumph of good management teams over flash-in-the-pan invention. Nesmith's adaptive presence of mind led her to realize she was not the person who could manage the business success of Liquid Paper. She smartly sold the rights of the technology to Gillette in 1975; Newell Rubbermaid bought Gillette's stationery products division in 2001.

Wang, on the other hand, fell victim to one of the cardinal sins of entrepreneurism. The genius founder rode his invention right into the ground, along with the company, when it probably had the time and resources to adapt to the rise of the PC and to own the market for word processing software.

Although it is easy to lapse into a sentimentalized view, we must always remember that the entrepreneurial organization is first and foremost a business. The entrepreneur's task is no different whether the company in question has fifty employees or fifty thousand; its primary task is to build shareholder value. The management team must secure a market position capable of sustaining growth over time, using its skill and discipline to constantly adapt to market circumstances.

The ability to attract, motivate, and retain a strong management team is the entrepreneurial company's most important asset. High-tech-sector investors often debate the relative merits of a great management team versus a great idea. Of course, investors should not have to choose. But if you ever have to, put your money on management.

The reality underlying this debate isn't really all that complex. Look no further than Microsoft, which is perhaps the textbook example of value-based entrepreneurism. From its beginning, Microsoft wedged its way into nascent markets using management expertise when it lacked superior technology (which was most of the time). Strategically smart and practical, Microsoft executives established a strong position rooted in market reality and an internal culture with the cohesiveness of a military boot camp. It continues to outmaneuver competitors even when it might be expected to rely on sheer size and momentum.

There is no time in the life of an entrepreneurial company when this kind of managerial skill is dispensable. Even in a company's earliest developmental stages, when it may be busy showcasing its technology, its management must be skillful enough to surpass competitors who have not yet revealed themselves. While it's possible for a paradigm-busting idea to prevail in spite of mediocre market strategy or execution, it's not likely.

Since change is usually the impetus for entrepreneurism, it follows that adaptability to change is another critical asset for the entrepreneurial company. Volatility in the marketplace, in social trends, and in business technology all give rise to opportunities for the entrepreneur. In fact, one definition of entrepreneurism is the attempt to take charge of change through profitable enterprise. More than mere nimbleness, this requires the courage to face the unexpected and to let go of theories once they begin to weigh down the organization, no matter how heavily vested those theories may be. One prime example is Coca-Cola, which was originally developed as a tonic—a liquid suspension of a form of cocaine. Only when a friend of its inventor suggested repositioning it as a refreshing beverage was it freed to fulfill its global potential as "The Pause That Refreshes."

The biotechnology sector illustrates even more compelling examples of entrepreneurial management teams' ability to take original breakthroughs and successfully adapt and reapply them to new market opportunities. For instance, Centocor was able to successfully change its therapeutic area of focus while at the same time relying on the core strength of its technology. Its monoclonal antibody technology was originally focused on the sepsis market, but Centoxin ultimately failed in clinical trials. Recognizing the certain roadblock that it faced, Centocor chose to adapt its technology and take it in a different therapeutic direction. With its development of ReoPro, an antithrombotic therapy addressing the cardiovascular disease arena and the rapid growth of angioplasty, Centocor successfully launched and marketed this product, and the company was eventually acquired by Johnson & Johnson in 1999.

This kind of adaptability runs counter to the better-mousetrap school. Its adherents tend to believe that the world will conform to their vision and adopt their invention as presented, thus changing life as we know it. While some technologies and innovations actually do prove that powerful, successful entrepreneurs have learned a crucial lesson from chaos theory: extrapolating the results of change isn't easy. Your own success as a change agent may make it harder to predict the results of your own work, and harder to capitalize on it. To stay in business long enough to have impact, you must meet payrolls and the exigencies of changing market conditions with the unchanging principles of professional management.

It is this staying power that separates the entrepreneur from the speculator and the inventor. Start-up and takeover artists are not true entrepreneurs; they operate with a profitable endgame in mind. As with inventors, there is nothing wrong with this kind of profit per se.

But all too frequently the speculator seeks to start up, acquire fast, cash in, and get out—often strip-mining assets, spinning off divisions, dismantling or merging entities into oblivion. The entrepreneur, by contrast, seeks to build a new organization that will endure, grow, and add to the *world's* wealth, not just his or her own. When a true entrepreneur leaves such an organization, it survives because it remains in the hands of professional management.

There are dozens of entrepreneurial philosophies that legitimately differ from the one I've outlined here, which could be characterized as a purist's perspective. Probably none is tougher to fulfill than this one. But ironically, this model for entrepreneurism is especially timely in the volatile markets of the new millennium; it is countercyclical, succeeding best when times are toughest. When the economy is roaring along and access to capital is relatively unrestricted, many people obtain it—including some of the wrong people. But when times are tough and capital is hard to come by, that is when funders find renewed appreciation for managerial excellence. And that's when the true entrepreneurs get going.

INNOVATION AND COMMERCIALIZATION: UNLOCKING THE VALUE OF INTELLECTUAL PROPERTY

Amiel Kornel

The power of invention is one of the overblown business myths of our time. In today's technology-enamored society, many people believe that an ingenious idea guarantees business success. But if this were so,

- How have commercial powerhouses such as Sun, Cisco, and Oracle achieved industry dominance with so few seminal inventions?
- Why have invention powerhouses such as Bell Labs, Xerox PARC, and Interval Research failed to generate rich returns for their investors?

To be sure, some powerful inventions result from leaps of insight and creativity, and they sometimes even create fortunes for their inventors. Such breakthroughs, however, are few and far between. Fostering them is an important but different subject. Here the question is how to extract value from the *other* 99 percent of intellectual property (IP) and intangible assets generated by companies.

One company that has solved this riddle is IBM. The information technology giant has ranked as the number one patent engine in the United States since 1993, averaging nearly eighteen hundred patents granted each year. Fully one-third of patents awarded to IBM in 2000 generate revenue via licensing or as part of new products and services. Following former CEO Lou Gerstner's decision to assert patents more aggressively, IBM shifted from being a net payer of licensing fees in the late 1980s to generating nearly $1.9 billion in revenue from licensing by 2000. Licensing contributed 23 percent of IBM's profit that year, as business development specialists—rather than lawyers—trolled for opportunities to secure licensing agreements for noncore IP.

In the normal course of business, most companies routinely generate potentially valuable intellectual property, work processes, and intangible assets. But, unlike IBM, few companies have the resources or strategies in place to effectively develop these into business opportunities. In a difficult economic environment it is important that companies work to tap into this latent revenue stream.

How can that be achieved? In large firms, the custodians of invention—typically R&D engineers and product managers—continuously hone internal processes. Team management, budget setting, incentives and rewards, and project tracking, for example, receive tremendous attention.

Our research and experience reveal that, while important, the choice of internal tools and processes correlates poorly with commercial success. Neither does the number of patents filed or the amount of money spent on R&D serve as a reliable predictor. An experienced engineer can draft a patent application in a couple of hours. The U.S. Patent Office awarded nearly 165,000 patents in 2000 alone. How many disclosures ever result in products? For large organizations, only 15–25 percent. How many actually generate significant revenue for their owners? Only a tiny fraction.

In fact, decisions and activities typically occurring *outside* the lab most affect a firm's ability to create value for both customers and shareholders. They determine whether a firm makes money from its patents and know-how or simply accumulates underleveraged assets at considerable cost.

This does not mean that companies should reduce investments in R&D. Rather, it means those investments will be squandered without careful attention to commercialization strategy. Long-term success demands aligning innovation focus and approach with commercialization processes and strategies. Examples abound.

■ Oracle, the world's second-largest software company, is known as a market leader in relational databases. While the initial breakthrough inventions opening the market for relational databases emerged from IBM and university labs in the 1970s, Oracle, more than any other independent software company, has effectively applied the technology to the needs of customers in such industries as pharmaceuticals, financial services, and logistics. Under founder and CEO Larry Ellison, its success has been built on developing commercially attractive database solutions.

■ Cisco, the world's leading provider of networking equipment, can justifiably lay claim to inventing the network router. It faced stiff competition from other equipment players, however, until successive CEOs (John Morgridge and John Chambers) brought a near-obsession with customer focus to the firm and launched an aggressive acquisition strategy, starting in 1996, to expand its portfolio of products. Cisco's ability to incorporate newly acquired ventures without losing sales momentum became widely recognized as a core competence.

Further Evidence

While every company must organize innovation and commercialization around its own unique structures and circumstances, there are certain core principles or best practices. In a recent survey of corporate innovation, the McKenna Group found a tight correlation between these best practices and a company's ability to benefit from their investments in innovation.

Nearly fifty U.S. companies were surveyed, including business-to-consumer companies such as Ford and Procter & Gamble, technology companies such as Intel and Genentech, major multinationals such as GE and Dow, and pure research firms including Bell Labs Innovations and Rockwell Scientific.

The survey questionnaire and follow-up interview led the participant through a self-diagnostic of the firm's effectiveness at innovation and explored drivers and inhibitors of success. Survey participants demonstrated a high degree of intellectual honesty. Their overall assess-

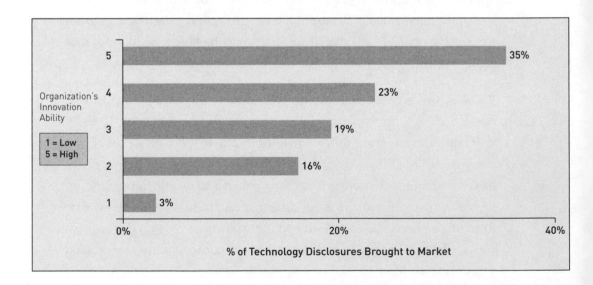

ments correlated strongly with the percentage of technology disclosures actually embodied in products their firms brought to market (a reasonable proxy for effectiveness).

What we learned was startling. While investing heavily in innovation—through tools, processes, and people—most companies neglect two of the fundamental rules of commerce: (1) ensure customer-centric solutions by continually gleaning external inputs, and (2) mitigate market risk by multiplying revenue streams.

Customer-Driven Innovation

Successful innovators do more than pay lip service to customer-centricity. They ensure that a constant flow of market intelligence informs R&D decisions. A common mistake is asking customers what they want. Instead, successful innovators investigate customer needs, pain points, and behaviors that shape requirements. Only this level of customer intimacy can generate insights about winning solutions.

And even once development is under way, customers should be involved in the process. Product engineers need to know the customer at least as well as those working in after-sales customer service do. According to our survey, effective use of customer input doubles a company's ability to bring IP to market.

Beyond involving a few key customers in development, successful companies design partner relationships with an eye to building and managing rich information channels. They never allow partner firms who own the customer relationship to shield them from key market intelligence. And internally, corporate R&D is aligned with customer-facing business units.

In one case, Sun Microsystems under founder and CEO Scott McNealy has maintained a laser focus on developing IP that can be commercialized quickly. Small teams of three to five people work on most

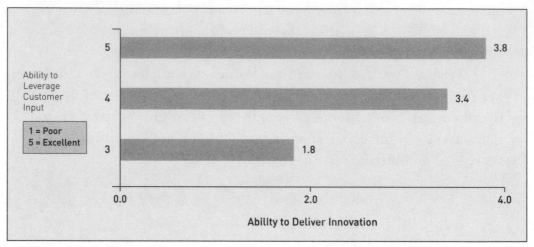

Source: McKenna US-50 Survey

R&D programs, which are constantly tested against the objective of transferring technology to product divisions. To tightly link R&D to commercial groups, roughly 10 percent of lab personnel are transferred each year to product divisions. The migration is usually temporary, although not always.

Managing Market Risk

Several options exist for monetizing IP and other assets such as relationships or brand. Companies might make product extensions, deliver services, spin-off ventures, make acquisitions, license IP, sell and auction patents, or even donate assets in return for certain tax benefits. Successful innovators use four or more types of monetization pathways. They emphasize licensing and venturing to a higher degree than less effective, more product-focused companies. Less successful companies rely on just two or three types of transaction to generate revenue. The operating and economic structures of those companies are tuned to delivering these outcomes—usually product extensions—most efficiently, and so perpetuate the neglect of other options.

At Procter & Gamble management is agnostic relative to monetization methods. New products, product extensions, spin-offs, and licensing are all fair game—whatever works. The company seeks licensing opportunities for all patents within five years if they are not used in a P&G product, or within three years if they evolve into products, whichever comes first. This acts as a powerful incentive for business units to quickly apply new technologies and to keep revitalizing old products.

Multiplying ways to cash in on IP provides researchers with more incentives to create commercially viable inventions while encouraging product and service organizations to "use it or lose it" (the company's IP, that is). And using options such as licensing or auctions mean that IP viewed as marginal can nonetheless generate returns.

The message: if you want your firm to be successful, focus not on seeding invention but on harvesting it. Creativity cannot be managed. Commercializing and monetizing products, solutions, and services aligned with real market needs can be.

TOOLS FOR COLLABORATION

Victoria Griffith

In his best-selling 1999 book *Business @ the Speed of Thought,* Microsoft chief Bill Gates chastised managers for not taking full advantage of electronic networks. Future winners, he wrote, will be those who "develop a world-class digital nervous system so that information can easily flow through their companies."

The exchange of all information within a company should be "over e-mail so workers can act on news with reflex-like speed," according to Gates. Face-to-face meetings for the purpose of exchanging information are a waste of time, he wrote, and should be reserved strictly for negotiation. Gates exhorted managers to use computers to exchange information, not just within their company, but with their suppliers and distributors as well.

Remember that Gates is in the business of selling information technology, so this advice should probably be taken with a big grain of salt. Yes, technology has dramatically altered the way we work. E-mail allows us to communicate easily with colleagues overseas without fretting about time, distances, and long-distance telephone charges. Computer software makes it possible to conduct in just a few minutes research that might once have taken weeks.

ON THE PURPOSE OF INFORMATION
TECHNOLOGY

Business @ the Speed of Thought: Using a Digital Nervous System

BILL GATES

■ We have infused our organization with a new level of electronic-based intelligence. I'm not talking about anything metaphysical or about some weird cyborg episode out of *Star Trek*. But it is something new and important. To function in the digital age, we have developed a new digital infrastructure. It's like the human nervous system. The biological nervous system triggers your reflexes so that you can react quickly to danger or need. It gives you the information you need as you ponder issues and make choices. You're alert to the most important things, and your nervous system blocks out information that isn't important to you. Companies need to have that same kind of nervous system—the ability to run smoothly and efficiently, to respond quickly to emergencies and opportunities, to quickly get valuable information to the people in the company who need it, the ability to quickly make decisions and interact with customers. ■

From Bill Gates with Collins Hemingway, *Business @ the Speed of Thought: Using a Digital Nervous System* (Warner, 1999).

Yet the biggest promise of data exchange via the Internet—that of vast efficiency savings based on increased knowledge—has also been the most elusive. Like so much associated with the Internet, fans of enterprise networks—computer software that mines vast quantities of data to manage a company more efficiently—seek to break with old rules.

In this world, transparency is the name of the game. When the concept is taken to its extreme, managers find they're expected to share information with everyone, from workers to suppliers to customers. It's not always the most comfortable of situations. "Prepare to be naked," author Don Tapscott is fond of saying about the production chain revolution.

Here's how the striptease works. Let's imagine a product, say, coffee. Enterprise management enthusiasts believe they can use business-to-business e-commerce to manage every aspect of the product's life cycle, from bean to cup. Café waiters in Milan might feed information on every customer order into a vast computer data system. A farmer in Brazil would then know just how many beans to grow to satisfy demand. Roasters would know precisely how much coffee to buy and process. Everyone would know the best price to charge, because they would know what competitors are charging.

By making all participants in the production process omniscient, the theory goes, we can eliminate glitches, bottlenecks, misled pricing, and erratic deliveries. Of course, much could go wrong. The Italian waiter might get distracted by a beautiful girl and enter the wrong number of orders on his electronic notepad. The Brazilian farmer's bean pickers could go on strike, foiling his plans for a timely harvest.

Despite the obvious pitfalls, a number of companies are moving in the direction of total production management through computer software. Through supply chain management, executives make sure precisely the right number of parts arrive at exactly the right time. Through customer relationship software, they ensure the right goods are delivered to stores at the right time.

There may be something to it. General Electric has promised to save hundreds of millions of dollars a year simply by making sure relevant data is available to any worker who wants it. When its lighting division wants spare parts, for instance, it solicits bids from suppliers via its computer software. Bidders reply the next day, instead of two weeks later, as they did when the division relied on paper responses.

Dell has built its manufacturing system on supply chain management. Suppliers must be hooked into a Dell database that tells them how many widgets are in the bins. When numbers run low, they automatically send out a truck with more. The process is so streamlined, say Dell managers, that bins are often filled just hours before the parts are needed.

By buying at the last minute, Dell keeps its inventory at a minimum. That means the company doesn't have to pay interest charges to finance stocks it may not use for many weeks. In 1997 the company's founder, Michael Dell, bragged that the company had reduced days in inventory to just twelve. It has fallen to even less since then. The CEO also vowed to build new factories that would have no storage space for inventory at all.

Wal-Mart automatically records every sale it makes in its stores in a huge data warehouse. The company uses the information to constantly reevaluate its marketing and distribution targets, boosting supplies of products that are selling well and cutting supplies of those that are not.

All this sounds good, and no doubt efficiencies have been achieved. Yet using software solutions to micromanage the production chain is far more complicated than it may at first seem. The biggest challenge is the cost of installing the technology in the first place. Enterprise networks can cost several million dollars to install, and rarely run less than a few hundred thousand dollars.

Managers are often at a loss as to what kind of information to put into the systems. They are forced to choose from a vast number of confusing options. Should they track customers by geographical location, name, or account number? Should they monitor payments by invoice number or supplier name?

Companies are also plagued, not surprisingly, by human error. Computers work only when the input of information is correct and timely. Brother Industries, the American arm of the Japanese-based word processor manufacturer, found this out the hard way when the company switched to an enterprise system in 1996. One glitch occurred when all of the company's paperwork—even the out-of-date stuff—was loaded into the computer. Managers got a nasty shock when they discovered the system was listing parts Brother hadn't used for years. Other parts were listed in duplicate. Sorting out the problem turned out to be a nightmare. Brother also found that certain plants were chronically low on supplies because no one had fed the computer information about the amount of time it took to receive parts from China—six weeks, far more than from other suppliers.

Nike blamed kinks in its customer management software for a profit shortfall in early 2000. Because of faults in the program, said the company, too many shoes were delivered to some stores, not enough to others.

Problems are magnified when companies try to include outside organizations in their networks. In the late 1990s Dell was powerful enough to insist its suppliers hook up to its supply chain system at their own expense. Suppliers didn't mind that much, because they could be assured of sufficient volume to justify the expense. If Dell begins to lose clout in the market, however, it could be a very different story.

Other troubles can occur when corporations become too transparent. A customer that can see right through the supply chain may gain knowledge a manufacturer doesn't want to reveal. If inventory looks too tight, for instance, the buyer may decide to go elsewhere. If stocks look plentiful, they may not be in a hurry to place new orders.

The picture is further complicated when suppliers are also competitors. This happens a lot in the computer industry—for instance, where Dell purchases from IBM but also competes with it. How much information should they exchange?

Even if the computer data is nearly perfect, outside events can—and often do—mess things up. A delivery truck that is supposed to pull up at 12:15, for instance, may be held back by an unforeseen flat tire or too many red lights. The more widely the system casts its net, the more unpredictability is introduced into the system. A drought in Brazil can choke off the coffee bean supply, for instance, no matter how carefully the farmer tailored the harvest to consumer demand.

Such troubles help explain why, despite the promise of massive savings from enterprise systems, most companies have refused to move their operations entirely online. Almost half of the executives interviewed in a Jupiter Research report released in March 2001 said their company expected to do less than 20 percent of their procurement online, at least for the next two years. After the September 11 attacks, many executives trimmed their planned expenditures further.

Even in the far more mundane world of e-mail communications, things can go wrong. Gates found that out when a message he sent in May 1997 was later used against him in the government's antitrust trial. Gates told subordinates he was "hard-core about not supporting" Sun Microsystems technology. Perhaps he should have confined his comments to paper.

WILL CEOS UNIONIZE?

Victoria Griffith with Paul Osterman

W e're seeing the rise of a new generation of labor organizations in the United States. While traditional unions continue to play a role, people are finding creative, alternative ways to organize for collective bargaining.

There are reasons for this. Older-style labor unions have a hard time addressing the needs of many in today's more flexible workforce. Knowledge workers, people who provide a company with intellectual brawn, now account for much of the workforce. Yet professionals have always been less interested in joining unions.

People have new concerns. With more women in the workforce, child care and flexible work hours have become an issue. Rising health care costs also make health care benefits a bone of contention. Americans are also more likely to hold temporary jobs or hop from one job to another. The loosening ties of workers to a single job or a single line of work make it harder to bring together employees under the umbrella of traditional labor unions.

Workers have not given up on bargaining for a better deal. But the negotiations are taking place in a different way. We see the rise of professional groups, loose coalitions of knowledge workers. We see the rise of living wage campaigns, which often bring together people from different parts of a community—clergy, politicians, social workers, and traditional unions—to demand decent wages and working conditions. We see civil rights and gay and lesbian rights groups calling for better treatment by employers.

We see the new type of collective bargaining all over. Take IBM. It would be very difficult to win the majority employee vote required to form a union at that company. Traditionally, professionals are difficult to organize from a labor point of view. But that doesn't mean workers there can't have a voice.

Two years ago IBM tried to change its pension structure in a way that favored younger workers at the expense of older ones. The employees didn't like it. Workers organized themselves through e-mail and the Internet to mount a challenge to the shift. That's not technically a union, but it's an organized employee group that has a collective voice. So it has a similar effect.

Something similar happened when Enron employees collectively accused managers of misleading them over the health of the company, the safety of their pension, and their own job security. And there's the Washtech organization in Seattle, which has tried to pull together temporary software workers to make demands for overtime pay and other benefits.

We see the continued strength of living wage campaigns. The grassroots movement began in Baltimore in 1995, where a coalition of churches and social workers forced local government to promise to pay a wage higher than the national minimum to allow city workers a higher standard of living. Around the country we're seeing votes for citywide living wages. The campaigns have sparked similar demands in at least seventy other cities in the country.

Justice for Janitors has been remarkably successful. That group took on a long-standing problem—wages for cleaners at commercial buildings. In the past it was impossible to organize labor in this area.

Many of the workers were immigrants who spoke little English. And it was impossible to mount a challenge to contractors on a one-by-one basis, because if one contractor gave in, the building's owners would simply switch to another. Justice for Janitors solved the problem by going after buildings' owners. Not only did they organize themselves into a single collective bargaining voice, they effectively organized the group sitting at the other side of the table.

Economics do sometimes get in the way. After September 11 the hospitality industry—including hotel workers—was badly hit. There were many layoffs, and it wasn't a good time for labor to fight. But these things move in cycles, and workers will gain more control again.

New tools are playing a role. In the case of Enron and IBM, for instance, workers depended heavily on the Internet to organize themselves. That's an interesting phenomenon, because it goes against traditional methods of labor organization, which depended on talking with each other and having a personal relationship with others in the group. It remains to be seen whether these groups will go on to become stable, long-term associations.

We also see a lot going on in the work/family area. It's nothing new that women are a big part of the workforce and that families need more time and help to raise children. But the political side is getting more active. Ted Kennedy wants to mandate that part-time workers be able to take family leave. How the Bush administration will respond isn't certain, but it's now a part of the political discussion.

Outrage over the high levels of executive compensation is also fueling demand for workers' rights. The anger became more subdued in the late 1990s as so many people began to feel rich themselves. But it's reviving in the slower economic environment.

While the groups are clearly having a big impact on local and corporate communities, it's uncertain how long it will take for the movement to reach a national scale. But it's unlikely that this new generation of organized labor groups will simply go away.

As people find new ways of voicing collective concerns to employers, the new generation of labor organizations will gain ground. The issue needs to be on managers' radar screens or they may find themselves caught off guard when employees try collective bargaining. Workers are less represented by traditional unions these days. But that doesn't mean they are not represented.

WILL THERE BE CAPITAL TO VENTURE? THE EVOLUTION OF THE INDUSTRY THAT FUNDS INNOVATION

Peter Rothstein

After unparalleled growth from the mid-'90s through the beginning of the twenty-first century, the venture capital industry is in a crisis. During the last several years many venture capital firms raised huge amounts of money under a model of large investments and fast, billion-dollar flips. By their own admission, venture investors abandoned the basic principles that had been responsible for the industry's long-term success. Discussions of back-to-basics investing models and portfolio transparency are seen widely in the press and on the agenda of private equity conferences. But with the huge increases in the amounts of capital committed and still flowing into venture capital funds, no one expects the future venture capital industry to resemble the early days of venture capital from twenty years ago. So how can we interpret recent trends and their implications for the future of venture capital?

The Evolution of Venture Capital

Venture capital (VC) has evolved over the past dozen years in significant ways. From a cottage industry in the 1980s to the high-flying superstars of the dot-com bubble, and more recently as the focus of articles on the rapid rise and fall of venture capital firms, the VC industry has compressed several generations of industry change into a very short time span.

The Cottage Industry

Venture capital in the 1980s and much of the early 1990s was in many ways a cottage industry. The number of firms grew from less than a hundred to several hundred, most with fewer than five investing professionals, and many with funds with as little as $10–25 million. The venture capitalist was almost unknown outside a small community of entrepreneurs, technology insiders, investment banks, and a handful of active strategic acquirers. They were mostly "deal guys" who carefully invested small amounts of capital in a small number of deals, knowing that total write-offs were much more common than public exits.

The Superstar Trend Spotter

In the mid to late 1990s venture capitalists went through a stage of huge growth in numbers, attention, and reputation. Venture capitalists began to show up on the cover of magazines. They replaced large corporations and market research firms as the prognosticators of new innovation and new emerging markets and trends. Every pronouncement was about revolutionary technology, new multibillion-dollar markets, and start-ups competing at Internet time against the dinosaurs of slow-moving industry. Indeed, many VC firms struck it rich for themselves and their investors on companies that went public in the late '90s bubble, producing returns of ten to a hundred times the invested capital. The feeding frenzy the public saw as Internet stocks doubled, quadrupled, and more after their initial offerings carried over into the VC world as well. Venture firms raised record amounts of funds in 1998–2000. Established VC firms that had previously raised and invested funds in the range of $50 million to $200 million now raised new billion-dollar funds, which practically became a threshold for the top-tier, big-league ranks. These billion-dollar funds were accompanied by big bets, with $50 million or more going into start-ups with forecasts of quick, multibillion-dollar exits.

The No-Risk, No-New-Deal Era

The late '90s bubble ended in the inevitable crash, and nearly every aspect of venture investing changed from high promise to uncertainty and high risk. Venture capitalists changed from rosy prognosticators to deer in the headlights, unable to evaluate all the venture risks. They saw the full range of risks in declining valuations, lack of paths to revenue and profitability, lack of exits, inability to create new syndicates for coinvesting, and lack of partner time for venture development. Investments in new ventures nearly ground to a halt. And VC business models and investing stages changed, especially for the billion-dollar funds, as the venture capitalists saw low valuation opportunities across all stages and types of equity, even in public markets.

The Aftermath and Next Incarnation

The no-risk stage has raised fundamental questions and uncertainties about venture capital models, industry structure, and portfolio analysis and reporting.

Many large investors in VC funds got burned in the late 1990s and its aftermath. The large pension funds, endowments, and foundations (known as limited partners) whose capital is the major source of most venture funds thought they were committing their capital to early-stage VC funds. As these billion-dollar funds have shifted their investing model to later stages and even investments in public companies, these investors have seen their risk profiles and target returns change. Some of these huge VC funds have reduced the size of their funds, although they are still significantly above historical sizes.

Although the large funds and their investors collaborated in the raising of billion-dollar VC funds, many now admit it was a myth to assume venture capital can scale. Most of the billion-dollar funds were raised with little accompanying growth in the VC investing teams. So how did this happen? Greed was certainly a factor. Many large endowments, pension funds, and foundations were making significant returns and needed to grow their asset commitments. They all wanted in on the brand-name funds. And VC firms started competing with each other in a period in which new funds had to have billions of dollars to be in the big leagues.

But the economics don't work without a significant change to the VC business model. A typical venture capital team of six partners that has the ability to invest $5 million to $10 million per venture from the seed and early stages can't invest a billion-dollar fund. They need to either vastly increase their investment per deal (moving into big-bet and later-stage models), significantly increase the size of their team (and take on running the VC firm as a much larger company), radically reduce the size of the fund, or try some combination of all three options. These are difficult business strategy decisions being made across the venture capital industry.

The amount of available capital that large investors want to put into VC funds has not radically declined. However, limited partners are asking for much more insight into the changing structures and strategies of the VC firms. They are also asking for more insight into real portfolio valuations.

So how can the venture market react and move forward in a manner that can still aim for superior returns and meet the needs of large investors for greater clarity? There are three themes that will characterize transitions in the VC market in the coming years: back-to-basics investing, specialization, and transparency in reporting.

Back-to-Basics

Venture capital is back to being hard work. If entrepreneurs sweat every payroll, every product development milestone, every big customer deal, in a back-to-basics venture capital world, VC firms sweat every detail for all their entrepreneurs, and also for every expectation of their limited partners, who have entrusted millions of dollars to their venture fund.

Going back to basics means modestly sized venture capital firms risking modest amounts of capital per deal, aiming for profitability as a pre-exit milestone. It means investing at early stages, where exits are assumed to be three to seven years out. Back-to-basics investing means that VC firms will return to playing active roles helping their portfolio companies reach critical milestones, use capital wisely, do the deals they need for validation, and grow to profitability and target returns. It means these firms will focus less on first-mover advantages and much more on companies that have long-term viability with unique technology that solves significant customer needs. It means that the partners in the VC firm will need operating and business development experience and will allocate significant time to a modest number of ventures. And it means that the firms will focus on building companies to last—the only solution to uncertainty.

Specialization Within the VC Asset Class

With the huge increase in recent years in VC firms and fund sizes, back-to-basics won't be the model for all firms. The venture capital industry has grown substantially to the point where specialization and fragmentation are producing a range of different types of VC firms. Some are specializing by stage—seed, early, later—and some that participate in VC investments should really be called private equity firms, based on the diversity of their planned investments.

Others are specializing by markets and areas of technology. There is increasing technical complexity in certain fields such as life sciences and nanotechnology. R&D processes, capital investment requirements, competitive barriers, and exit strategies all differ considerably across many fields, further leading to specialization.

VC firms are establishing much clearer distinctions. For example, seed-stage funds invest at riskier times in a venture's life cycle. In contrast with large funds, which need to put large amounts of capital to work and manage many deals per investing partner, small seed-stage funds are structured to identify and invest in only one to two deals per partner per year, often with small amounts invested and risked in stages. In contrast to large funds that are dependent on multibillion-dollar public market exits for attractive returns, the modest-capital, seed-stage investing model can provide significant exit opportunities and superior returns even in modest acquisitions, and the potential for benefit from, but not dependence upon, the return of the IPO market.

Some of the firms that are closer to the billion-dollar size are transforming themselves into diversified private equity firms. These funds are going beyond minority investments in early-stage ventures and sometimes taking positions in buyouts, public companies, and operating spin-offs. And other specialization funds are focusing on market segments such as energy and life sciences, where industry experience and relationships are critical.

This fragmentation within venture capital is being accompanied by alignment of the VC firm business model and team background and expertise with their area of focus. This fragmentation also means that the myths of "bigger is better," "early-stage is risky," and "later-stage is safer" can all be evaluated much more discreetly. And for the large limited partners who invest across all equity stages, clear distinctions and specialization give them a much better ability to tune their investment commitments in alignment with their risk and return preferences.

Transparency and Reporting

For limited partners to more carefully manage their capital commitments across multiple funds, their combined risk profile, their true diversification, and so on, much more information and transparency into the investment portfolio needs to be provided. VC firms invest their fund's capital in ventures over the three to six years after a fund is raised. VC firms have to nurture their portfolio companies for many years, to proven success, before their companies can be acquired or go public and allow investors to realize returns. It usually takes five to ten years for investors to have reliable insight into the true valuation of one of their VC fund investments. During these long years VC portfolio valuations are often based on the last time individual portfolio companies raised money, and these valuations may have little to do with changing burn rates, sales cycles, competitive positions, profitability milestones, product strengths, and other operating and strategic metrics. This makes risk analysis, portfolio positions, and new asset commitments increasingly complicated for the large limited partners.

Given the large capital commitments to venture capital and the significantly growing effort to provide visibility into financials, operations, real value creation, and real risk across all asset classes, the venture capital market also needs to develop metrics that give greater visibility into the value, risk, and diversification of their portfolios.

A number of recent efforts such as the Bell Mason Diagnostic (developed by Gordon Bell and Heidi Mason) and the Paths to Value model (developed and published by PricewaterhouseCoopers) aim to provide frameworks that can evolve to provide the needed visibility. The Paths to Value model captures and reports on variables that are much better leading indicators of value creation than simple trailing quarterly financial reports. This model deals with factors that can be summarized and reported on a periodic or real-time basis and that are better predictors of value creation, specifically:

1. Strategy factors—market size, competitive position, business model
2. Resource factors—strength of management team, cash flow position, investor role, and value contributed
3. Performance factors—customer acquisition, product development, channels/alliances

We can and should expect that models that provide more transparency and deeper levels of investor reporting will evolve and become an accepted part of the way investors and VC firms communicate about portfolio risk and value. These models and metrics will also be used by VC firms and by their portfolio companies as management tools to focus on the operating and strategic imperatives critical to the building of their companies.

Venture Capital Matures?

Venture capital has probably had a disproportionate share of media attention given the relatively small number of professionals in the industry. But if invention, entrepreneurship, and capitalism are major themes of the modern Western economy, then venture capital is a unique part of their intersection, and is a telling picture of both the successes and the excesses of these themes.

The venture capital industry, by its very definition and focus, is prone to excess. Excess can lead to too much money fueling bubbles and fads, and we should expect bubbles to come again. After all, the Internet bubble wasn't the first. Investment bubbles go all the way back to the tulip bubble in the seventeenth century, with a number of other bubbles occurring across various markets and industries over the years. But the late-'90s bubble was the first bubble in which the relatively new venture capital industry played an important dynamic. So the VC market will be taking some lessons to heart from its rapid rise and fall as it moves forward into the next stage of maturation.

Will venture capital leave behind some of the excesses and mature as a more disciplined industry with clearer models, methodologies, structures, and reporting metrics? Or will discipline be a transitory period before the next boom-and-bust cycle? Only time will tell for sure. But with greater segmentation, clearer distinctions across segments concerning VC business models and practices, and greater transparency throughout the investor value chain, the industry should weather future cycles in a much more robust fashion.

7. How to Be a Leader

and Live to Tell About It

YEARS AGO, WHEN I EDITED A SUNDAY OP-ED COLUMN in the business section of the *New York Times,* a well-known academic said he wanted to write an article for the paper about leadership. "Leadership?" I said. "That topic is over. Extinct. No one is interested in leadership anymore. Pitch me another idea, one with staying power."

Not only was I seriously wrong, but the academic in question went on to publish several best-selling books on the topic.

The attraction to the concept of leadership is the belief that anyone can learn to do it. Americans, the social scientist and pollster Daniel Yankelovich once observed after conducting global research into national values, differ from their European counterparts in one crucial way: Americans believe strongly in self-improvement. They believe, in other words, that any schmo can rise to the top of society, through hard work, guts, and moxie.

Americans, of course, are not wrong. A great many schmos *have* risen to the top—to the White House, even.

But how do they do it? How do leaders lead?

This section—another of my favorites—examines leadership, difficulties and all. This section makes clear that a little bit of self-improvement can go a very long way. It also makes clear there are no easy answers.

J.K.

LEADERSHIP IS 1 PERCENT INSPIRATION AND 99 PERCENT PERSPIRATION

Ronald Heifetz and Marty Linsky

At the beginning of the twenty-first century the toughest challenges facing businesses, such as globalization and the technological revolution, demand not merely the application of expertise or the use of the resources of authority, but the orchestration of ongoing changes that disorient the habits and values of people throughout the workplace.

This is the domain of leadership.

Most discussions of leadership are framed in the positive—an exposition of the personal traits or skills needed to get people to follow you through good times and bad. And this is understandable, because leadership can be thrilling and meaningful. But what makes leadership different from good management is leadership's dark side: the inevitable attempts to take people who lead out of the game. Discussions of leadership focus far too exclusively on the inspiration side and not enough on the perspiration and hazards. To right the balance and pay respect to the costs of leadership, we focus in this short article on the challenges of leading and staying alive.

Exercising Leadership Is *Difficult* and *Dangerous* Work

Leadership is *difficult* because it focuses on the most intractable challenges of change, the ones that defy easy solutions because they involve deep-seated conflicts, value-laden issues, and strongly held loyalties.

Leadership is *dangerous* because people resist refashioning their innermost concerns, surfacing conflicts, and questioning long-held assumptions. They push back in an effort to resubmerge the issues that the person who leads tries to help the organization address.

Any change that is truly transformational, in a corporation, public organization, or community, asks people to give up some of the things they hold dear: their views of themselves, their ways of doing business, their understanding of where they fit in the wider scheme of things. That is why at its heart, leadership is about loss. People exercising leadership are asking others to abandon something that is important to them for some uncertain possibility.

Contrary to conventional wisdom, people don't resist change per se. People resist loss. Nobody we know gives back a winning lottery ticket. People love change when they know it's beneficial. People resist when they face the possibility or reality of loss embedded in change.

Such deep transformation is termed "adaptive change," something very different from the "technical change" that people in positions of authority address daily. Technical problems may be very complex, like a broken arm or a failure in a nuclear reactor, but existing know-how and problem-solving processes can solve them. Adaptive problems cannot be attacked with experts or standard routines. The problem lies within the people in the organization themselves, who must learn new ways and give up old, familiar, comfortable habits. That process is inherently disruptive, causing disequilibrium and distress in the organization as it takes place. Adaptive work challenges people to clarify what's precious and essential and distinguish it from what's expendable.

It's no wonder, then, that people in authority, colluding with their organizations, shy away from leadership challenges.

The most obvious manifestation of avoiding an adaptive challenge is treating the problem as if it were a technical issue. For example, when a company lurches into financial difficulty, people in authority often respond with some kind of across-the-board belt-tightening, whereas tackling the underlying problem might require giving up certain lines of business, the firm's independence, or even its very existence.

By treating an adaptive challenge as a technical problem, people in authority can do what they know how to do best: meet the expectations of their constituents by taking the problem off other people's shoulders and fixing it themselves. The rest of the organization can relax under the illusion that the problem will go away without any real wrenching or dislocation on their part. Across-the-board cuts may be painful, but not as painful as rethinking a company's strategy. Tough trade-offs need to be made between legitimately competing priorities.

Cost cutting may even work for a while. But the underlying dysfunctionality will inevitably resurface, again and again, until someone exercising leadership has the courage and skill to accept the responsibility for helping the organization take on the deeper issue directly.

Authority is a contract for services. Authority relationships are about entrusting people with power in exchange for the performance of some set of services. While authority relationships will take different specific forms in different environments (every job description is an authorization), the core organizational functions of authority are direction, protection, and order. As long as those in authority perform those functions well, they will be rewarded and stay in power. People in authority are almost never authorized to exercise leadership, however; they are almost never expected to raise deep, difficult, value-laden issues that are likely to cause their authorizers and constituents distress and surface conflict.

There is a fundamental paradox here, really more of a clever seduction. People in authority usually aspire to be seen as leaders; they want the *L* word on their forehead. So one of the typical ways that organizations and communities ensure that their authority figures will never exercise leadership, will never disturb them by mentioning the unmentionables or forcing them to face up to difficult issues, is by calling them leaders. Calling them leaders is a reward for exercising authority really well, for meeting and exceeding people's expectations. By conflating really terrific exercises of authority with leadership, everyone is happy. People in authority have the label they desire, and the rest of the community can go along without being disturbed.

When someone, in or out of authority, does have the courage to raise the difficult issues, however, to point out the gap between espoused values and behavior, to surface deep-seated conflict that holds back progress, that person puts him- or herself at risk. Danger lurks in the form of the resistance that exercising leadership inevitably generates.

The danger is compounded because people exercising leadership often don't see it coming. Caught up in the cause, and in the rightness or even righteousness of the cause, they get swept up in the action on the dance floor and have difficulty standing on the balcony, above the fray, to observe systemic patterns of behavior not easily visible from the ground.

Resistance can manifest itself in a variety of ways. Some of the most common faces of danger are (1) personal attack, an attempt to shift the debate from the challenging issue to the character or style of the person taking the initiative; (2) marginalization, forcing people who seek to lead into being so identified with the issue that they are dismissed as too narrowly focused with little of value to say on anything else; (3) seduction, especially by allies and supporters, who use the granting and withholding of their approval to make sure that they do not have to make any difficult compromises or suffer any painful losses themselves; and (4) diversion, for example, filling up the in-box so that the immediate always forces out the important.

Each of these thwarting tactics aims to reduce the organizational disequilibrium created by the effort to confront the difficult challenge. By attempting to silence the person exercising leadership, the system hopes to restore order, maintain what is familiar, and protect itself from the pains of adaptive change.

Leadership, then, requires the diagnostic capacity to get on the balcony and distinguish the adaptive from the technical aspects of a complex challenge, and then the strategic and tactical ability to orchestrate conflict so that it produces experimentation and learning rather than dogma and entrenchment. To lead and stay alive demands reverence for the pain of change so that you can challenge people with the wisdom to appreciate why and how they will fight back.

SEVEN MYTHS ABOUT LEADERSHIP AND WHO SHOULD BE CEO

Jeffrey Sonnenfeld

Two decades ago CEO succession was often portrayed as a simple passing of a baton between exiting incumbents and their hand-picked replacements. Leadership succession in general was seen as winnowing a pool of contestants competing for hierarchical advancement into narrowing pyramids of opportunity. At that time fewer than 10 percent of CEOs of major corporations came in from outside the company as external recruits.

Relying upon the External Labor Market: Making Versus Buying

Since then the number of external recruits has risen to 50 percent, thereby undermining the reliance upon internal loyalists and exaggerating the value of the frequently recycled external celebrity executive names. During these twenty years the average CEO's compensation grew from twenty-five times that of the average employee to 419 times that of the average employee. The justifications ranged from escaping decades of insular cronyism in mentor-protégé models of internal succession to the need to shake up complacent corporate cultures through dynamic, fresh-blooded leaders.

The downside of such a shift in succession from internal to external sources is that it can undermine morale as rising incumbents feel a diminished sense of career mobility. Bypassed internal candidates may feel less interested in taking future risks on behalf of their firms. Why should a prospective CEO volunteer for unpleasant assignments and groom protégés who may become rivals in logjammed career paths when their own career path is suddenly limited?

Furthermore, the genuine performance skills and character of an external recruit are far harder to verify. Fraudulent credentials have surfaced recently among the top leaders of such firms as Bausch & Lomb and Veritas Software, while the unsavory past employment history for a CEO of Sunbeam was not revealed until years after he was removed. Finally, the recruitment of CEOs from across industries and corporate cultures has often led to the hiring of once admired leaders unable to repeat their past successes in settings that require unfamiliar skills, new relationships, and different knowledge.

The Pathology of Messianic Succession Goals

With the demise of so many of these celebrity CEOs due to failed performance in their newly adopted firms, we see a reconsideration of charisma. Once widely admired heroes such as former Apple CEO John Scully, who arrived from Pepsi; former Xerox CEO Richard Thoman, from IBM; and former Kodak CEO George Fisher, from Motorola, all failed when transplanted to different soil. On top of this, at firms such as Enron, WorldCom, and Qwest outsiders brought in as CEOs presided over meltdowns in character, as evidenced by excessive pay packages, short-term stock manipulations, fraudulent financial reporting, the theft of billions of dollars of investor assets, the liquidation of pensioners' funds, and other such reprehensible conduct. It is not surprising that there has been a profound reassessment of the embrace of the "imperial CEO." Recent academic studies match the swelling media critiques of celebrity CEOs, suggesting that the embrace of charismatic leadership led to this infatuation and overestimation of the value of external CEOs as saviors.

The difficulty of understanding the changing conventional wisdom and scholarly research regarding CEO succession is that sweeping conclusions are rapidly reached through a spiral of analyses based on a blurring of issues. For example, corporate performance is often measured by either return on investment, increase in revenues, increase in profits, increase in market share, or increase in stock price, with little correspondence between measures. Furthermore, trade-offs in leadership qualities are often confused into false dichotomies. For example, management staffing dilemmas that involve internal development versus external recruiting are distinctly different from the governance debate over insiders versus independent board directors, which in turn is quite different from charismatic versus transactional leadership. To unravel such confusion, it is helpful to reveal seven new and dangerous myths regarding the process and outcomes of CEO succession.

Seven Myths About Top Leadership Succession

Myth 1: There Is a Shortage of CEO Talent

There is no diminished pool of talent for top leadership. Skilled and ambitious aspirants for top office have not lost their eagerness or been bred out of existence. There has been a profound change in where boards fish for their talent, however. Being an insider has become a liability. Whereas in 1980 the top two hundred U.S. firms hired merely 7 percent of their CEOs from the outside, the rate is now 50 percent.

Over this period the number of top jobs that open up each year has not changed that much, but the salaries have soared. This is because the restricted search for CEO candidates among current CEOs leads to a false scarcity. Thousands of available and ready management committee members are bypassed for consideration in filling the roughly one hundred open jobs each year.

Myth 2: It Is Generally Better to Hire CEOs from the Outside

Boards reason that a firm in need of a radical transformation is not likely to have the necessary talent ready and trained, let alone bold enough to shatter the expectations of colleagues with tough strategic and personnel moves. In reality, however, the process of taking charge is far faster for internally selected CEOs. Being current on the strategic issues faced by the firm, knowing where the bodies are buried, and knowing whom can be trusted are all key resources that boards undervalue in CEO candidates.

Accordingly, successful companies such as United Parcel Service, Wal-Mart, Procter & Gamble, General Electric, American Airlines, Intel, and Thomson Publishing routinely promote from within. At United Parcel Service, for example, internally groomed CEOs Oz Nelson, Jim Kelly, and Mike Eskew were able to transform their firm from its roots as a domestic trucking company into a global logistics business operating in two hundred countries, not to mention a communications technology leader and one of the world's largest airlines.

Internal CEO successor Robert Crandall at American Airlines pioneered the integration of technology into loyalty marketing, yield management, and reservation systems that revolutionized the industry. Another internal successor, Richard Harrington, transformed Thomson Publishing from a large newspaper publishing empire into an electronic business and professional data content provider and knowledge-driven

ON STRATEGIC ALLIANCES

The Prince

NICCOLÒ MACHIAVELLI

■ Here it ought to be noted that a prince should avoid joining forces with someone more powerful than himself for the purpose of attacking another unless necessity compels him to do so, as I explained above; for by winning he then becomes the prisoner of his ally. As far as possible, a prince should avoid being left at the mercy of someone else. The Venetians joined France in attacking the Duke of Milan when they could have avoided it, and that was their downfall. But when such an alliance cannot be avoided (as was the case with the Florentines when the Pope and Spain sent an army to attack Lombardy), then a prince should take part for the reasons already discussed. And let no state suppose that it can choose sides with complete safety. Indeed, it had better recognize that it will always have to choose between risks, for that is the order of things. We never flee one peril without falling into another. Prudence lies in knowing how to distinguish between degrees of danger and in choosing the least danger as best. ■

From Niccolò Machiavelli, *The Prince*, translated, edited, and introduced by Daniel Donno (Bantam, 1966).

software provider. Andrew Grove, an internal successor to Intel's founders, is renowned for his self-doubting, "paranoid" style of leadership, which led the company to profound technological shifts. Under Grove, Intel shifted its focus from commodity memory chips to premium microprocessors at strategic crossroads he called "points of inflection."

Firms I have labeled "clubs" and "academies" regularly succeed by developing great pools of internal leaders. Clubs are firms that promote from within and tend to value cross-functional generalists in their internal grooming and succession (e.g., Ford, GM, UPS, Hewitt Associates, McKinsey & Co., Coca-Cola, Pepsi, and Aramark), while academies also rely upon internal talent but value specialty expertise more (e.g., P&G, IBM, Intel, and GE).

Clubs tend to groom generalists and rotate executives through key assignments in an effort to broaden and create general managers. These businesses tend to sell products and services known more for their reliability than their innovation. Utilities and automakers may be such examples. By contrast, academies tend to groom specialists within distinct, parallel pipelines, with rare lateral career movement. These firms tend to sell house knowledge as a distinctive competence. Consumer products firms and electronics firms have often fit this model.

Myth 3: It Is Generally Better to Hire CEOs from the Inside

This once-preferred option also has its limits. Companies frequently need fresh blood. Those firms classified as clubs and academies (see above) can suffer insularity. It mattered that Robert Wood left Montgomery Ward frustrated by its smug focus on the catalog business and took over Sears as CEO, where he introduced his new company to the idea of the suburban store. IBM had lost its way until outsider CEO Louis Gerstner came in to shake up this complacent technology icon through an enhanced customer management process, focused research and development, consulting services, and Internet-driven commerce.

There are businesses that regularly go to the outside labor market to hire CEOs. I have labeled these firms "baseball teams" and "fortresses." Baseball teams regularly go to the outside labor market, as if they were recruiting free agents from rival sports teams; those who slip in such companies fall back to minor league employers. This is regularly the case for entertainment and technology companies, where there are clearly preferred employers (e.g., the broadcast networks, major studios, and top magazine publishers; technology leaders such as Microsoft, eBay,

The Functions of the Executive

CHESTER I. BARNARD

■ The coordination of efforts essential to a system of cooperation requires, as we have seen, an organization system of communication. Such a system of communication implies centers or points of interconnection and can only operate as these centers are occupied by persons who are called executives. It might be said, then, that the function of executives is to serve as channels of communication so far as communications must pass through central positions. But since the object of the communication system is coordination of all aspects of organization, it follows that the functions of executives relate to all the work essential to the vitality and endurance of an organization, so far, at least, as it must be accomplished through formal coordination.

It is important to observe, however, that not all work done by persons who occupy executive positions is in connection with the executive functions, the coordination of activities of others. Some of the world of such persons, through organization work, is not executive. For example, if the president of a corporation goes out personally to sell products of his company or engages in some of the production work, these are

and Yahoo); a second tier of firms (local TV stations, technology start-ups, niche studios, etc.) is filled with disenchanted alumni of the major leagues, along with rising aspirants.

The baseball team firms regularly hire specialized outside experts such as researchers, programmers, attorneys, consultants, fashion merchants, designers, journalists, and entertainment stars. The strategic imperative of these firms is to provide invention and novelty in products and services. The fortress firms, by contrast, hire outsider generalists who can fluidly handle crises and are prepared to cut across functional not executive services. If the president of a university gives lectures to a class of students, this is not executive work. If the head of a government department spends time on complaints or disputes about services rendered by the department, this is not necessarily executive work. Executive work is not that *of* the organization, but the specialized work of maintaining the organization in operation.

Probably all executives do a considerable amount of non-executive work. Sometimes this work is more valuable than the executive work they do. The intermixture of functions is a matter of convenience and often of economy, because of the scarcity of abilities; or there may be other reasons for it. As a result of the combination of executive with non-executive functions, however, it is difficult in practice merely by comparison of titles or of nominal functions to determine the comparative methods of executive work in different organizations. If we mean by executive functions the specialized work of maintaining systems of cooperative effort, we may best proceed for general purposes to find out what work has to be done, and then, when desirable, to trace out who is doing that work in a particular organization. ■

From Chester I. Barnard, *The Functions of the Executive* (Harvard University Press, 1938).

barriers. They move easily around and across the functions of marketing, operations, finance, engineering, and human resources to handle cost-cutting challenges. These fortress firms have usually slipped into a distress mode where survival or liquidation is the strategic focus. They must constantly defend themselves against competitors and creditors, not to mention headhunters and recruiters. They may also be within industries such as airlines, forest products, and retailing, which face episodic expansion and contraction periods in response to business cycles and seasonal patterns.

Myth 4: Charisma Is Just Empty Corporate Cheerleading and Self-aggrandizement

As scholars decry the empty boosterism of failed celebrity CEOs and the champions of now vanished cyberspace concerns, many are simply overreacting. They've concluded that the "great person" theory of history is wrong.

Our research on fifteen hundred CEOs of major firms, however, suggests that when properly defined, the CEO's charisma can contribute as much as 15 percent of the firm's performance as measured by investor returns, increases in sales, increases in market share, and increases in earnings. Critical, however, was realizing that flamboyance was not the essence of CEO charisma. The core dimensions were personal dynamism, empathy, authenticity, goal setting, and risk seeking.

Colgate-Palmolive CEO Reuben Mark is the perfect example. Mark is sometimes referred to as the "anonymous CEO," given his penchant for avoiding the press and studiously resisting the temptation to steal the credit for contributions made by his employees. At the same time, he is viewed as powerfully charismatic by his key constituents—shareholders, customers, suppliers, and employees. A $10,000 investment in Colgate in 1984 at the beginning of his reign as CEO would have returned $335,000 by 2001—a premium of over $85,000 over the same dollars invested in GE over the same period of time, with a lot less fanfare.

Myth 5: Maverick CEOs Are Better Performers

We have seen an era of swashbuckling, self-anointed "serial acquirers" destroy their own firms through a confusing pileup of unrelated businesses after initially mesmerizing Wall Street with the excitement. Tyco, for example, moved its headquarters to Bermuda as a tax dodge, though it operated out of Exeter, New Hampshire. The CEO, Dennis Kozlowski, mesmerized the investment community with a dazzling number of deals lacking any long-term management vision. However, virtually every major strategic pronouncement from Tyco was eventually reversed. Even before his legal problems, he flip-flopped over breaking up the firm. He flip-flopped over whether a major business unit, CIT, a financial services firm, would be sold to an investment bank or to the public. Originally a government-supported laser research lab, Tyco accumulated a heap of unrelated businesses, including health care products, security systems, telecommunications equipment, baby diapers, and financial services. Kozlowski was proud to be labeled "Deal-a-Day Dennis" for the seven hundred major firms he bought over three years—only to be followed by an 81 percent loss of market value.

The flawed logic of these serial acquirers—the CEOs of Tyco, WorldCom, Global Crossing, and Adelphia—repeats the failures of their predecessors from the 1970s. Such conglomerateurs as Harold Geneen of ITT, Charles Bludhorn of Gulf & Western, Gerald Tsai of American Can, and Peter Grace of W. R. Grace presided over the unraveling and dissolution of the tangled strategic messes they had inherited. ITT, originally a phone company, became a base for buying hotels, bakeries, and heavy industry. Gulf & Western, originally an auto parts seller, became a platform for buying steel mills, sugar refineries, sports franchises, and film studios. The old-line packaging company American Can opportunistically but fatefully moved into retail, stocks, and insurance.

These maverick CEOs were impatient and believed that they could allocate financial resources more efficiently than the external financial markets could. A recent Yale School of Management–Gallup Organization survey found that 26 percent of CEOs from major companies believed that "great leaders are born and not made." It is CEOs who believe in greatness anointed at birth who can be the most dramatic and the most destructive.

Myth 6: Failures Derail Careers of CEO Candidates

We are regularly treated to recipes for leadership success as well as proud CEO autobiographies presenting tales of unbroken triumph. The unspoken debris left out of accounts such as Jack Welch's *Jack*, Al Dunlap's *Mean Business,* and John Scully's *Odyssey* seemed to surface soon after the books hit the bookstore shelves. The process of leveraging failure remains a mystery because the intricacies of failure are not studied with the same intensity as is the siren song of success. We are often afraid of a contagion of failure through association. The victims of defeat are often angry with themselves and ashamed. Others around the victim are similarly embarrassed. Furthermore, people often lack the resources needed for career restoration. In reality, the work of anthropologist Joseph Campbell documents that a core human quality of folk heroes through the ages is not their flawless resumé but rather their resilience through adversity.

Failure is often the missing ingredient in genuine success sagas. The experience of failure reminds us of our human vulnerabilities and our vital interdependencies. The humbling nature of career setbacks also builds confidence and character strength. As Nietzsche declared, "What does not kill me makes me stronger." The genuine comeback stories of such executives as Home Depot founder Bernard Marcus, communications entrepreneur and New York City mayor Michael Bloomberg, Apple Computer founder Steve Jobs, and real estate developer Donald Trump, along with such historic figures as Gandhi, Mozart, and Churchill, provide for inspirational accounts of how vital this career stage is for self-awareness and the development of internal resources.

Myth 7: Departing CEOs Should Immediately Leave the Board to Allow Successors and Fellow Directors a Clean Slate

There are certainly high-profile examples of CEOs who cannot surrender the throne. These CEOs, whom I have dubbed "monarchs" in my book *The Hero's Farewell*, are unwilling to relinquish control. They undermine genuine successors in the pipeline because they are troubled by unfulfilled needs for heroic immortality and the establishment of an identity independent of their role as CEO. Often other life roles have atrophied over the years, and they look fearfully at a late-life abyss of insignificance without more personal life goals beyond their mission for the enterprise. Such CEOs do not leave office other than feet first—through death or overthrow.

Similarly, there are also those CEOs I call "generals" who initiate an insincere departure process and then reverse course, undermining their successors after the supposed transfer of power. For these executives, it is far more the loss of heroic stature than the quest for a specific mission that leads them to retake the seat of power. A genuine failed successor or a temporarily weakened successor presents the opportunity for such mothballed leaders to jump back into office. Often in times of crisis it is helpful to have former CEOs informed and ready to serve in a transitional role. In general, however, both monarchs and generals as predecessors on the board are dangerous.

There are two other types of departing CEOs who actually make superb board members. I call them "ambassadors" and "governors." These are the former CEOs who leave gracefully but serve as wise advisors. They continue to be interested in new leadership positions beyond the CEO suite. Such brilliant and visionary leaders as Bernie Marcus at Home Depot, Andy Grove at Intel, Jim Kelly at UPS, and Herb Kelleher at Southwest Airlines were adroit, unobtrusive mentors with unrivaled knowledge to share with their heirs. Research in psychology shows that any reduction in reaction time as we age is more than compensated for by the advantages age brings in terms of greater expertise, improved reliability, enhanced judgment, and breadth of perspective.

Succession as a Continuous Process

Decades ago CEO succession processes often looked deceptively simple. Using succession tables and replacement charts, it was as easy as moving chess pieces on a chessboard. But these approaches were often myopic and failed to consider changing strategic needs of a healthy firm and fresh perspectives needed for a troubled enterprise. At the same time, the messianic impulse of contemporary boards to rush to external saviors with marquee names is not the answer either. The challenge of CEO succession is not an issue of the "good ol' boy" obligation of honoring unwise promotion commitments to cronies or the marketing challenge of finding perfect branded resumés to dress up a firm's image. The challenge of CEO succession is realizing that it is an ongoing partnership between the CEO and the board to match the right individual with the right business conditions.

WHERE HAVE ALL THE LEADERS GONE?

Bill George

T hank you, Enron and Arthur Andersen.
  The depth of your misconduct so shocked the world that it awakened us to the reality that the business world was on the wrong track, worshiping the wrong idols, and headed for self-destruction. Like the proverbial frog that dies when temperatures are gradually increased but immediately jumps out when tossed into a boiling pot of water, we needed this kind of shock therapy to realize that something is sorely missing in many of our corporations. What's missing? In a word, leadership. "Authentic leadership."

What began as a few executives charged with violating the law morphed into issues of corporate governance and the failure of our governance systems. Even after enacting Sarbanes-Oxley and other governance reforms, corporate governance gurus are clamoring for additional laws and regulations. The reality is that it is impossible to legislate integrity, stewardship, and good governance. As we begin to understand the never-ending spate of corporate scandals, we realize that the missing ingredient is corporate leaders committed to building authentic organizations with enduring value and values.

Every generation has corporate thieves who break the law to

reward themselves. This time around the excesses are not limited to a few. The vast majority of corporate CEOs are honest leaders dedicated to building their companies, but unfortunately, far too many yielded to the short-term pressures of the stock market and the opportunities for personal wealth. As a result, they wound up sacrificing their values and their stakeholders.

Our system of capitalism is built on trust—trust that corporate leaders and boards of directors will be good stewards of their resources, providing investors with a fair return. There can be no doubt that many leaders have violated that trust. As a result, investors lost confidence and withdrew from the market. In the process, many people got hurt, not just the perpetrators.

A survey by the *Wall Street Journal Europe* reported that only 21 percent of European investors believe that corporate leaders are honest. A similar Time/CNN poll reported that 71 percent of those polled feel that "the typical CEO is less honest and ethical than the average person." In rating the moral and ethical standards of CEOs of major corporations, 72 percent rated them "fair" or "poor." In the midst of this crisis, we ask ourselves, "where have all the leaders gone?" Where are today's versions of James Burke of Johnson & Johnson, Walter Wriston of Citicorp, John Whitehead of Goldman Sachs, and David Packard of Hewlett-Packard? These people not only built great enterprises but were statesmen in the business community and leaders in addressing societal issues as well.

In contrast, today's corporate leaders remain silent. Are they afraid that by speaking out they may invite scrutiny of their companies? In so doing, they give the impression that they have something to hide or are also part of the problem. Only a few CEOs, such as Henry Paulson of Goldman Sachs and Henry McKinnell of Pfizer, have been willing to condemn these practices publicly, recognizing that the larger issue is one of public trust in the capitalist system. Paulson's acts were doubly courageous, as he risked not only criticism from his peers but his customers as well.

Capitalism—Victim of Its Own Success

How did we get into this situation? Is this a recent phenomenon, or have these activities been going on all along?

We are witnessing the excesses of the shareholder revolution that began fifteen years ago. In its early stages, pressure from shareholders did much to improve the competitiveness of American corporations, as companies trimmed unnecessary expenses, improved profitability, and increased cashflow. However, the financial rewards from their actions, both corporate and personal, were so great that companies and share holders alike developed an inordinate focus on short-run results. In a booming stock market, it all seemed to be working.

Then capitalism became the victim of its own success. Instead of traditional measures such as growth, cashflow, and return on invest-ment, the criterion for success became meeting the expectations of the security analysts. Investments were cut back to reach earnings targets, limiting the company's growth potential. Driven by speculators and security analysts, expectations kept rising, just as companies were strug-gling to make their numbers. Companies that met or exceeded the "magic" earnings number were handsomely rewarded with ever-rising stock prices. Those that fell short, even if they recorded substantial increases, were inordinately punished, and shareholders demanded the replacement of the CEO. No wonder many CEOs went to extreme mea-sures to satisfy shareholders.

However, revenues and earnings do not escalate forever, especially in the face of economic downturns, events like September 11, and oper-ating problems. To offset financial problems, many executives stretched the numbers and the accounting rules well beyond their intended limits. Some of these accounting schemes, like calling operating expenses capi-tal equipment to avoid the P&L and booking revenues before they were earned, violate even the most basic rules of accounting.

In the past five years stock options went from modest perks to mega-grants for top executives, especially CEOs. Because options had no cash impact and were not charged against profits, many executives and boards viewed these grants as free. The effect was to shift CEOs' focus almost entirely to getting the stock price up—by whatever means necessary. Realizing they could not sustain their earnings, many CEOs cashed in their options for huge gains just before their stock collapsed.

The general public played a role in this tragedy as well. In idealizing the high-profile personalities that ran these companies, we made them into heroes. We equated wealth with success and image with leadership. To our dismay, we have learned that these celebrity CEOs have been filling up their personal coffers at their shareholders' expense, while destroying the pensions and life savings of thousands of people.

The media turned these short-term earnings artists into the folk heroes of the business community. While making wealth, image, and star power the criteria for success, the media overlooked the many solid corporate leaders building quality companies for the long-term. Ken Lay, Bernie Ebbers, and Dennis Koslowski were the focus of intense media worship before their fall. Just one year before he was led off to jail in handcuffs, *BusinessWeek* put Koslowski on its cover as the CEO of the top company on its Nifty Fifty list of top stock performers. These three executives alone have destroyed over $300 billion (€268 billion) in shareholder value.

Back in 1998 I met Koslowski to talk about acquiring one of his companies. In our brief meeting he explained how his offshore headquarters enabled his company to avoid U.S. taxes, how he automatically issued pink slips to 25 percent of the workers on the day he acquired their company, and how he shut down every research project or investment that didn't pay off in the first year. As I walked out of his office, I held on to my wallet and decided to cancel further talks with him. You cannot do business with people you do not trust.

The Case for New Leadership

Somewhere along the way we lost sight of the imperative of selecting leaders that create healthy corporations for the long-term. The lessons of building great companies like 3M, British Petroleum, Coca-Cola, Johnson & Johnson, General Electric, Pfizer, and Procter & Gamble were lost in the rush to get the stock price up. We forgot that those of us who are fortunate enough to lead great companies are the stewards of legacies we inherited from past leaders and the servants of our stakeholders.

The lessons from this crisis are evident: If we select people principally for their charisma and their ability to drive up stock prices in the short-term instead of their character, and shower them with inordinate rewards, why should we be surprised when they turn out to lack integrity?

We do not need executives running corporations into the ground in search of personal gain. We do not need celebrities to lead our companies.

We Do Not Need New Laws. We Need New Leadership.

We need authentic leaders, people of the highest integrity, committed to building enduring organizations. We need leaders who have a deep sense of purpose and are true to their core values. We need leaders who have the courage to build their companies to meet the needs of all their stakeholders, and who recognize the importance of their service to society.

To get out of the never-ending string of corporate scandals and back to building enduring companies that can succeed over the long run will take a new generation of leaders to step up and lead in an authentic manner. More than ever before, we need leaders of character, integrity, and values atop our corporations. The future of our system of capitalism depends on them.

8. Marketing

"Find Out What They Want and How They Want It and Give It to 'Em Just That Way"

TO SHOW THE POWER OF A DISHWASHING DETERGENT, an award-winning creative team at a Madison Avenue advertising agency dipped a crystal chandelier in cookie batter, put it into a dishwasher, poured in their product, and switched the machine on. They must have been pretty desperate.

Few people really understand the difference between marketing, advertising, and sales. I know this to be the case because marketing and sales budgets are usually the first to be cut during a downturn. When senior executives see a drop in sales, their reaction is to lower the profile of the products they sell! To them, advertising in a downturn seems foolhardy. They equate it with fluff.

Trouble is, building awareness—as marketing gurus such

as Benson P. Shapiro have shown—is more like an investment than an expense. Awareness for a product or company needs to be built up over years, and it usually grows incrementally over time. Great brands need to mature, but when they do, they command customer loyalty and premium prices long after the spending to promote them has stopped. Extinct brands from decades ago—Ipana toothpaste, Indian motorcycles, and Bugatti automobiles, for instance—still have value and awareness in the marketplace because of investments made in years gone by, which is one reason why advertising and marketing people speak of brand equity and not just brand.

Informing the customer about who you are and what you are selling is the first step in the sales process. Great marketing and advertising opens doors, creates relationships, and makes it easier to close a deal.

With marketplaces for products becoming increasingly crowded, the need for differentiation has intensified. Whereas once there were fifteen to twenty automotive brands, now there are hundreds. Whereas once there were three TV networks, now there are dozens. Every sector is becoming more crowded.

Crowded markets are great for customers. The laws of economics dictate that perfect markets attract new entrants that compete by offering roughly equivalent products. They try to win market share by lowering prices and adding features. Adding features means higher costs. Lowering prices means thinner margins. You do the math.

Great marketing is one way in which great companies have been able to keep their prices and margins high. Not only has IBM been a technological powerhouse, it has also been a high-performance marketing beast. Procter & Gamble makes great toothpaste, but it also makes great marketing, advertising, promotion, and product placement decisions. The ingredients in most beer are pretty much the same. But what makes Anheuser-Busch's Budweiser brand number one is the way it understands and communicates with its market.

This section takes you from the company to the customer. Reaching those customers and making them understand why you're different and why they should love you is worth real money. The sophisticated way in which Coca-Cola understands and is able to communicate with its market is one reason why brands such as White Rock and Royal Crown were eclipsed long ago.

Marketing and advertising are investments, not simply expenditures. They are not too dissimilar from investments made in factories, plants, and even R&D. They should be treated that way.

J.K.

THE TEN COMMANDMENTS OF MARKETING

Yoram (Jerry) Wind

In a world afflicted with massive information overload, the role of marketing has undergone a tectonic shift for corporate strategists. No longer relegated to functional status, marketing has become the corporate oxygen, the central mechanism for a business's fortunes. Business bookshelves overflow with marketing tomes aimed at embracing these new attitudes toward marketing and its massive impact. Executives, frantically searching for a competitive edge, continue to seek out gurus and consultants to shore up real or perceived weaknesses in marketing strategy within their organizations, often with mixed to poor results.

In truth, there are no quick fixes when it comes to developing sound marketing principles for an organization. Understanding the fundamental and underlying premises of building an effective marketing strategy in this new, Internet-driven millennium cannot be overlooked. There has been much talk over the past decade about new rules, new drivers, and new paradigms. Yet this is a time, perhaps more than ever before, when the essential rules, rules that have stood the test of shifting markets over many decades, become vital to creating effective marketing strategy.

Marketing strategy focuses on understanding the changing needs of target customers and other stakeholders, and developing and offering products and services that meet these needs. The effectiveness of this external focus and matching process often means the difference between business success and failure. The increasing recognition of the importance of marketing strategy to business and corporate strategy can be seen in the emergence of the CMO (chief marketing officer) role and an increasing number of CEOs who view marketing as central to their role.

The complexity of marketing strategy has increased with the emergence and increasing importance of the Internet. At the same time, organizational demands for links to financial performance have increased, as reflected in the current interest in measures such as return on marketing expenditures. These changes mean that a coherent marketing strategy has never been more important.

Ten Guidelines for Effective Marketing Strategy

What is needed for effective marketing strategy in today's environment? Marketing strategy clearly needs a broader perspective than the traditional focus on the marketing mix strategy of the four P's (product, price, place, and promotion) and their interdependencies. The following ten guidelines offer insights from research and practice on the key components of a rigorous, coherent, and effective marketing strategy.

1. Begin with customer insight. Ensure thorough and ongoing understanding of and insight into consumers' changing needs, expectations, and behavior. All marketing strategy begins with customer insight. The centrality of the customer is well recognized. Yet to be truly customer-oriented, it is important that the firm understand the changing needs, expectations, buying processes, and behaviors of their customers. Managers also need to understand the heterogeneity of the market and its changing segments, extending their focus beyond current customers to prospective customers. This understanding, which can benefit from the rich conceptual and empirical knowledge on consumer behavior and the firm's own experience and research, can lead to insights that in turn can help strengthen the current position of the firm and identify new business opportunities. The understanding and insights are obtained from a variety of sources—client contacts and partnering, marketing research, results of experiments, and so on—and should be continuously validated.

2. Understand the scenarios. Understand and make sense of the broader context—the changing needs, expectations, and behaviors of the other stakeholders, changing technology, competitive dynamics, government regulations, and other forces of change both external to the firm and internal—and construct key alternative scenarios. In very uncertain and rapidly changing environments, the market is shaped by a complex set of factors, many of which are external to the firm. How quickly will a new technology emerge? Will customers accept it? How rapidly? Fortunes were won and lost in the emergence of innovations such as the personal digital assistant (PDA)—as seen in the very different results of Apple's Newton and the Palm Pilot—based on how well companies read customers and designed products to meet their true needs. How could regulations reshape your markets? Consider how shifts in financial services regulations opened up competition in credit cards to powerful nontraditional players such as automakers (GM) and telcos (AT&T). The shifting environment can create new opportunities and open new markets, draw in new entrants, and create new industries (such as biotech) or reshape existing ones.

The firm needs a process to continuously gather, analyze, and interpret intelligence on customers, competitors, and other key stakeholders and the changes in their needs, objectives, expectations, and behaviors. The firm should ensure that its mental models allow it to make sense of the changing environment without biasing it in favor of its current assumptions.[1] The firm can effectively undertake a scenario-building process. This can be either a structured formal process such as the one initiated by Shell or a brief and more informal process to identify a few key future scenarios.[2] Ideally, this process of examining the external environment should lead to the selection of target segments and the identification of the key factors needed to succeed in specific competitive markets. One can choose either a robust strategy that can succeed across any scenario *or* a selected strategy for a target scenario with accompanying contingency plans if an alternative scenario is triggered.

3. Shape the vision. Determine the vision, business paradigm, and stretch objectives for the firm, business, product, and market units. Key to any strategic (marketing and business) planning is the determination of a vision and associated business paradigm and stretch objectives for the firm, the business, and the product and market units. It is important that the vision not only be determined by the firm's current position and aspirations but also reflect the type of firm that could be successful under the changing business environment.[3] Having established a vision, it is critical to develop its associated business paradigm. A pharmaceutical firm, for example, may define its vision as enhancing wellness and shift its business paradigm from selling pills to providing wellness solutions while helping the customer and other stakeholders meet their financial objectives. This vision and associated business paradigm have significant implications for the definition of the market and approach to marketing and business strategy.

Once a vision is established and its desired business paradigm defined, the firm is ready for the establishment of stretch objectives. These objectives should ideally be customer-oriented and include, in addition to the traditional financial measures of revenue and profit growth, newer measures such as maximizing the lifetime value of the customers and other relevant measures centering on the customer (loyalty, attrition, recurrent revenues, etc.) and other stakeholders. These measures can be structured as part of a balanced scorecard and linked to their drivers. Whatever the objectives, the key is to set them high enough to stimulate reexamination of current strategies and the undertaking of innovative ways of achieving the objectives. In setting and communicating these objectives, it is important to ensure that they are taken seriously and perceived as achievable.

4. Generate growth. Generate and evaluate a set of growth strategies, and create a portfolio of short- and long-term growth engines that capitalize on the market opportunities and the firm's competencies. Profitable and sustainable growth is key to the survival and success of all firms. It is important though, that the firm focus its attention on the generation, evaluation, and selection of value-creating growth strategies (as opposed to growth for its own sake, which can often be unprofitable). The marketing perspective is critical in evaluating strategic growth opportunities to ensure that they capitalize, to the greatest extent possible, on technological advances and other market opportunities. Companies should also look at developing a portfolio of growth engines, ensuring there are growth engines at all stages of the product/business life cycle. Some are the current engines of growth, some are at early launch stages, and some are in development as future value-creating growth engines.

5. Target a portfolio of customer segments. Select a portfolio of target segments and for each a positioning, branding, and associated value proposition. At its core, marketing strategy focuses on target customers and the right positioning and associated value proposition for each. Given the heterogeneity of all markets, a critical phase in the development of strategy is the selection of a portfolio of segments (and their associated positioning and value proposition). The portfolio enables the appropriate resource allocation among the target segments. In this context, it is important that the market is segmented dynamically, reflecting not only its current needs, expectations, and behavior but also expected trends and changes in the customers, the competitors' proactive and reactive strategies, and other environmental forces. In developing this segmentation, managers should also consider including an aggregate segment that

The Organization Man

WILLIAM H. WHYTE

■ For a future capitalist, the organization man displays a remarkable inability to manipulate capital. His handling of "debt consolidation" is a case in point. The growing popularity of loans for this purpose conjures up a picture of chastened citizens tightening their belts and cannily reducing total interest charges. The picture is quite misleading. It is true enough, of course, that in taking out one large loan from a bank, a person can cut down the interest he has been paying on a variety of purchases from 25 to 30 percent to a low of 12 to 18 percent. But this is not the reason most purchasers take out the loan. In actual practice, their consolidating is a sort of check-kiting operation by which they can square themselves away for yet another round of commitments. When these are halfway digested, they will be back again. And again.

They pay dearly for the convenience. Consider, for example, a possible alternative. A mythical couple we will call the Frugals decided to defer all but necessary purchases for enough months to accumulate an

is a collection of "segments of one"—those that justify a one-on-one approach.

The positioning for these target segments should go beyond the traditional focus on benefits to customers, instead establishing an *emotional* link between the customers and the firm and its product and service offerings.[4] The positioning should be consistent with the value proposition for that segment and be linked to the branding strategy of the firm. The branding includes global, regional, and local brands as well as private brands, co-branding, initiatives, customized brands, and all brand extension strategies. The portfolio of brands, and any other portfolio of countries, businesses, and so on, should be driven to achieve extra $500. They will then have a revolving fund of their own that they can use for cash purchases, and instead of paying out a fixed amount each month in installment loans, they will use these sums to replenish the $500.

Now let's take a normal couple. The Joneses, with precisely the same income, don't put off purchases but instead commit themselves to a combination of installment loans and revolving credit plans. At the end of ten years, the Joneses will have paid out somewhere around $800 in interest. The Frugals, by contrast, would have earned interest—roughly $150. Not counting the extra benefits they would have

reaped by being able to buy for cash, they would be, in toto, almost a thousand dollars better off.

The Frugals, to repeat, are somewhat mythical. Most suburbanites fail to accumulate capital to produce capital, and they fail to manipulate what capital they do have. It rarely occurs to them, for example, to use their savings as collateral in taking out a loan. Were they to do this, they would frequently get an actual rate as low as 4¼ to 4½ percent instead of the usual 10 to 12 percent—and their savings would still earn them the regular rate of interest. ■

From William H. Whyte, *The Organization Man* (Simon & Schuster, 1956).

the vision, objectives, and business strategy and thus maximize the brand equity and value of the firm.

6. Create integrated, innovative offerings. For each target customer (account, segment, segments within a geographic unit) set realistic objectives and generate and evaluate strategies and creative product and service offerings, including integrated pricing, distribution, communication, and customer experience and relationship. For each target customer (whether a segment, an account, or a cluster of target segments within a defined geographic area) effective marketing strategy requires the creative generation and rigorous evaluation of integrated product and service offerings and associated pricing, distribution, communication, and customer experience and relationship strategies.

In developing such an integrated offering, it is important that the focus be on the right unit of analysis. In most business-to-business markets, and in a number of business-to-consumer cases, account strategy is a must. If the firm wants also to focus on customers for which individual account management cannot be justified, the portfolio of segments should reflect both the segment of individual accounts and the selected target segments.

It is important as well to look across brands. The traditional focus on brands often ignores the opportunities in focusing on customers who have the need for multiple brands. Consider, for example, the case of pharmaceutical firms that are notorious for their brand focus despite the fact that most consumers who suffer from a given ailment have other ailments as well. A company that offers an integrated wellness solution to diabetes patients who also have high cholesterol (a very frequent co-occurrence)—including information and education—will achieve higher levels of customer satisfaction, loyalty, and profitability than a company that sells its diabetic brand and a cholesterol-reducing brand in isolation. Yet this integrated approach requires a shift from brand focus to customer focus that is difficult for many organizations to implement given their current structures.

The offering often needs to be tailored to the local needs of the segments. While the natural tendency of most firms is to develop a national, regional, or even global strategy, in an increasing number of cases in which local markets differ greatly from each other the more appropriate approach is to develop a local strategy reflecting the idiosyncratic demand and supply characteristics of the local market.

Managers need to go beyond the simplistic focus on the four P's or even their customer counterparts, the four C's—customer selection, customer cost, convenience, and communication—to fully explore innovative strategic options to meet changing customer needs, take into account likely moves by current and new competitors, and capitalize on emerging marketing practices such as brand placement in movies, writing movies and books around brands, sport sponsorship, and so on.[5]

7. Design the organizational architecture. Develop or modify the required organizational architecture and cross-functional value-creating processes (such as new product development and integrated global supply network) to support the marketing strategy. To effectively implement a marketing strategy, the organization needs an architecture that is designed to support it. A customer-centric approach will be hard to implement in an organization that is organized around rigid functional silos or inflexible brands. A focus on developing relationships with customers will be only lip service if the organization doesn't have the technological "memory" to capture customer interactions, and an emphasis on customer satisfaction will fall flat if front-line employees are not in a culture that empowers them to act quickly on behalf of customers to correct mistakes. This organizational architecture goes beyond a focus on structure to encompass the interrelated architectural building blocks of corporate culture, physical facilities, corporate governance, value-creating processes, people and competencies, technology, financial and other resources, information and decision support systems, and performance measures and incentives.

8. Build the informational infrastructure. Develop the databases, information, research, and modeling infrastructure driven by user and customer needs rather than technology. The technological infrastructure, while part of the organizational architecture, is such a key component of marketing strategy that we consider it a separate point. A good technology architecture can provide the data and models to make timely and informed decisions about marketing strategy. At the same time, technology can be part of a valuable, real-time interface with customers.

More often than not, however, initiatives in this area are driven by technology strategy rather than marketing and business strategy. The result is that the focus tends to be internal rather than on the needs of the customers. As an example of this shift in focus, consider the emergence of customer relationship management (CRM). While relating to customers is an important concept of any marketing strategy, the focus of CRM is company-driven, not customer-driven. CRM uses data to reach the "right" customers with the "right" message at the "right" time with the "right" offerings. If one redefined the process to be customer-centric, the focus should be on the design of a *customer-managed relationship* (CMR), a process in which the platform enables the empowered customers to structure the relationship they want with the firm and others. We see the beginning of such an approach in customer-designed interfaces such as MyYahoo!, where customers are given the tools to design their own relationships.

In addition to forging better relationships with customers, information technology can help managers make timely and better decisions by harnessing rich data sets in real time. The integration of diverse databases, the development of powerful marketing research and modeling, and the creation of broader decision support systems (DSS) all contribute to quicker, more rigorous decision processes. Many of these tools are being integrated into coherent "executive dashboards" that offer managers real-time information on key performance measures and their interrelated business drivers. In addition to these key components of the informational infrastructure that are designed to make better and faster marketing strategy decisions, the infrastructure should also accommodate processes such as ERP (enterprise resource planning), SCM (supply chain management), CRM (customer relationship management), and other technologies for value creation processes.

9. Focus on convergence. Reexamine the other guidelines to ensure capitalizing on the opportunities offered by integrating the Internet and other advances in information technology into a coherent marketing strategy using the five C's of convergence marketing. One of the great strategic misconceptions of the dot-com revolution was the concept that the Internet would replace other channels. The idea was that the customer would never again visit another bookstore, wouldn't have to bother with grocery shopping, and would never again have to go through the hassle of going to a bank teller. Online grocer retailers such as Webvan, which offered a single electronic channel for delivery, crashed and burned based on this misconception. People still like to shop. They sometimes prefer to pick out their oranges in the store. They make a one-click order on Amazon *and* they enjoy browsing the shelves and sipping cappuccino at Barnes & Noble. These customers are not completely different animals, as some imagined, but instead are like centaurs, running on the fleet hooves of the new technology but with the same human hearts. Companies need to understand how customers integrate new technology and channels into their lives and appreciate how these various channels complement one another. Just as the radio didn't get rid of print advertising and television didn't destroy radio advertising, new channels more often than not are integrated into the existing portfolio rather than replacing existing channels.[6]

When these new channels arrive, managers need to develop strategies focused on convergence of the old and the new rather than the typical focus on choosing one or the other. The power of this strategy can be seen in the approach of UK retailer Tesco, which built a very successful online retailing business on the foundation of its existing network of physical retail stores. This convergence strategy allowed it to leverage its brand and marketing presence facing customers as well as its infrastructure for warehousing and delivery.

Channels are perhaps the most obvious aspect of convergence. Managers should consider the broader implications of convergence as reflected in the 5 C's of convergence marketing:

- **Customerization.** While new technologies allow for customized products as well as customized communications with customers (a combination called "customerization"), customers still seek standardized offerings and messages as well as customized offerings and messages. This requires a convergence strategy, combining both standardized and individually tailored offerings and communications.

■ **Community.** Customers are part of both virtual and physical communities, yet these are often separate worlds. Companies need to understand when customers prefer to be part of physical versus virtual communities, and look for ways to draw together these two worlds and incorporate them in the firm's marketing strategy.

■ **Channels.** As discussed, companies need to create strategies across channels, rather than separate strategies for different channels. Effective combination of these channels requires an understanding of customers. For example, a major financial services firm found that even investors who conduct most of their transactions online prefer to set up their account at a physical office. This convergence leads to a seamless strategy that allows customers to click, call, or visit.

■ **Competitive value equation.** Pricing has been reshaped by online auctions (eBay), name-your-own-price setups (Priceline), and other dynamic pricing models. These new models, however, live side by side with traditional fixed-price offerings, both online and with physical retailers or travel agents. Companies such as eBay have recognized this by creating convergence models that allow customers to participate in an auction *or* buy a product for a fixed price. The competitive value equation is built both as a new mixture of value-based pricing models *and* the value drivers as affected by the 24/7, anytime/anywhere convenience and interactivity.

■ **Choice tools.** New technologies offer customers the opportunity to use search engines (Google); a variety of decision tools, such as comparison engines (Bizrate), customer evaluation engines (Zagat.com), or expert evaluation engines (ConsumerReports.com); and life management tools. But customers still desire a combination of online and expert advice. Companies need to develop convergence strategies that allow customers to ask questions online or, if they prefer, pick up the phone or walk into an office to talk to an expert advisor.

10. Engage in adaptive experimentation. Develop an implementation plan based on the principle of adaptive experimentation and continuous learning. Implementation of marketing strategy is critical to success, but in a rapidly moving environment a rigid approach to implementation can lead to the very effective execution of the wrong plan. By viewing the implementation of marketing strategy as a process of adaptive experimentation, managers can continue to learn about their markets and the effectiveness of a given strategy as it unfolds.[7] This allows them to gain the insights needed to make midcourse corrections that increase the effectiveness of marketing initiatives. Companies need to be able to capture and share this learning across the organization. The implementation plan also needs to address the likely resistance to change by internal and external stakeholders.

Conclusion: Putting It All Together

The ten guidelines are interrelated. They highlight both the interrelated substantive aspects of marketing strategy (segmentation, positioning, branding, the various marketing mix elements, etc.) and the processes required to design and implement an effective marketing strategy. They also highlight the importance of marketing perspective in the design of business and corporate strategies.

While integrating these ten guidelines may seem complex, particularly in today's fast-changing, global environment, the fundamentals of marketing strategy are still straightforward:

- Focus on changing customer needs, wants, and expectations (guidelines 1 and 2).

- Develop the firm's value proposition, product and service offerings, and associated strategies (guidelines 3, 4, 5, 6, 9, and 10).

- Create the capabilities, organizational architecture, and infrastructure to support the strategy (guidelines 7 and 8).

The core of any marketing strategy is understanding the changing needs of the customer and the opportunities to shape these needs. This provides the basis for designing the firm's value proposition—product and service offerings. These in turn provide guidelines for the design of the required infrastructure that facilitates the design and implementation of the firm's offerings and related strategies.

HUNTERS AND FARMERS: CREATING THE CUSTOMER-CENTRIC SALES AND MARKETING TEAM

Ben Shapiro

To other functional departments such as finance and operations, the sales and marketing functions look alike. After all, both are outward-looking, focused on the customer and the market. But creating a strong marketing/sales team has proven difficult in practice and is getting even more difficult.

Why the Concern About Marketing/ Sales Coordination?

Every business exists for financial performance—making money. We know generally how to measure it across different companies and industries, and use metrics such as return on investment (ROI), earnings-per-share (EPS), growth, and earnings before interest, taxes, depreciation, and amortization (EBITDA).

Financial performance is the result of operating performance. Operating performance includes all the things that a company must do to win the competitive battle in its industry to attract, retain, and profitably serve customers. It varies greatly among industries but generally includes activities such as customer acquisition, on-time delivery, developing new services and products, and running efficiently.

But operating performance is also a result; it is derivative of human performance. Human performance involves many things but is primarily dependent on three: the personal capabilities of the individuals in the business, their individual motivation, and their ability to work together harmoniously.

Nowhere is the need to work together more important than in the twin customer-facing functions of marketing and sales. Sales and marketing look similar at a distance, just as Americans think of Singapore and Shanghai as similar and close. But when you get near the functions, you begin to understand the differences and to appreciate the challenge of coordinating and integrating them for improved operating performance and outstanding financial performance.

If marketing and sales do not cooperate, the company's strategy will be inconsistent and weak, and execution will be flawed and inefficient. In today's hypercompetitive world the sales and marketing functions must yoke together at every level, from the core central concepts of the strategy to the minute details of execution.

The Central Coordination Issues

When companies generally made their money in a large number of midsized accounts, marketing was typically seen as the strategic function that concentrated on product and service lines, market segments, and competitive positioning. Marketing did the thinking, managed the brand and consumer franchise in consumer goods companies, and provided support to the sales force. In this simpler world, sales did the execution in the field and sold to end users and distributors in business markets and to the trade (wholesalers and retailers) in consumer goods markets. Marketing was cerebral, creative, and long-term-oriented; sales was action-oriented, relationship-focused, and short-term.

But the world has changed. Now in most industries there is a relatively small number of large accounts, some midsized ones (the previous focus of the field sales force), and often a bunch of little ones. And accounts are complex collections of diffuse buying teams involving different customer functional departments (purchasing, engineering, information technology, operations, finance, etc.), different levels in the customer's organizational hierarchy, and different customer regional and line-of-business organizations.

Customers are reached through complex overlapping means, including global and national account teams; field sales, including product and market specialists as well as territorial generalists; telesales and telemarketing; service specialists; distributors; dealers; value-added integrators, resellers, and packagers; wholesalers; retailers; direct mail; and e-commerce. Procter & Gamble, for example, has well over one hundred people on the ground in Bentonville, Arkansas, to sell to and service Wal-Mart. Large individual accounts are now separable market segments and even profit centers supported by their own multifunctional organizations. The days of easy separation of sales and marketing are gone along with the homogeneous, simple midsized account base.

At the top of the customer base pyramid, where the accounts are huge, marketing and sales must make joint decisions about product, price, brand, and all kinds of support. When heavyweight distributors demand private-label merchandise, both organizations need to be involved. Pricing, product customization, and service customization cannot be entrusted to either group alone. The impact on economics, the whole account base, and corporate strategy requires an integrated approach.

At the small-account end, the sales force competes with and is often complemented by telemarketing, direct mail, catalogs, advertising, and other distribution channels. In the past these were often the sole purview of the marketing people. Now the marketing and sales organizations must make joint architectural policy and execution decisions. Without coordination, the decisions will be shortsighted, suboptimal, and conflict-ridden. For example, when field sales, telesales, and customer service people all interact with the same account, the objective is flawless, efficient, timely service, but the real result can be chaos, infighting, expensive duplication, and terrible service.

Industrial firms have traditionally had closer sales-marketing ties than consumer goods companies, especially consumer packaged goods companies. Even the traditional industrial goods ties are not strong enough for the current challenges. But in consumer packaged goods the changes are proving cataclysmic. The sales force can no longer passively accept and execute plans from marketing. Account managers, product managers, and advertising managers need to work together to protect profits and enhance volume in the harsh world of customer power, intense competition, and overcapacity. Most of all, the product managers and advertising managers need to develop a new respect for and understanding of individual customers, account managers, and sales managers. No longer will headquarters reign supreme. As power shifted from seller to buyer, it also shifted from headquarters to the field.

The Solutions: An Integrated Approach to Integration

There are many approaches to improving integration. They work best when they themselves are well integrated (big surprise). Thus the stress here will be on mixing and matching the individual elements of coordination to get a robust, efficient program.

All programs must begin with two hallmark approaches. First is a common understanding of the need for integration and for both sales and marketing to focus on productive sharing of power, information, and resources. Neither the field force nor headquarters managers can say that pricing, for example, is their purview only. It is an issue that involves both.

The second hallmark is a clear, unified, explicit strategy. Here such topics as custom product or service programs for large customers and coordinated messages for all dealers and end users can be specified. A major underlying point of contention will be the freedom for people in the field to customize policies for individual customers. The limits of such customization must be set and the processes for approvals clarified. Otherwise there will be constant tension and infighting between headquarters and the field.

Once the common understanding and the strategy are developed, major integrative tools include organizational structure, formal management processes, information technology, the informal social network, and people. Organizational structure is a natural beginning, but most people expect too much from it. There is no perfect structure. Instead, there are many trade-offs to be made. And, almost invariably, each option will have both strengths and weaknesses. The important thing is to organize to accomplish the most important strategic objectives given the current environment. As the objectives and the environment change, as they inevitably will, the structure must change. One major point of contention is with organizational units whose purpose it is to coordinate field and headquarters around issues such as regional promotions. At one time Campbell Soup had eighty-eight regional promotion managers scattered across the country, with one person for each of four product lines in twenty-two regions. Such approaches are very expensive and often create a barrier rather than a conduit for good field-headquarters communication. At other times such field-positioned marketing people work well. At one point Hewlett-Packard had a large number of market development managers scattered in the field to facilitate the introduction of complex new products. Subtle decisions such as the location of such boundary-spanning units and the level and experience of the people appointed have a big impact. A unit located at headquarters will have access to different information, involvement with different people, and a self-image that is quite different from the same group sprinkled throughout the field organization.

Formal management processes such as planning and budgeting approaches, compensation schemes, training programs, coordinating committees and task forces, and review procedures are very important. Some companies have found that a standing committee including both marketing and sales representatives to discuss a specific issue, such as pricing and discounts, goes a long way to ameliorate conflict over normally contentious topics. Of course, such approaches can also add to a bloated bureaucracy and slow, constipated decision making.

Information technology is probably the only really good news here. It enables sales and marketing to gather, catalog, analyze, and share such information as current sales rates, customer response to new initiatives, competitive activity, and marketing communication literature, including brochures, proposals, and presentations. Companies have found success and/or failure with large integrated customer relationship management (CRM) systems, depending upon design and implementation. And, increasingly, the integrated systems can be supplemented with powerful point solutions such as those designed to manage marketing literature and disseminate it to the field.

The final two items are very important but very subtle: the informal social system and the people who populate the organization. Typically the field force is made up of more-independent, free-spirited people who idealize a fighter-pilot mentality. Headquarters marketing is more buttoned down and idealizes a more sophisticated, centralized approach. Each often looks down on the other.

Anything that can be done to bridge the gap is very useful. Several things can be done to encourage informal social ties between marketing and sales. Rotation of people from marketing to sales and vice versa helps. So does co-location. Of course, as the company grows larger and more global, co-location becomes difficult. And there are conflicting needs. Should, for example, the product managers be located near head-quarters sales management, with the benefits of coordination around customer needs and information, or near the research and development people, with the benefits of coordination around technology and new product launch? The appropriate trade-off will depend upon the current strategy, challenges, and opportunities as well as feasibility issues such as space availability. But activities that are clearly dysfunctional, even such benign-seeming ones as a sales-versus-marketing golf tournament or softball game at the national sales meeting, are to be discouraged. They only contribute to the schism.

The nature of the demands on sales and marketing means that different people are appropriate for each function. Even different sales jobs require different personality profiles. "Hunters" who can open new accounts are more ego-driven and less relationship-oriented than "farmers," who are outstanding at servicing and developing existing accounts. These differences limit the opportunities to develop people who are dual-faceted, good at both the sales functions and the marketing functions. Still, some companies try to hire people who have good crossover skills and can team well. Some companies have also found that rewarding and promoting people who can team and actively work across the marketing/ sales boundary leads to a cadre of more-balanced managers. These same companies often explicitly punish salespeople and marketing executives who callously disregard the importance of the sister function.

Marketing and sales should not be the same because the functions they perform require important differences. But they can be comple-mentary and operate in such a way that customers are efficiently and effectively acquired, developed, serviced, and retained.

HOW MASS CUSTOMIZATION GETS THE RIGHT STUFF TO CUSTOMERS

Paul Taylor

Have you ever looked at old photographs and admired the hand-fashioned clothing people wore? Until the industrial revolution, producers catered to consumers one at a time. Sophisticated machine tools hadn't been invented, so almost all consumer products were made to order.

But the age of custom-made wasn't as romantic as it may seem in retrospect. Such items were labor-intensive and often prohibitively expensive. The typical American was lucky to possess one suit of clothes and one pair of shoes.

Industrialization changed that. Machines began to make clothes, shoes, furniture, utensils, and other goods. A wide range of new products swept Europe and North America into the era of mass production. The shift suddenly meant that ordinary workers were able to afford items that had once been out of the reach of even much of the upper classes.

Mass production also had a downside. Consumers rarely came into direct contact with producers. Goods were made on assembly lines in huge factories, shipped over great distances, and sold in impersonal places such as department stores. To achieve economies of scale and lower the cost of each item, manufacturers made large quantities of identical items. Consumers sacrificed the luxury of personal attention for affordability. Off-the-peg clothes might not be a perfect fit, but at least they were cheap.

Assembly line efficiencies enabled workers to produce more, justifying bigger pay packets, which in turn fueled personal consumption. The industrial revolution changed the economics of manufacturing. Mass production made things more affordable, but at the cost of sameness.

The American genius of the assembly line was Henry Ford. Ford's great contribution to the American dream was the Model T, which rolled off his Highland Park, Michigan, assembly lines at the rate of one every twenty-four seconds.

By introducing mass production techniques to his factories, Ford built his fortune and brought the car within reach of America's emerging middle class. To extend the efficiencies, Ford and those who followed him also created vertically integrated manufacturing systems that produced everything from the steel for the chassis to tires and headlights.

Assembly line production at Ford was fine-tuned to deliver goods at a price people could afford to pay. But it was not very flexible, so all Model T's looked alike. As Ford himself famously declared, "The consumer can have any color he wants, so long as it's black."

Ford's success was so compelling that managers began to apply the philosophy to other sectors. At midcentury William Levitt believed he could turn out houses with an assembly line approach. In 1947 he pioneered mass production of homes on potato fields twenty miles from Manhattan. Differences between the nearly 17,500 two-bedroom houses he built were slight. By standardizing the units, Levitt was able to put up more than two dozen a day, helping meet the enormous postwar demand for housing. Nevertheless, even today, the name Levittown remains a kind of shorthand for the sameness of mass production.

Neither Ford's nor Levitt's take-it-or-leave-it attitude would be welcomed by consumers today, who are used to choosing from an ever-expanding variety of goods and services. By the 1950s U.S. consumers had become accustomed to having a bigger say in the types of products they bought. Cars no longer came just in black, but in mint green and chartreuse. And the movement to personalized products has accelerated.

If the last century belonged to mass production, the new one belongs to "mass customization." The term was coined in a 1997 book by Stan Davis called *Future Perfect*, and refers to a continuous feedback loop between a manufacturer and customers that helps a company react quickly and smoothly to shifting consumer tastes.

"From clothing to computers, businesses are working to become more consumer friendly," said the authors of a 1998 Federal Reserve Bank of Dallas essay. "They do it to gain new sales and stay competitive. They do it because pleasing the customer isn't just about producing more stuff. It's about producing the right stuff."

So, just what is the right stuff? The same authors define it as "more of what we do want and less of what we don't want." The problem for companies lies in divining what consumers will want at some future date. If they produce a wide range of products or a large volume of one product on spec, they risk being saddled with unsold inventory.

How can companies give customers what they want while keeping the cost of production low? Information technology has begun to provide some of the answers. Computers provide companies with a valuable peek into the minds of consumers. Even before the Internet, workers collected data from shoppers by telephone and at stores, then fed the information into the company's database. In the 1980s the Italian clothing manufacturer Benetton used this insight to accelerate or decrease production of certain items and to home in on popular colors.

The Internet has made this kind of interaction easier. By studying consumer patterns fed automatically into their online databases, companies can adjust production to meet popular demand. The new information means companies can finally tailor their production with some certainty of getting it right. But how can they do so rapidly while keeping manufacturing costs under control?

Enter Michael Dell of Dell Computer. In the 1990s Texas-based Dell Computer grew from a start-up into one of the biggest makers of personal computers in the world by building systems to order. Michael Dell started his $32 billion computer business in a University of Texas dormitory room in 1983 on the basis of low fixed cost. His mantra was to build to order and do it quickly.

Dell realized that customization would lose value if consumers had to wait months for their orders. He also perceived that telephone and online sales could be used as a cheap and instant method of finding out what buyers want. Here's how it works: Dell's customers configure and order their systems over the telephone or via the company's Web site. Customers can create the system they want, right down to the speed of the microprocessor, the amount of RAM, and the capacity of the hard drive. At one time Dell estimated there were almost sixteen million possible combinations for desktop models alone.

The company begins assembling a computer only after it receives an order, then ships the finished product directly to the consumer's home or business within a few days. Dell uses information technology to streamline the assembly process as well. Its own suppliers are notified electronically of component requirements. Most of them have set up satellite plants close to Dell's main manufacturing sites to ensure they meet the group's tough delivery schedules.

Cargo doors line both ends of Dell's plants. On one side suppliers deliver components throughout the day. On the other workers load finished products onto trucks. The practice has been dubbed "continuous-flow manufacturing."

Actual assembly takes about twelve minutes. Even adding time for loading software and testing for quality, a computer can be put together in just four hours. By economizing on product inventory, delivery, and every other step of the process, the company provides a customized product at a competitive price. Michael Dell has been lauded as the Henry Ford of mass customization.

Dell isn't the only company to have discovered the advantages of direct sales and low inventories. Cisco Systems, the leading manufacturer of networking equipment, has gone a step further and outsourced most of its manufacturing operations as well. Similarly, Amazon.com, the online retailer that helped define the Internet shopping revolution, ships books and other goods ordered online directly to customers from a central warehouse, or asks its partners to fulfill orders directly from their own stocks.

Futurist Alvin Toffler, who predicted the coming of mass customization in the 1970s, warned: "If you have a company and you're not moving toward automation on demand, you'll have a competitor one day soon who will put you out of business."

Mass customization seems to be what consumers want. A survey conducted in 2000 by J. D. Power and Associates, the market research group, revealed that 17 percent of North American car buyers would purchase a customized car, provided they did not have to pay extra for it and got what they ordered in eight weeks or less. But the shift to mass customization poses challenges. In particular, customization requires corporations to be far more agile. Being agile means being fast as well as flexible. In order to increase speed without driving up costs, companies need to change the way they manufacture.

Joseph Pine, author of a book on the topic, points out that with mass customization, low costs are achieved through economies of scope, not scale. "Economies of scope are realized by the application of a single process to produce a greater variety of products and services more quickly and cheaply," he says. The process needs to be comprehensive and involve adjustments in everything from manufacturing techniques to management styles.

A number of groups have made headway in becoming agile manufacturers. One way of meeting customer needs without going broke is to use parts in different combinations to get a product consumers want. Because the company always uses the same parts, economies of scale come into play. But the customer still gets a semitailored product.

Black & Decker used the technique to reconfigure 122 basic tools to be produced from a small set of standard components. As a result, the tool manufacturer was able to cut costs, increase its product portfolio, and force rivals from the market. Motorola has adapted its Bravo pager factory line in Florida to allow products to be put together from different combinations of modules. Orders are uploaded from sales representatives' laptop computers in the field.

Japanese eyeglass maker Paris Miki uses systems run on personal computers to take a digital photograph of a customer's face, then superimpose images of different spectacle choices. The customer can change the look and color of the eyeglasses before they are made.

Mass customization enables companies to reduce inventory, improve margins, and deliver greater customer satisfaction. It is the dividend of the information age, which has given managers new tools such as computers and the Internet. Wouldn't the people in those old photographs be surprised?

FROM ZERO-SUM TO WIN-WIN:

PERFORMANCE-BASED PRICING

Ben Shapiro

Because pricing is such a difficult and complex arena, it has confounded sales and marketing executives and scholars for centuries. In no other aspect of marketing is the two-sided conflict/cooperation nature of the buyer-seller relationship made so clear. Part of the relationship is a zero-sum game between buyer and seller in which one's gain is the other's loss. Pricing is at the center of this part. But there is a second, win-win part of most buyer-seller relationships, including almost all business-to-business relationships. The win-win part often includes improved products and services that simultaneously provide greater customer value and higher supplier profitability. We constantly strive to move elements of the relationship from the zero-sum conflict side to the win-win cooperation side to achieve business success and relieve personal angst on both sides. We have searched for ways to move pricing into the win-win category. In some situations performance-based pricing can make pricing a win-win element of the buyer-seller relationship.

Performance-based pricing is an arrangement in which the seller is paid based on the actual performance of its product or service. It is becoming much more popular. In the advertising industry agencies traditionally were paid 15 percent of the cost of the media they bought for a client. Now more and more agency-client relationships are moving to performance-based pricing—they are paid based on achieving certain client advertising and/or marketing goals. The contractor who rebuilt the Los Angeles freeway damaged in the 1995 earthquake received enormous performance incentives by completing the reconstruction early. Other industries as diverse as consulting, trucking, and heavy industrial services are seeing the same trend.

An Example

Before explaining the benefits, drawbacks, and application of performance-based pricing, let us describe an example involving a complex relationship between ABB and Ford.[1] Ford needed a world-class supplier to design and build a turnkey automotive painting facility in Oakville, Canada. Ford and ABB agreed to work together in an initial preparatory phase, rejecting the traditional approach of bids based on incomplete information.

The initial preparatory phase involved a significant exchange of information and perspectives between the two firms and led to a novel type of agreement. ABB would design and build the plant at a far lower cost than standard. Then if ABB could reduce the cost even further, it would receive a preagreed percentage of the savings. This innovative, performance-based approach left both parties significantly better off than under conventional bidding or a negotiated price arrangement. Ford received a significantly lower cost at a lower level of risk: ABB received a share in the cost and design improvements it was able to create.

Advantages

One advantage of performance-based pricing is the often-mentioned alignment that can be achieved between the buyer's goals and the seller's goals. But that is only part of the story. There are two other major advantages.

Performance-based pricing ensures that the seller does not undercharge the buyer. When the final performance of the service or product is in doubt, the performance-based arrangement guarantees that as the seller provides more, it is paid more. Significantly, both institutional and individual buyers also receive assurance that they will not overpay. No person or organization wants to pay more for a product or service than it is worth. Again, when performance delivery is in doubt, performance-based pricing enables the buyer to pay only for the amount of performance that is actually delivered. Most important, the individuals responsible for the actual purchase decision do not want to absorb the career risk of overpaying. In our personal lives we suffer some marginal consequence if we overpay for a product. In business it can literally end the job security of a procurement executive. Performance-based pricing creates a greater sense of fairness for both buyer and seller.

The third benefit may be even more important than the first two. We often see performance-based pricing in highly uncertain situations and where both buyer and seller must make complex trade-offs among conflicting objectives. Simple contractual arrangements do not force the buyer and seller to communicate in depth. Performance-based pricing arrangements are generally very intricate. The parties are forced to deal with each other's limitations, objectives, and trade-offs. The very process of discussing, in precise detail and with great discipline, these issues develops wide-bandwidth communication between buyer and seller. Each has the opportunity to precisely present its objectives and to explain its own issues.

This process of open communication encourages a great degree of buyer-seller cooperation and coordination and a much broader agreement. More issues are raised and factored into the high-sensitivity problem-solving process. When the two parties involved are buying and selling committees representing different organizational jurisdictions within their organizations, and perhaps different levels of management, the necessity for precision and discipline in communication helps the process *within* buyer and seller groups as well as between them. In fact, it leads to better agreements that provide more value to the buyer and lower cost to the seller. Customers receive and pay for only what they value, and suppliers can reduce costs by removing non-value-added service and product components. The win-win aspect of the relationship increases and the zero-sum aspect decreases.

Applications and Limitations

Performance-based pricing is growing because (1) its economic logic is so powerful, (2) it provides new opportunities for buyer-seller communication, and (3) it has been proven in practice. After successful deployment by credible players (e.g., EDS in systems integration and outsourcing, services such as waste cleanup and welfare recipient job placement for government agencies, and many advertisers and advertising agencies), it is clear that the approach is implementable. Even Procter & Gamble, the last major consumer packaged goods advertiser to stay with a 15 percent fee, is moving in this new direction. It is sometimes a pragmatic pathway to managing risk, uncertainty, and performance for the long-term benefit of both parties.

Advertising has been a fertile field for performance-based pricing. The September 14, 1998, issue of *Advertising Age* reports that the percentage of marketers who compensate agencies on billings (media purchases) dropped from 71 percent in 1983 to 35 percent in 1997. The average profit margins of large agencies, according to a study by Morgan Anderson Consulting, went from 13 percent to about 19 percent. This demonstrates how profitable performance-based pricing can be. The trend toward broader agency involvement with clients beyond traditional advertising has made it both possible and appropriate for the move to a new pricing approach—one that provides the agency with more opportunity in return for greater risk and broader, more integrated responsibility.

But performance-based pricing is *not* for all pricing situations. In fact, it is appropriate in only a limited number of situations, albeit some very important ones. Still, some limited variants can also be useful. Point guarantees, such as penalty clauses that involve a discount when delivery is late, are a simple form of performance-based pricing. Penalty clauses are becoming typical in major construction projects.

Performance-based pricing is complicated. As with usage-based pricing and point guarantees, the actual amount to be paid cannot be determined until after delivery of the product or service, and often not even until after usage. Thus, for example, time-of-day pricing (e.g., restaurant early-bird specials or cheaper cinema matinee pricing) does not fit into the performance-based pricing model. Neither does stratified service pricing such as first class and economy in air travel. This is similar to product line pricing and can be considered service line pricing.

Performance-based pricing differs from usage-based pricing in that it charges for the *quality of performance* as well as the quantity of usage. If the telephone company charged a performance premium for better sound quality or faster connections as measured in use, these would become performance-based prices. Both performance-based and usage-based pricing, however, set the price after service or product delivery, when the customer value is clear. These are both wonderful examples of using the pricing approach to clarify value for the customer and expand the spread between customer value and cost.

It is useful to consider the risk embodied in various pricing approaches. Pricing that is openly based on costs plus a predetermined profit margin (often referred to as "time and materials") involves no vendor cost risk or price risk. The customer pays for all cost overruns, and the supplier's profit is established before delivery. Typical fixed-price sales involve only cost risk for the seller. The price is set before the product or service is made or provided. Performance-based pricing moves both the cost and price risk to the seller. Neither is established before the deal is made. But the vendor then obtains the opportunity to better manage the spreads among value to the customer, price, and cost to its advantage. With risk comes added opportunity. The vendor who uses performance-based pricing must thus be willing to accept greater, two-sided (price and cost) risk for added reward opportunity.

Finally, performance-based pricing is not good for sellers who desperately need short-term cash flow. Because the price can be determined only after delivery, and often not until after usage of the product or service, payment is often delayed longer than normal. A software start-up, for example, might desire to price on the basis of the value-in-use of its software, such as cost savings to the customer. Such an approach might make the sale easier because of the alignment, insurance, and high-quality communication benefits of performance-based pricing. The problem is that the savings from the software utilization might take months to determine, thus delaying payment to the software vendor. Most start-ups can't wait that long for payment.

A possible solution in some cases would be progress payments, including early fixed payments and later performance-based payments. The trade-offs here, including revenue recognition, are quite complex, and might force the vendor away from performance-based pricing.

Application Guidelines

The complexity and custom nature of the performance agreement mean that performance-based pricing is applicable only to relatively large, important transactions or relationships for both buyer and seller. The up-front cost of exchanging information and negotiating the performance goals and measures as well as the cost of applying the measures mean that this isn't for small or trivial situations. The power of the approach really comes to bear only when there is a mutual need to focus on joint objectives, and the abilities to meet those objectives are fraught with significant uncertainties. Performance-based pricing must be implemented with care and vigor. It is not a halfway solution.

Experience provides pragmatic guidelines for implementing performance-based pricing:

1. Invest the time up front to carefully and fully define the objectives of the project and exchange all the relevant information. Both buyer and seller must understand their own situation as well as the other party's, including overarching business goals and strategy. If there are serious functional or other internal fractures on either side, the process won't work.

2. Broaden the negotiation perspective to encompass all elements of the situation. That way each party can bring to bear its most complete arsenal of tools and approaches.

3. Explore a wide range of outcomes and consider what is controllable by the seller, the buyer, and neither. The exploration of outcomes, and the broadening of the negotiation perspective (number 2 above) require substantial creativity.

4. Take the time to negotiate completely. Do not rush because important details can and will be lost in haste.

5. Develop clear measures of achievement for each objective. Specify precisely what "performance" means.

6. Enumerate an explicit formula to relate payment price to performance outcomes.

7. Specify a mechanism to adjudicate disagreements over outcome measurement.

The paradox in applying performance-based pricing for both buyer and seller is that it is most appropriate where outcomes are fairly cloudy, and thus where the performance-based agreement is often hardest to negotiate. But the process of carefully specifying objectives, performance, and measures and of broadening the negotiation perspective is what makes the approach so powerful. It enables the parties to shed light on the sources of the uncertainties and to illuminate new ways in which they can cooperate for their mutual benefit.

SPEND 90 PERCENT ON THE WHO,

9 PERCENT ON THE WHAT, AND

1 PERCENT ON THE HOW:

THE ART AND SCIENCE OF BRANDING

Sam Hill

A brand is a relationship between a product or a service and a customer.[1] A successful brand is a win-win proposition for everyone involved. For the buyer of the product or service, brands save time, convey copious amounts of information in very abbreviated form, and contain an implicit or explicit promise of performance. For the seller of the product or service, brands provide tangible economic premiums.

The most visible form of brand premium is price—getting more for essentially the same product than a competitor does. For example, in late 2000 McKinsey & Co. analyzed the fate of two identical cars made in the same factory at the same time.[2] They found a Chevrolet Prism had a manufacturer's suggested retail price of $15,315 but actually sold for $14,315 after the manufacture's rebate. A similarly equipped Toyota Corolla listed for slightly less, $15,223, but sold for considerably more,

$14,973. Two absolutely identical products, save the nameplate, and yet they sold for a substantial difference in price. In general, pure bulk products such as gasoline can recognize price premiums of 1–3 percent, industrial products such as jet engines 5–10 percent, and consumer products up to 30 percent.

Of course, every price difference is substantial in that it falls straight through the P&L to the bottom line. But Toyota's price premium of 4.6 percent is actually relatively small. Is this because Toyota is leaving money on the table? Not exactly. Toyota chooses to take its premium not in price but in another form—market share. This is not uncommon. For example, the top three or four products in any category, from the supermarket to mining equipment, will have very similar prices. However, the category leader often has two to three times the sales volume of the weaker brands in the category. Market share is the most common form of brand premium.

Share is particularly valuable in complex consumer or industrial products and services, where additional services or products are purchased to complement the original purchase. Often the initial sale is made at a very low price, but additional high-margin products and services are then purchased without competitive bids. In the auto industry, where price premiums tend to be low, on-sells have long meant the difference between success and failure. For the two cars discussed above, in addition to the increased volume and price difference, Toyota will also receive additional revenue from options, financing, insurance, and ongoing maintenance services.

On-sells are becoming common, though, in virtually every category. To take a very simple example, American Express makes little providing me with a standard-issue green charge card. However, as a part of that they also automatically deduct a trip insurance fee on every flight I book and pay for with that card. (Now that I think about it, I'm not even sure what "trip insurance" is.) This and other little add-ons could well deliver more profit than the card itself. For a slightly more complex example, look at the recent highly publicized example of auditing firms, which make little on the actual auditing but millions on the consulting services to address the issues surfaced in the course of those audits.

The results of both types of premium are the same—a greater top line, higher margins, and better financial performance.

Brands and Low-Differentiation Products and Services

Until very recently only a few companies explicitly developed brand strategies. Sure, makers of consumer packaged goods, such as mouthwash or soda pop, paid a great deal of attention to brands. But most business-to-business and services companies shared the view of Bob Herbold, formerly of Procter & Gamble and Microsoft, who said brands are the result of images created by massive levels of TV advertising targeted at consumers.

Reasonably enough, companies that did not sell mass-market products direct to consumers or that had a low reliance on TV image advertising did not think of their marketing in terms of brands. Instead they spoke of "industrial marketing," often a euphemism for solution selling, or "commodity marketing," which often meant pricing based on benchmarks established through markets that traded standardized bundles of the product in question, such as money (London Interbank Offered Rate, or LIBOR), gold (London Metal Exchange, LME), wheat (Chicago Board of Trade, CBOT), etc.

However, increasingly even the most industrial companies are becoming interested in brands. They have come to realize that brands are not just for heavily advertised consumer products. For example, McKinsey, Goldman Sachs, Datek, Intel, Alcoa, Boeing, and Cargill are not consumer companies, but all have very well established and profitable brands. Indeed, these brands are stronger than many of those in traditional branded consumer categories. Airlines, bread, shampoo, and minivans are in fact more price-sensitive and have less-loyal consumers than the most competitive commodity, such as wheat.[3]

Ah, but now comes the hard part. The challenge is how to achieve brand premiums, especially in today's world of increased price transparency, falling customer loyalty, and ultrasophisticated buyers. The rest of this chapter is devoted to how to do it, and especially how to do it in products and services in categories where branding has traditionally not received a great deal of attention. Let's get started. How, then, are brands created? And beyond that, since all brands are not created equal, how are strong and powerful brands created?

Who, What, and How

Brands develop naturally around good products or services over time. Buyers use the product, become loyalists, and even evolve into brand advocates who tell others, gradually growing the brand. Many of the great brands were built through this simple formula: usage, loyalty, and word of mouth.

For example, consumer research says most American consumers are aware of and have a high regard for lawn mowers built by Briggs & Stratton. But the company has spent microscopic sums on advertising of any sort. Not only that, but they have never produced a single lawn mower. They make the engines for most mowers, and because their logo sits atop the engine, many consumers naturally assume they have a Briggs & Stratton mower. But a century of visibility and association with a reliable and well-performing product has created a powerful and valuable consumer brand.

There are many examples of these slow-growth, organically grown brands, including Starbucks, Linux, REI, Iams, Midwest Express, Google, Mossy Oak, and others.[4] However, natural brand building can be risky, especially in today's hypercompetitive markets. For example, for years Evian has relied essentially on an excellent product and great word of mouth supplemented by a modest outdoor and print advertising budget. For over two decades this made them the leader in the U.S. bottled water market.

However, Evian has now slipped to a distant fourth, well behind the two leading brands, Aquafina (made by Pepsi) and Dasani (a product of Coca-Cola). Through massive investment in product development and advertising and leveraging the clout of their massive distribution systems, Pepsi and Coke have quickly built brands that have overtaken and surpassed the market leader. When most of us think of brand building, the Pepsi/Coke approach is what we have in mind: an accelerated process of creating relationships with new consumers and deepening relationships with existing ones.

Every consulting firm and advertising agency has its own proprietary process to rapidly build brands. At the core of every brand-building process are three basic steps, which can be simply summarized as who, what, and how? More formally, *who* means the process of identifying the core target market for the brand, *what* means specifying a major point of differentiation,[5] and *how* involves development of a marketing plan, with formal steps, milestones, and budgets.

Who

There are two ways to identify the core market for a brand. For an established brand, it is often possible to accomplish this by simply working inside out. To quote Shailesh Mehta, formerly CEO of Providian Financial, "Identify your most profitable and loyal customers and go find more like them." This approach is particularly powerful for brands that have traditionally been limited geographically, that have just begun to take off in their growth cycle and have lots of inherent upside left in them, or "sleeper" brands. Sleeper brands are brands that have tremendous brand awareness and regard but which have never been aggressively marketed. For example, Rigid long made tools for professional plumbers. Working with Home Depot, they have now extended that to a very successful line of power tools.[6]

However, working inside out is not always an option. For example, for completely new brands and even for many existing ones, it is often necessary to search out new customers with whom to build relationships. The process of identifying potential groups of new users is called targeting, and begins with segmentation.

Segmentation is systematically carving up a market into groups with distinct buying needs. Segmenting a market begins with basic manipulation of off-the-shelf statistical data. Product sales are broken out by who buys the item. For consumers, segment descriptors might include age, sex, household size, income, zip code, and so on. For businesses, they might include firm size, SIC code or industry classification, location, or type of ownership. These segmentations are very useful for market sizing and are a good starting point. But they are only a starting point.

Look at an easy example. It's a safe bet that a family with a household income of over $100,000, four children at home, and an interest in skiing will own an SUV. But which brand of SUV? Chevy? Toyota? Land Rover? Mercedes? Cadillac? Basic statistics describe markets but are not sufficiently refined for brand segmentation purposes. Identifying the core target market for a brand requires a deeper level of segmentation.

Deeper segmentations are built around a multilevel understanding of what and why customers buy. First, marketers seek to understand how customer groups differ in their buying behavior. Then they seek to understand why these buying behaviors exist. Occasionally the underlying driver is a difference in attitude. More often, especially in considered purchases such as industrial goods, buying behavior is explained by differences in underlying customer needs.

For example, the Australian Wheat Board must sell its product against the highly subsidized grain produced by the United States and the European Community. It does so very successfully, in part because across the world the AWB has systematically identified the finickiest and most difficult purchasers, those who are the least forgiving of quality breaches or failure to meet specifications. Many, but not all, of these buyers are in Japan. These buyers are so picky because they understand the impact of impurities in wheat on the quality of baked products. They also appreciate the havoc variances in quality can have on the baking process, such as variations of a half inch or more in loaf height. By concentrating on this relatively small group of buyers that really get quality, the AWB manages to obtain premiums in one of the most difficult markets in the world.

Most marketers find it necessary to spend considerable amounts of time gathering data and talking to consumers to construct a useful segmentation, and even then they often consider several before settling on one that describes the market in a useful way. For example, upscale car manufacturers have found it useful to map the market along two dimensions, luxury and technology, but that conclusion required the generation of dozens of alternative market views. And once a segmentation that really describes the market is developed, there's still the matter of selecting which segment is best suited for your brand. Here are a few observations, based on experience, that might help.

First of all, the smaller the target market, the bigger the opportunity. Every marketer wants to define the largest possible potential market for his or her brand. There is a very natural and almost universal fear of defining the target too narrowly and, as a result, missing out on potential sales. This is one of those natural tendencies, like leaning uphill when skiing, that is absolutely, positively guaranteed to result in painful failure. Identifying the core market is not about identifying everyone who might possibly be attracted to the brand, but rather about finding the core group for whom that brand and no other will suffice. It is an exclusive exercise, not an inclusive one. Take the example of Dodge trucks.

In 1993 Dodge had only 7 percent of the U.S. pickup truck market. Desperate to change this, Bob Lutz charged designer Trevor Creed with creating a design completely different from any other on the market. The resulting design had an in-your-face grille and bulging fenders and looked more like a shrunken semi than a traditional pickup truck. When Dodge tested the design with consumers, they found that 20 percent of consumers loved the design and 80 percent hated it. Many Dodge marketers argued that aiming for one-fifth of the market was too big a risk and suggested toning down the design. Lutz overruled them, asserting that 20 percent was three times their current share. And in fact Dodge did sell three times as many of the new trucks. In 1993 sales were seventy thousand; in 1994 they leaped to two hundred thousand. But then, as the market became more used to the design, some of the 80 percent came over as well, leading to sales of four hundred thousand in 1998.[7]

As counterintuitive as it may seem at first glance, the case for a tight target is in fact very logical. In today's cluttered world, brands directed at an "average" customer will always be edged out by one tailored to the specific needs of a well-defined segment.

Here's another lesson learned the hard way: get the who right, and everything else will fall into place. The most common mistake in branding is to work the process backward. That is, companies often start with a decision on the how (say, a new advertising campaign or corporate identity program) and then try to work backward to the what. They often stop there. That's a huge mistake. Start with the who, spend 90 percent of the time there, then 9 percent on the what, and whatever is left on the how.

What

The objective of the what step is to identify a point of difference that can be turned into a point of differentiation. That is, find something different or potentially different about the product or service that the target segment cares about.

Deciding the what for a brand starts with a thorough inventory of the available options. Start by looking at each of the seven basic ways to differentiate any product or service: functionality (including appearance), underlying technology, quality, convenience, customization, risk management (including proxies for reliability, such as awards won and industry rankings), and image.[8]

Then within each category, list those differences applicable to your brand, and those already staked out by competitors. For example, most toothpastes are differentiated based on functionality. However, the category contains products that prevent cavities or bad breath or gum disease, whiten teeth or remove the stains of coffee and smoking. Some competitors, such as Sensodyne for sensitive teeth, have already staked out some of these so conclusively that it would be hard for a competitor to displace them.

At the end of the inventory most brands will find they have several minor points of differentiation and no single dominant one. That's okay. It is the role of marketing to magnify one of those differences and cement it in the target segment's mind.

As you tackle the issue of differentiation, here's the number one rule for success: don't be afraid to be different. In consumer audio, there is a plethora of high-end brands, such as Bang & Olufsen, Marantz, and Sherwood. Arguably the most successful is Bose, a billion-dollar privately owned corporation based in Framingham, Massachusetts.

When Amar Bose finished his coursework at MIT in 1956, he bought himself a set of the best audio components, took them home, and put on a record of a violin piece. It sounded terrible. After a great deal of experimentation and analysis, Bose, by then a professor at MIT, decided that the problem was that the sound a component makes in the laboratory has nothing to do with how it sounds in a home. The reason is simple: in a home, as in a concert hall, most of the sound we hear is reflected sound. Therefore, to get accurate sound, speakers need to be designed to bounce sound off things.

He tinkered for a few years, piling up patents. When he could find no one to license them, he started his own speaker company. His first product, the 901 Direct/Reflecting loudspeaker system, came out in 1964. Unlike most speakers of the time, it had no tweeters and no woofers. Instead it had nine drivers, most of which pointed away from the listener. Competitors laughed and said the speakers wouldn't work.

They did. The company grew like wildfire, became absurdly profitable, and has since won over fifty-five awards for its products. The hallmark of Bose is that they do things differently. They target ordinary consumers, not audiophiles and critics. They sell directly, unlike other competitors who go through audio chains. They sell different products. These include the Lifestyle system, tiny, almost invisible speakers that provide large-system sound but fit in the poshest living room. His award-winning Wave radio uses a complex system of tubes to provide stereo sound from a compact shelf radio. They've succeeded (and wildly at that—Wave retails for $600, twice the price of copycats) because at Bose, being different is celebrated. And as a result, they stand out from the wall of look-alike speakers in every audio shop's sound room.

Once your inventory of options is complete, it is necessary to choose a key point of differentiation. There are three criteria for choosing a point of differentiation: it must be meaningful to the target segment, it must be ownable, and it must be comfortable to the brand. Typically the most difficult test is ownability.

In any market category are two or three brands trying to genuinely carve out a point of differentiation and two or three dozen trying to copy the true innovators and cut price. Take laptop computers, where Sony, Apple, and IBM continue to work to develop differentiated products, and most competitors are satisfied to copy. For example, Compaq quickly matched Apple's colorful Internet-ready computer iMac with its own colorful Internet-ready computer, iPaq. There are two ways to defend differentiation. First, claim your differentiation point unambiguously, early, and often; second, invest in widening the gap. Using the example above, by the time iPaq hit the market, Apple was already preparing the Titanium G4, the next wave.

How

There are three basic sets of nitty-gritty tools in branding: iconography, or development of a distinctive look and feel for the brand identity elements; marketing communications, including advertising, PR, direct, online, events, promotion, and so on; and strategic alliances and co-brands, such as Kmart and Martha Stewart.

The key to using these effectively is to use tools that fit the brand. That is, select a set of tools that reaches the right target and delivers the right message. For example, Brooks Instruments, a tiny division of Emerson that makes process control equipment, has scored a big hit with a comic strip that appears on their Web site and chronicles the adventures of Dr. Direct. Dr. Direct solves thorny engineering problems with humor and élan (just the way we engineers think of ourselves). Their Web site is a huge hit with the engineers who spec their products.

In fact, Dr. Direct illustrates another important point about how: that it's how, not how much. Many highly publicized dot-coms spent millions on marketing but have nothing to show for it. Meanwhile, other companies have spent pennies to achieve excellent results by carefully targeting their market and being creative in their delivery. Take RIM, the relatively unknown Canadian company that introduced the Black-Berry pager in January 1999. Since then, over a million BlackBerry units have been sold. But they did it without a huge marketing budget.

Instead they carefully targeted a narrow group: traveling professionals (and their IT support). They recruited around fifty "evangelists" who visited Fortune 500 companies and set up over a thousand pilot programs where they provided pagers for trial without charge. By the end of the first year they'd built a beachhead into a difficult-to-crack market, and their core of loyalists helped them roll out the devices across the corporation. (They also loaned them to key journalists and received a mountain of PR in return.)[9]

Closing Thoughts

Who, what, how. That's it. The discussion above might suggest that branding is a simple straightforward process. Unfortunately (or fortunately for those of us in the business of helping companies build brands), it's not quite that simple. Customers do not wear T-shirts labeled with their segment, and points of differentiation are often elusive and hard to stake out. Nonetheless, it's essential that companies do work to develop their brands, and do so aggressively.

During the eighties and nineties top management's focus was on the bottom line—lowering costs by building scale facilities, squeezing suppliers, and reengineering every process to improve efficiency. But we have now reached a point where virtually every competitor has reached or has access to scale, has implemented strategic sourcing, and has reengineered every department in sight. Low-cost position is now part and parcel of being in the game. But it no longer plays a very large role in who wins.

Increasingly it is management of the top line that drives profitability. And successful top-line management is about the ability to achieve those brand premiums we spoke about.

FROM SOW'S EAR TO SILK PURSE: HOW TO TURN A COMMODITY PRODUCT INTO A SPECIALTY

Ben Shapiro

In this digital age everyone wants to draw sharp, binary distinctions. People love to make simple distinctions between commodities and specialties. Specialties are high-margin items, we are told, and commodities are undifferentiated and thus low-margin items. But the story is much more complex. Most products and services operate in the great in-between that has some characteristics of commodities and some of specialties.

Our purpose here is to clarify the differences between specialties and commodities, enumerate the four different forms of specialty markets, explore what's in between the pure forms of specialties and commodities, and suggest ways to manage margins and slow the natural decline of specialties to commodities.

Specialties Versus Commodities

Specialties differ from commodities along two dimensions. First, specialties create significant customer value. That is why people talk of being in the high-value-added section of the market. In any given market specialties generate more value in general for customers than commodities. But it is notoriously hard to compare customer value across markets, so one has to do the comparisons within markets.

Providing high customer value, however, is no guarantee that you will end up selling a specialty. Many commodities provide high customer value but low margins to the supplier. The other condition necessary for specialty status is high competitive differentiation. Without differentiation, your dumbest, most desperate competitor will set your price. Differentiation protects customer value from competitive degradation.

The Four Customer Values

Customers seem to place significant value on four attributes, which define the four kinds of specialties. First is *convenience*. Convenience specialties enable the customer to trade time and effort against a lower price. If you provide higher convenience than your competitors and if it is important to the customer, you can charge a higher price. Convenience stores that are close to the customer, easy and fast to shop in, and open long hours get to charge higher prices than larger, more remote stores. Of course, if two convenience stores are next to each other, they may end up beating each other up on price because they have no viable differentiation.

The second type is the *availability* specialty, which provides the only reasonable option for getting an urgently needed product or service. Spare parts for capital equipment are a typical availability specialty because the need is urgent if the machinery is not operable. Picture a large piece of industrial equipment or your own automobile. Some products that are usually a commodity can temporarily become an availability specialty. When demand outstrips supply, the price is driven up until supply grows or demand abates. In the late 1990s newsprint, which is typically a commodity, was in short supply, and prices and margins rose to the occasion for a period of over a year.

Convenience and availability can relate to both products and services and are very important forms of specialties. But when people speak of a specialty in hushed, reverential tones, they are typically thinking of the other two forms of specialty, functional and relationship.

The *functional* specialty is the product or service that can physically do a better job than its competitors. It is the biggest, fastest, or highest-resolution. The differentiation may come from proprietary technology, patents, or both.

Finally we come to the *relationship* specialty, which has its special value and differentiation from the personal, brand, or institutional relationship provided by the vendor. Here the differentiation is in the vendor or the vendor's people, not the product. The difference may be in the quality of the individuals providing service and sales, or in the value of the guarantee embodied by the brand.

The Dynamics of the Commodity Magnet

Almost all products begin as specialties with high margins. But two processes degrade the specialty into a commodity over time. When a product is first introduced, it has a combination of real unfamiliarity and perceived mystique or cachet to the customer. This enables the supplier to charge for support in helping customers define their needs and choose the right solutions. Additional help is often provided after the sale, including usage and maintenance support, to enable the customer to get full value from the purchase. Over time, however, the customer, whether individual or organizational, learns a great deal about the product and its use. Their familiarity diminishes the value of both the real expertise provided by the supplier and the mystique or cachet surrounding it. Then the product begins to move from specialty to commodity. The customer is thus the first culprit.

The second culprit in the degradation is competition. Competitors introduce imitations or, even worse, improvements. This process is more widely recognized than the customer's own development of expertise and familiarity.

Often, customer knowledge and power develop simultaneously with competitive imitation and improvement. The two processes interact in a combination of fragmentation and commoditization. Different market segments emerge with somewhat different needs. Various competitors position their products and service against those needs. The previously homogeneous market is now more fragmented and thus more expensive to serve. Increasing customer power and competitive intensity force prices down despite often higher costs. Margins suffer, competitors consolidate or fail, and the market matures.

The Great In-Between

Most products are not pure commodities or pure specialties. They exist in a mixture of functional and relationship specialties, with some aspects of convenience specialty, and even availablity specialty if there are major shifts in the supply/demand balance, and an amalgam of commodity pressure. The goal of most companies should be not to turn a commodity into a specialty but instead to constantly improve margin in an evolutionary fashion in this complex, mixed market. Breakthroughs are rare, but continuous margin improvement is a reasonable goal in many situations.

Moving Commodities Toward Specialties

The natural progression is from specialty to commodity. Thus it takes special intelligence and effort to go in the other direction. But it is possible. In California a company called Granite Rock has managed to differentiate itself in the crushed stone industry. And Perdue has done it in chickens. If it can be done in crushed rock and chickens, there is hope for most every product and service.

One key is to understand that customer value and differentiation can be created in three different phases of customer activity. Customers choose a product or service because it provides value in one of three ways:

1. During purchase
2. From ownership
3. In use

Successful value-adding differentiation can work at any or all levels.

During the purchase process convenience and risk reduction are important. In the business of industrial cutting tools for making precision gears and other such components, a division of Kenametal, a carbide tool supplier, has gone so far as to provide factory-floor "vending machines" to dispense tools when needed, with enormous availablity and billing convenience to the customer. In its supercharged heyday of the late 1960s and early 1970s, IBM made it safe for computer-illiterate CFOs to purchase Big Blue computers. It was risk reduction at the highest levels, and desperately appreciated by the customers, who were involved in high-risk, confusing purchases.

Much brand power comes from the sheer pleasure of ownership, without any special usage value. Versace ties and Vuitton luggage may not be functionally superior, but they provide a special cachet to those who own them. This is harder to apply in the organizational context, but it exists even there.

And, of course, there are many opportunities for value creation and differentiation in customer utilization.

Sometimes there are single large opportunities for creating customer value and differentiation. For example, Polaroid's introduction of the patent-protected instant photograph created a superspecialty for three decades, until electronics trumped chemistry. Most of the time the move from commodity to specialty is more like creative, meticulously executed trench warfare than business blitzkrieg. The critical things are to understand what is important to the customer in all three phases of the purchase/consumption process, what you can do significantly better than competition, and where you can repeat the process as customers grow more powerful and competitors flex their imitation and improvement muscles. The rewards in somewhat higher margins and returns, if not overwhelming, are usually very worthwhile. The only other high-profit option is to dominate the commodity part of the market, with lower costs and, generally, higher volumes.

9. Communication

"A Fool May Talk, but a Wise Man Speaks"

WHEN I WORKED IN THE NEWSROOM OF THE *NEW York Times*, I covered economics much of the time. Just after Saddam Hussein invaded oil-rich Kuwait, which led to the first Gulf War, I was asked by my editor to write a story about what the invasion meant for the economy. I had two days to get the views of several dozen people, create the story line, convince my editors I was right, and—oh yes—produce an article with charts, tables, pictures, and graphs. Needless to say, I was under a wee bit of pressure.

In the middle of this effort I got a call from a public relations woman who told me she had an important story to pitch, one that was right up my alley.

I told her I was crazy busy and could not talk. I was not impolite. Even though I told her things were nuts, she proceeded to call me once an hour, pleading to let her make her pitch.

"All right, all right," I groaned. "Make your pitch."

"Thanks," she said. "Here's my story, and I'll be brief. We're holding a contest in New York, sponsored by an insecticide company, to find the world's biggest cockroach."

"Here's my response, and *I'll* be brief," I said. *Click.* I hung up the phone.

There are three things you must know when dealing with the media.

The first thing is timing. There are moments when reporters sit in the newsroom drinking coffee, cleaning their fingernails with their letter openers, bending paper clips, telling jokes, reading mail. There are also times when they are insane. Get those two times mixed up and they will remember.

The second thing to know is that never in my career did I ever cover cockroaches. You have to know *who* covers *what.* Reporters and editors are specialists. The person who covers currency trading or the commodities markets or technology does not cover retailing or banking. The good, hardworking people who cover global economics do not also work on stories about Raid, Off!, or the Roach Motel.

The third item to know is that you can call reporters and other newsroom staff directly to make your pitch. But if you get the first two items wrong, the only thing you'll get is a click.

This section discusses not only media but communications in general. This is important because it can be argued that good communication—written, verbal, visual, and numerical—can make the difference between failure and success in management and even in business. It can also be argued that good communication has several levels and several focal points. At a minimum, success requires good communication between individuals and individuals, the company and itself, the company and its customers, the company and the capital markets, your company and other companies. Getting that right is what this section is all about. It is not about insects.

J.K.

IT PAYS TO TALK RIGHT: THE POWER AND INFLUENCE OF CORPORATE COMMUNICATION

Paul Argenti

The term "corporate communication" isn't new, but the notion of it as an integrated functional area of management (think finance, marketing, or production) is still an evolving one. Over the past twenty years senior managers at a growing number of companies have started to recognize that a unified communication function is a key ingredient to achieving business goals—and even strengthening a company's reputation.

By way of introduction to corporate communication, in this chapter we will:

- Define the term
- Look at some of the reasons organizations should care about corporate communication
- Offer a framework for results-oriented strategic communication

- Explore some of the key subfunctions of corporate communication

We can define corporate communication ("corp comm") as *the corporation's voice as projected to its various audiences, both internal and external.* These audiences—which I call "constituencies"—include customers, employees, the media, business partners, investors, special-interest groups, and local communities, to name just a few.

For a company to speak with one voice to all of its constituencies, many of which are both sophisticated and demanding, it needs a thoughtfully constructed corporate communication program that is also aligned with overall company strategy and mission.

Why Care About Corp Comm?

Every functional area at one time or another has had its day in the sun—it's been the most novel, the most cutting-edge, the most important. But as we enter the twenty-first century most of us can appreciate the enduring value of communication, for several key reasons.

First, the relationship between organizations and the general public over the past twenty years has become strained. People are generally more educated about issues (global warming, sustainable farming, fair trade) and more mistrustful of corporate intentions. Consumers see in the headlines enough high-profile cases of executive pay excesses and accounting fraud that a heightened sense of skepticism has become the norm. To attract customers, employees, and investors, companies need to be progressive leaders about a whole range of global issues and put their vision in a broader social context.

Second, organizations themselves have become inherently more complex over the past several decades. In earlier times companies could get by with much less sophisticated communications activities than what they need today—the traditional public relations "flak" juggled fending off the press with managing corporate advertising and directing internal communication. But in today's organizations, many with thousands of employees, there are just too many balls in the air to keep the show going without a coordinated corporate communication function.

And third, we live in a highly sophisticated communication age. Information travels virtually instantaneously from one corner of the world to another courtesy of technological developments such as satellite news feeds and the Internet. To capture the ever-waning attention span of the general public, companies are also focusing more on the visual component of their communications. From glossy annual reports to entire gas stations "designed" from top to bottom by high-profile New York agencies, the bar is even higher today for a company's message to stand out in the minds of its constituencies. These trends all speak for a sophisticated and strategic approach to communication.

Taking a Strategic Approach to Communication

From informing employees about the rising cost of health care, to convincing shareholders that the company is worth investing in, to simply getting customers to buy more of its products, the company that takes a strategic approach to communication is the one most likely to achieve its objectives.

Communication strategy is not a new concept. In fact, communication theories go back to the days of ancient Greece. We can trace the roots of modern communication theory to Aristotle's major work, *The Art of Rhetoric*.[1]

> [E]very speech is composed of three parts: the speaker, the subject of which he treats, and the person to whom it is addressed, I mean the hearer, to whom the end or object of the speech refers.

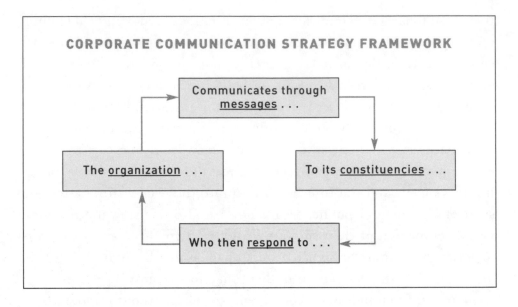

CORPORATE COMMUNICATION STRATEGY FRAMEWORK

Communicates through messages . . .

The organization . . .

To its constituencies . . .

Who then respond to . . .

Let's rework the philosopher's terms a bit to apply this same structure to modern-day corp comm. Instead of a speaker, the first component in a corporate communication strategy is the organization. The second component, in place of Aristotle's "person . . . to whom the end or object of the speech refers," is the constituency. And the final component, Aristotle's "subject of which he treats," we call messages.

Taking this a step further, we can create a framework for corporate communication (see the figure above) by synthesizing Aristotle's ideas with those of communications theorist Mary Munter.[2]

What do you notice about this framework? For one thing, it is circular. This may be surprising if you think about communication as a one-way information flow; in fact, it is anything but. Organizations should set clear objectives for every communication and then measure their success in meeting those objectives: Was the message understood? Did our constituency (consumers) take the action we wanted them to take (buy more products) as a result of the communication (an advertising campaign)? Only when the flow of communication comes back to the organization in this circular pattern is management really communicating strategically.

Of course, this framework is not much help to the organization that does not know the constituencies it's targeting with a given message. For instance, how much do they know about the company? What is their attitude toward it? Do all constituencies share the same view? XYZ Inc. might have a consumer constituency that has a negative view of the company because they feel it's not environmentally responsible. At the same time, its investor constituency might be fans of its history of strong reported earnings and lean cost structure and be busily accumulating shares of the company. XYZ needs to craft communications to these different groups with these predispositions in mind.

So who are all of a company's constituencies? The answer to that will depend partly on the nature, size, and reach (i.e. global or domestic, local versus regional or national) of their businesses. But most organizations share some key primary and secondary constituencies. Take a look at Table 1.

Table 1
KEY CONSTITUENCY GROUPS FOR ORGANIZATIONS

PRIMARY	SECONDARY
■ Employees	■ Media
■ Customers	■ Suppliers
■ Shareholders	■ Government
■ Communities	□ Local
	□ Regional
	□ National
	■ Creditors

In reality, these constituency groups are not as fixed or separate as they appear on paper. They can change over time and as circumstances vary. In a time of crisis, for example, a company might do best to focus more intently on its relations with the media (which it may consider a secondary constituency under normal circumstances) to manage its reputation and attempt to minimize negative press in a time when it is most vulnerable.

Organizations should also resist thinking about constituencies in silos, because the lines between them can be blurry or sometimes even nonexistent. One common example of this is employee shareholders in a company. Starbucks employees who receive "Bean Stock" are simultaneously members of two constituency groups: employees and shareholders. Given the blurry lines we just mentioned, it's important that these subfunctions stay in close coordination, since they will often have some constituencies in common.

Managing Identity, Image, and Reputation

Reflecting the reality of the firm through visual images and the right choice of words is the most fundamental function of a corporate communication department. The study of identity and image has taken off in recent years as design agencies work with more companies to develop the right look for a particular approach to the marketplace. And as consumers and investors take a more holistic view of companies and their noncore activities (e.g., corporate social responsibility), corporate reputation is also moving into the spotlight.

Some of these terms are used almost interchangeably, but in fact they mean quite different things. How do we best distinguish these concepts? We can define *image* as the corporation as seen through the eyes of a particular constituency. Just as an organization has different constituencies, it can have different images with each of them. For example, cigarette companies are often the target of consumer ire but a delight to their shareholders, who may sit back and watch international sales of the same product soar, along with their account balances.

The Nature of Managerial Work

HENRY MINTZBERG

■ The manager uses five basic media: the mail (documented communication), telephone (purely verbal), the unscheduled meeting (informal face-to-face), the scheduled meeting (formal face-to-face), and the tour (visual). Certain fundamental differences exist among these. Documented communication requires the use of a formal subset of the language and involves long feedback delays. All verbal media can transmit, in addition to the messages contained in the words used, messages sent by voice inflection and by delays in reaction. In addition, face-to-face media carry information transmitted by facial expression and by gesture.

The most significant finding concerning media is that managers demonstrate very strong attraction to verbal media. Virtually every empirical study of managerial time allocation draws attention to the great proportion of time spent in verbal communication, with estimates ranging from 57 percent of time spent in face-to-face communication by foremen (Guest 1956) to 89 percent of episodes in verbal interaction by middle managers in a manufacturing company (Lawler, Porter and Tennenbaum, 1968). Rosemary Stewart (1967), who collected the most extensive data, found that her middle and senior managers average only 34 percent of their time alone, most of the rest in informal communication, and Burns (1954) found that conversation consumed 80 percent of the middle managers' time. My own findings bear this out. ■

From Henry Mintzberg, *The Nature of Managerial Work* (Harper & Row, 1973).

A corporate image is not something to be taken lightly. An organization may not have a dedicated department for crisis communications, for example, but it had better have a plan and a SWAT team of sorts in place to deal with communications during a crisis. Members of the crisis comm team should include corporate communication professionals, senior management, and representatives from media relations. Communication professionals should be involved in crisis planning and crisis management every step of the way—often, how a company communicates during a crisis is a key determinant of how it emerges (or doesn't) from that crisis.

In the early 1980s, for example, Johnson & Johnson dealt with the fallout of several people being poisoned by cyanide-laced Tylenol capsules. In what would become a textbook example of effective crisis communication, J&J mounted a quick and coordinated response and demonstrated a concern for the public that only strengthened its reputation as "the caring company." Not only did J&J immediately pull the product from store shelves nationwide, but thousands of the company's employees made over one million personal visits to hospitals, physicians, and pharmacists around the nation to restore faith in the Tylenol name.[3] Effective communication was a key factor in allowing J&J to emerge stronger than ever from what could have been an irreversibly damaging crisis.

Identity consists of a company's defining attributes: people, products, and services, for example. An organization has some kind of identity whether it wants one or not, based in part on the visual components it presents to the world. People all over the world know Coca-Cola's red can and white script lettering and McDonald's golden arches in front of a store, whether it's in Beijing, China, or Providence, Rhode Island. Unlike its image, the organization's identity shouldn't vary from one constituency to another.

Determining how a firm wants to be perceived with different constituencies and how it chooses to identify itself is the cornerstone function of corporate communications. If the firm is making serious changes in its image or identity, this subfunction can easily be a full-time job for a team of corporate communicators while that process is under way.

Finally, *reputation* consists of the collective images of *all* of an organization's constituencies, and is built up over time. We see reputation scorecards in many places today: *Fortune*'s Most Admired list, *BusinessWeek* and Interbrand's "Best Global Brands" ranking, and Harris Interactive and the Reputation Institute's Reputation Quotient (RQ) Gold study, featured in the *Wall Street Journal,* are just a few.

These highly publicized rankings have gained so much attention that some corporate public relations executives' bonuses have actually been based on *Fortune*'s list of America's Most Admired Companies.[4] For many public relations firms, this has translated into a burgeoning business opportunity—reputation measurement and management services are becoming more and more prevalent as companies work to climb the "best of" scoreboards and stay off the "worst of" lists.

So what's motivating this level of interest? Companies now recognize that a solid reputation can provide them with an intangible but powerful source of competitive advantage: they can attract and retain the best talent, generate a loyal customer base, and be sought after by the most desirable business partners. And all of these things are ingredients for growth and commercial success.

The table on page 380 summarizes key definitions from this section.

If identity and image are the building blocks of reputation, then corporate communication plays a key role in constructing an organization's reputation—yet another reason for corporations to focus on ensuring that a strong corporate communication infrastructure is in place.

Conclusion: The Corp Comm Connection to Mission

The days of the PR flak keeping nosy reporters at bay are over. Today's business environment is vastly more complex than it was decades ago. The constituency groups of the modern corporation have grown both in

Table 2
DEFINITIONS OF TERMS

TERM	DEFINITION	QUESTION
Identity	Consists of a company's defining attributes, such as its people, products, and services.	Who are you?
Image	A reflection of an organization's identity—the organization as seen from the viewpoint of **one constituency.** Depending on which constituency is involved (customers, investors, employees, etc.), an organization can have many different images.	What do **I** think of who you are and who you tell me you are?
Reputation	The collective representation of **multiple constituencies'** images of a company, built up over time and based on a company's identity programs, its performance, and how constituencies have perceived its behavior.	What do **we** think of who you tell us you are and what you've done?

number and in sophistication; their demands on companies are greater and their mistrust of them higher. Information is available more quickly and through more outlets than ever before. Against this backdrop, organizations have no choice but to speak with one voice to their constituencies, and to do this they need a strong corporate communication effort.

In analyzing companies with the most effective corp comm areas, we see a striking commonality. In all of them, communication strategy is closely linked to overall company strategy and mission.

Sam Walton: Made in America

SAM WALTON

■ All I know is that nothing ever makes me feel better than when I visit a store and some department head comes up to me with pride and shows me all her numbers and tells me she's number five in the company but she plans to be number one next year. I love meeting all these merchants we've got on our team out there. When they show me an end-cap display they've got loaded up with charcoal or baby oil or lunch boxes and then tell me they chose that item because of its high profit margin, and then go on to brag about all the volume they've done with that item, I get so proud for them I can hardly stand it. I really mean that. It is just the proudest I get. Because if we, as managers, truly dedicate ourselves to instilling that thrill of merchandising—the thrill of buying and selling something at a profit—into every single one of our associate-partners, nothing can ever stop us. ■

From Sam Walton with John Huey, *Sam Walton: Made in America* (Doubleday, 1992).

Johnson & Johnson's management of the Tylenol crisis demonstrated how a company was able to resolve a dire situation in a way that actually *strengthened* its reputation and brand. Despite its decentralized structure, Johnson & Johnson's management is bound together by a document known as "the credo." The credo is a 308-word company-wide code of ethics that was created in 1935 to boost morale during the Depression, and it is literally carved in stone at company headquarters in New Brunswick, New Jersey, today. It acknowledges: "We believe our first responsibility is to the doctors, nurses, and patients, to mothers and all others who use our products and services." James Burke, CEO at the time of the Tylenol crisis, made sure that the principles of the credo guided the company's actions during that period, helping J&J react to tragedy without losing focus on what was most important.

Too often in the past, corporate communication has been thought about as a means to an end rather than a function itself. This viewpoint has changed as more and more companies recognize the power and influence of corporate communication. Developed within the framework of a company's overall strategic plan and given focus and support from senior management, the corp comm function is an invaluable resource for any company that hopes to succeed and reach its fullest potential in today's business environment.

IT'S NEVER SMALL TALK:

HOW TO TALK TO THE PRESS

Geoffrey Moore

You're the CEO of the Acme Corporation. Having worked your way up the corporate ladder through several divisions, you know the business inside and out. Of course, there are some areas you trust to people with specialized skills—the general counsel, the controller, the head of human resources. Your executive vice president of corporate communications takes care of a wide range of functions including publicity and sponsorships, advertising, press relations, speechwriting, community relations, and employee communications as well as coordinating with investor relations, government relations, and corporate philanthropy.

But as the most visible public face of Acme, there's one specialized communications task you can't duck, even though they didn't teach it in business school: talking to the media. Sure, you have press relations people who deal with the press every day and know how to handle their questions. Inevitably, however, you'll be in the media spotlight. Consider these situations:

■ It's 6 A.M. and you're roused from a sound sleep by the telephone. The caller identifies himself as a reporter for CNN and, after a not-very-sincere apology for calling you at home, says he's going on the air this morning with an exclusive report that Acme is having merger discussions with Consolidated Industries. He wants you to confirm it. In fact, you *are* in merger talks, but no one is supposed to know. What do you say?

■ Or it's a reporter from the *Washington Post* who asks you about a rumor he's heard that the Department of Justice will today file an antitrust suit against Acme in federal court. What do you say?

■ Or a local radio news reporter greets you by explaining that you're on the air live and he's just seen a report on the wire that two people have died after eating Acme snack foods. What do you say?

There are many ways you could respond to these unexpected intrusions, but there are two things you should never do: don't lie, and don't ever say "No comment."

The safest response to such unwelcome calls is simply "I'll get back to you." You have no obligation to provide an instant sound bite, and a statement like "I'll get back to you" is unlikely to be published or broadcast. You're entitled to some time to think and consult before you say anything of substance. But always ask for the reporter's phone number and e-mail address and agree on a deadline for your response.

The Art of Talking to Journalists

Conversations with journalists are unlike conversations with anyone else. It's a highly structured dance in which your partner is a professional trained in the art of extracting from you precisely the information you don't want to disclose. Neophytes at this dance have as much chance of emerging unscathed as they do of beating Tiger Woods in a friendly weekend game of golf.

This chapter won't make you a press relations professional any more than an article on health tips will make you a doctor. But it just might help you avoid seeing your name on page one of tomorrow's newspaper in an unflattering context.

Let's start with your rights and the reporter's rights. A free press is the bedrock of our liberty and serves an incalculably important role by shining light in dark places. They have a near-absolute right to say whatever they want, as long as it's reasonably truthful or at least isn't said maliciously. You may think it's malicious when they call you an incompetent scoundrel, but that's not the way courts see it. And that's good—you wouldn't want to live in one of the many countries where reporters go to jail for merely saying negative things about people in power.

Reporters are free to research any and all information about you, to call you, to ask outrageous questions, to infer anything from your answers or from your refusal to answer, and to use as little or as much of what you say, even if it is out of context. But you have rights too, and nowhere is it written that you must give the press the rope with which to hang you. You can decline to speak, or speak subject to certain ground rules, or limit your remarks to certain subjects. You can expect courtesy, honesty, and some level of directness from a reporter. You may ask if it's okay with the reporter if you record the interview. (It's always okay.) You may ask the reporter to call you back after he or she writes the story to check statements of fact and direct quotes. If the reporter agrees, you have the right to correct errors but not to change the wording of statements that you now wish you hadn't said. You may ask the reporter to clarify the intent of the story. But you can't demand to know who told the reporter what, and it's unlikely the reporter will tell you about others he or she plans to call.

When a broadcast organization wants to talk to you, you can ask for (but won't always get) a live interview, which gives you somewhat more control over what goes on the air than a prerecorded session that can be heavily edited. You have a right to ask who will be interviewing you and who else will be interviewed on the same program. Any producer who refuses to give you this information should be told politely that you'd rather they pass you by this time. If you have video of your products or facilities, you might offer it to the producer as "B roll" that can be played while you're speaking.

Reporters use the forms of polite social discourse to get you to say more than you intended. At a dinner party, if there's a lull in the conversation, you often feel an urge to fill it. But a press interview isn't a social chat. After you've said exactly what you want to say, shut up. The reporter will sometimes remain silent, hoping the awkward pause will impel you to expand your comments. That's when you're most likely to slip up. It never hurts to be polite, but resist the urge to keep talking.

When you don't want to respond to a question, you can always find more graceful words than a curt "No comment." Making an effort to sound as pleasant and cooperative as possible, you can say something like, "That's not an area I want to discuss today, but I'll get back to you if anything changes."

Even though the reporter takes the lead in asking questions, you should always have your own agenda and a short, well-thought-out list of points you want to deliver no matter what is asked. You may want to jump right in by saying, "Before we get to your questions, I'd like to give you a quick overview of Acme's position in the industry." During the questions and answers, know how to use "bridging" techniques, a staple of sophisticated communication that you'll see politicians using every Sunday on the TV talk shows. When the reporter asks about something you'd rather not emphasize, make your answer very short and polite before you morph in midsentence to the subject you really want to discuss.

No matter what questions are asked, make every effort to stay on your positive message. As Henry Kissinger once joked at the beginning of a press conference, "Does anyone have any questions for my answers?" No one will read the exact transcript of the interview, so it's fine if you repeat your main points several times in slightly different words. Just keep them short and easy to understand.

Beware the mousetrap question that makes it sound as if the reporter already knows something you consider confidential and then waits to see if you deny it. When the reporter says, "I know that Acme is going to be canceling its line of green widgets, so could you tell me how many you've sold?" you have no obligation to confirm the rumor. The reporter could be fishing without any firm knowledge. It is entirely acceptable to respond, "Jane, you know Acme never discusses speculation about future product plans." Then, without missing a beat, take the opportunity to bridge over to something else: "But on the subject of our product line, we're very proud of the way the flamtraps we introduced last year have captured the public's imagination. Sales are up thirty percent this quarter."

There are situations, however, where it's best not to duck behind a practice of avoiding speculation. If you must deny something, don't leave any wiggle room. Slam it to the ground as hard as you can: "That is 100 percent false. We do not do it. It violates our corporate policy and is grounds for immediate dismissal."

"But It Was Out of Context!"

Executives who haven't had much experience talking to the media often complain that they were quoted out of context. Tough luck. It's not the reporter's job to accept your context. The reporter is looking for a few colorful words to plug into his or her own context. So if you talk for an hour and say ninety-nine positive things about a subject, with only one less-than-positive aside, guess which one will appear in print.

Be careful about assuming an interview is over when the reporter turns off the microphone or puts the notepad away and says, "Thank you for your time." What you say in an unguarded moment as you walk the reporter to the elevator may be the only thing used in the story.

Going "off the record" or speaking "on background" are techniques best left to communications professionals who have a close relationship with the reporter. You should generally not attempt to segregate your comments into different categories. Assume that you'll read everything you say, under any ground rules, in the article. There are exceptions to this rule, but don't try them without competent communications counsel. And never say anything like "Just between us . . ."— a meaningless phrase that only shows your inexperience.

Like football, press relations is played on offense and defense. A marketing communications representative promoting a product typically exudes chumminess in an (often futile) attempt to become the reporter's best buddy. But in most cases you'll gain little by trying to be a pal. Cordiality can't hurt, but the tone of the interview should be one of crisp professionalism, tinged with a hint that you expect the facts to be reported correctly. (One way to deliver that hint is to put a tape recorder on the table.) If the subsequent article screws up the facts, react immediately by demanding a correction of factual errors and space for a published letter to the editor disputing every erroneous interpretation.

The purpose of the correction is not so much to set the record straight in the minds of readers who saw the original article. Rather, it gets the facts into the publication's editorial system so they pop up in research for all future articles. And, more subtly, it tells reporters that they damn well better get things right the next time. There are few experiences more dreaded by reporters than having their journalistic skills maligned by their own editors in a corrections column.

Never worry that you'll hurt your relationship with a publication by demanding a correction in the most forceful terms. If they got the facts wrong, they'll want to know about it. If a newspaper says Acme was fined $10 million for a toxic waste spill and the actual amount was $100,000, you're entitled at the least to a published correction. The problem is that the correction just reminds readers that there was a fine and it makes little difference to them how many zeros are after the dollar sign. Furthermore, a less-than-ethical editor might employ subtle retaliation by printing the correct amount and then adding a gratuitous bit of new negative information not in the original story, like the fact that one of your executives was charged with perjury related to the waste spill. That's why a letter to the editor can be more effective than a simple correction.

Letters to the editor should be short and need not repeat the specific error. They should add some positive information to mitigate the reputation damage. For example, in the above case the letter could say, "On March 20, the *Daily Blatt* incorrectly reported the amount of a fine assessed by the Environmental Protection Agency against Acme Corporation fifteen years ago. Without admitting or denying liability, Acme settled the matter with a payment that was only 1 percent of the amount published in the *Blatt*. A more complete and balanced report would have noted the thirty-seven awards Acme has earned in the last decade for its pro-environment initiatives. As citizens who breathe the same air and drink the same water as the *Blatt*'s readers, we are proud of the many contributions the people of Acme have made to cleaning up the environment."

If the letter hasn't been published within a week, send an e-mail to the letters editor with a copy to the editor of the editorial page noting that they have an obligation to report facts correctly. Ask pointedly whether they intend to publish your letter or leave the distorted record unchanged. If another week passes, call the editor of the editorial page, the executive who usually has ultimate responsibility for letters. This approach won't always work, but it's often effective. There's no need to write to the reporter or editors on the news side. News editors can only publish corrections—they have no authority to run letters, which is the province of the editorial page.

Keep It Short

Learn to speak in sound bites, even if you're talking to a print reporter. If the question is "Where do you think the economy will be in six months?" don't launch into a twenty-minute dissertation on productivity, the money supply, and interest rates. While one-word answers such as "up," "down," or "flat" are overly cute, it's seldom necessary to speak for more than the length of this paragraph. If the reporter wants more specifics, he or she will ask.

The practice of press relations has changed over the years, and technology now gives you more options for providing information. E-mail, for example, allows you to control exactly what you say while meeting the reporter's need for quotable statements before the deadline. It's often an excellent middle ground between the risk of a live interview and the lost opportunity of an interview denied.

E-mail is particularly useful when the proposed interview covers subjects about which you have many things you want to say, but where you are vulnerable on follow-up questions because of related negative facts. Such a good news/bad news situation might occur, for example, where sales have been excellent year to date but where next year's prospects could be negatively impacted by pending legislation, a competitor's product announcement, or an expiring labor contract. It's quite acceptable to respond to a reporter's telephoned request by saying you're not able to talk right away but you'll get back to him or her before the deadline. Then ask what kinds of things the reporter wants to cover, and be sure to get an e-mail address. Closer to the deadline, respond with a detailed e-mail saying everything you want to say on the subject. You can attach related documents or refer the reporter to a Web site that contains additional information. The reporter may be frustrated by his or her inability to ask follow-up questions but, given no other choice, is likely to quote some of your carefully crafted words.

Of course, there are pluses and minuses to this tactic. The press may tag you as aloof and unapproachable. On the other hand, you don't risk misstatement, interruption, or the bad impression of hesitation in your voice. And you don't need to feel guilty—you're not being manipulative by exercising your right to respond on your terms. After all, you didn't call the reporter; he or she called you for help with a story. And it's likely that the reporter hasn't put all his or her cards on the table either.

You can also mitigate the aloofness label by making your e-mail especially friendly and helpful: "Hi, Jim, I appreciated your call, and since then I've given quite a bit of thought to your questions about Acme's sales. Knowing how important it is for you to get all the data down accurately, I've assembled a report for you that's attached to this e-mail. And you may quote me as saying . . ."

You're Not Running for Office

Keep in mind that it's perfectly all right to have a reputation among the media as an executive who's fairly tight-fisted with information and tenacious in pouncing on any errors. Press relations isn't about winning the congeniality award; it's about advancing the corporate agenda while protecting the interests of stockholders. Sure, there are executives who pride themselves on being regular folks who go out with the press crowd for a few beers after work while carefully observing the line between personal and business information. It doesn't happen as often as it used to, and I don't recommend it. But there's no law saying you have to be a stiff corporate suit. Just be very careful.

There are times, especially when a reporter has been newly assigned to your company or industry, when you might want to invite him or her to an informal lunch or a get-acquainted chat. The purpose isn't to influence the news in the sense that you expect subsequent coverage to be more favorable or less negative. Professional journalists aren't that malleable. But it doesn't hurt to establish mutual trust, and it helps to ensure that the reporter has a fuller context of facts about you and your business the next time you're in the news.

Any article that quotes you is also likely to include comments from "objective" third parties—industry consultants, security analysts, academic experts, and others. Every reporter has a list of these "influentials" in his or her Rolodex. It's a good idea to brief them periodically so they understand your strategy and can comment knowledgeably. Ask your communications advisor to compile a list of people who are most often quoted in the media. Then carve out time to meet them and share information they'll find useful.

There are times when you can be the influential. Offering to be a background source for industry information is a great way to stay on friendly terms with the press. You can tell a reporter to call you anytime for a chat about industry trends if you can do it as "a senior industry executive" or some other designation that doesn't identify you or your company.

You'll always earn points with the media by respecting their deadlines. Reporters love sources who help them meet the intense pressure of filing their stories on time. They even appreciate it if you're calling back only to tell them you'd rather not be in the story. They'll act very disappointed and try to make you feel guilty. The fact is, they probably didn't expect you to cooperate. They'll just cross you off their list of possible sources for that story and move to the next name on the list. But they'll remember that you were courteous enough not to ignore them.

Sometimes you aren't the most qualified person to do the interview. If you think another executive should represent the company, never just tell the reporter to call the other person. Take the contact information and promise that someone will call back before the deadline. Then call the other executive. This not only saves the reporter's time, but also gives the new source a chance to think about the inquiry before he or she is put on the spot.

Softballs, Hardballs, and Beanballs

What if you're doing an interview and a question comes out of left field that you consider improper? For example, you're discussing business prospects and the reporter says, "There's a lot of concern these days about integrity in corporate leadership, so I'd like to ask if you've ever smoked marijuana." Whether or not you were ever a pothead has nothing to do with your answer. It's important to dismiss the legitimacy of the question without showing the slightest irritation that could be interpreted as confirmation. Simply smile and in a calm voice say something noncommittal, like:

- "You know, John, that's a provocative question. Now if you'd like to continue our discussion of Acme's business, I'll be happy to continue this interview."
- "John, I'll make you a deal. I'll forgive you for asking such an irrelevant question if you'll forgive me for not responding to matters unrelated to Acme's business."
- "Nice try, John. Now, do you have any other business-related questions?"

Never mislead a reporter, no matter how penetrating or awkward the question. If you can't supply the answer, say so and explain why: "Charlene, I'm afraid you're getting into areas of our business that we consider proprietary. We've consistently declined to discuss that."

Don't underestimate the importance of the press. You may get a request for an interview at a particularly busy time, and you could be tempted to brush it off as a low-priority annoyance. Or worse, you agree to do the interview without adequate preparation. In most cases, talking to the media demands no less preparation than you'd give to a board of directors presentation. Inconvenient as it may be, you should drop what you're doing and sit down for a strategy session with a communications expert. Ask for a background fact sheet, a printout of previous articles written by the same reporter, and a set of confidential questions and answers that pull no punches. The most useful questions are those that are the most difficult, annoying, sensitive, or embarrassing.

For important interviews, schedule a rehearsal where a communications rep plays the role of the reporter. And follow the example of trial lawyers by making a video recording of the rehearsal and studying your answers. A good way to check your body language is to turn the sound off for one of the playbacks.

Never try to impress the reporter with your importance, high position, wealth, fancy office, or perks. Reporters are smart, but they're paid less than most business executives and some of them resent that fact. Anything within the bounds of dignity that you can do to humanize yourself will pay dividends. The late Thomas Watson Jr., the aristocratic chairman of IBM, once began an interview by removing chewing gum from his mouth and tossing it in the wastebasket. "You know," he said with his eyes twinkling, "my mother always told me not to chew gum in public." The enchanted reporter wrote one of the most favorable articles about IBM in years.

This brief chapter has merely skimmed the surface of some media relations techniques. Professional communications counsel can help you make the experience of talking to the press successful and satisfying. It's well worth the effort to prepare carefully. As Abraham Lincoln said, "Without public sentiment, nothing can succeed; and with it, nothing can fail."

10. There's Many a Slip 'Twixt the Cup and the Lip

Good Ideas Gone Awry

BUSINESS IS FILLED WITH MISTAKES, WHICH IS ONE reason why we learn and also why it is so much fun. What I mean by that, to be more precise, is that business is really only fun when you are learning from somebody else's mistakes.

Let me illustrate what I mean by picking on the big boys.

Pity the poor marketing Einstein at General Motors who came up with the name Nova, for a new model of Chevrolet, only to learn when they tried to sell the car in Mexico that it meant "no go" in Spanish.

Or the genius at Intel who designed a first-generation Pentium chip that could not do complicated math.

Or the bonehead at Coca-Cola who launched a new, sweeter-tasting Coke, called Coke II, just as the dieting craze and diet Coke were taking off.

Or the whizzes at Motorola and Teledesic who invested billions in satellite technology to support expensive 7-pound satellite phones to serve a customer base of a few hundred foreign correspondents and a few thousand shepherds.

Learning from slip-ups is how we learn. This section examines them in the technology and service sectors.

J.K.

REENGINEERING

Des Dearlove

Reengineering was the big business idea of the early 1990s. Among its chief proponents were James Champy, cofounder of the consultancy company CSC Index, Michael Hammer, an electrical engineer and former computer science professor at MIT, and to a lesser extent Thomas Davenport, a professor at the University of Texas.

In their hands reengineering became a crusade to tackle internal inefficiencies and the bureaucracy that had grown unchecked in many large companies. Thanks to the popularity of reengineering, CSC also became one of the largest consulting firms in the world.

The fundamental idea behind reengineering is that organizations need to identify key operations and make them as lean and efficient as possible. Peripheral processes (and, therefore, peripheral people) need to be discarded.

In its aim to integrate the flow of work across functions, reengineering echoed other ideas such as Total Quality Management. But where TQM was an evolutionary approach, requiring the active participation of the workforce, Champy and Hammer presented reengineering as a revolution. They urged companies to start from a blank sheet of paper. Workers were shouldered out of the way.

Reengineering, they claimed, was not just a technique to stream-line the flow of work but a potent strategic weapon. The ultimate goal was to create a uniquely efficient process architecture that competitors could not replicate. Reengineering became a movement. Every movement needs a mantra, and Hammer obliged with his clarion call: "Don't automate; obliterate."

It suited the times. Arnold Schwarzenegger movies were popular in the early 1990s. Reengineering provided a theoretical underpinning for the cost-cutting initiatives of the period. A wave of downsizing followed as corporations throughout the world obliterated in the name of reengineering.

As the downsizing bandwagon gathered momentum, *reengineering* became a euphemism for layoffs. In many cases it was used to bolster profits by cutting headcount and was pursued with such vigor and disregard for the human cost that its victims and survivors alike came to regard it as little more than a flag of convenience.

The human side of reengineering proved its greatest stumbling block. To reengineering purists, people were objects that handled processes. Depersonalization was the route to efficiency. By 1995 Champy, Hammer, and Davenport had all issued public apologies for the human cost of reengineering.

The reengineering movement wasn't bad in and of itself. The trouble lay in the way it was applied. In too many cases it was used cynically to justify an ulterior purpose. While the concept of reengineering was simple, actually turning it into reality proved immensely more difficult than its proponents suggested.

Chainsaw Al

With his white hair and dapper suit, Albert J. Dunlap was the very picture of benevolence. Yet his management of companies such as Scott Paper and Sunbeam earned him the nickname "Chainsaw Al." His book was called *Mean Business*. Interviewed on ABC's *Nightline*, Dunlap explained his narrowly focused business philosophy: "The reason to be in business is to make money for your shareholders. The shareholders own the company. They take all the risk."

From a shareholder's perspective, Dunlap's business record was impressive. His resumé boasts eight turnarounds. The most notable of these was at Scott Paper, whose stock price rose 220 percent in the first nineteen months under Dunlap's control.

At Sunbeam, the mere naming of Dunlap as CEO produced an overnight rise of 59 percent in the stock price. Dunlap's managerial mantra was simple cost-cutting. He could be relied upon to strip an organization to its bare bones. At Sunbeam it took Dunlap a year to reduce the company's factories from twenty-six to eight and to cut costs by $225 million.

"There are really three types of executives," Dunlap once explained. "There are people like myself who go into the most troubled of situations and rescue the company. There's the Jack Welch type of executive who, year in and year out, runs a very good corporation. There's the Bill Gates type of executive who founds a technology and creates a corporation."

In a poignant coda, Dunlap was himself downsized in June 1998 when Sunbeam ditched him—the company was making a loss and its share price was plummeting. "We lost confidence in his leadership and his earnings forecast," Dunlap's replacement coldly noted. Dunlap now treads the boards as a conference speaker. Sunbeam went into bankruptcy early in 2001.

By the mid-1990s public anger at excessive corporate bloodletting led to downsizing being reinvented in the more politically correct guise of "rightsizing." No one was fooled. The corporate world had overplayed its hand, generating a backlash.

Recent research by one consulting firm suggests that downsizing had limited success. It examined 288 Fortune 500 companies that weathered the last recession. It found that the share prices of companies that laid off more than 3 percent of their employees performed no better over a three-year period than those of companies that made smaller cuts or none at all. Companies that announced job losses greater than 15 percent of their workforce—such as Pan Am in 1991 and Lucent Technologies between 2001 and 2003—actually performed significantly below average. Companies that announced repeated rounds of layoffs, such as Digital Equipment in the early 1990s, fared even worse.

—DES DEARLOVE

THE REAL IMPACT OF THE INTERNET

Paul Taylor

At the height of the Internet mania in the late 1990s, time-tested rules of good business were thrown out the window. A clear view on how to achieve profits became far less important than conceiving a Big Idea. Planning based on conservative estimates of growth was replaced by wild ambitions resting on unrealistic notions of market potential.

The gold rush got under way in earnest in 1996, when Netscape, the first popular Web browser, was floated on the Nasdaq stock exchange. Interest in the stock surprised even its founder, Jim Clark. The spike in Netscape's price—it climbed 107 percent in a single day—inspired fortune seekers large and small. The miners grabbed their picks.

Inexperienced investors scrambled to fund business plans hastily scribbled on the back of coffee shop napkins by college kids between lectures. Venture capitalists were thrilled with the change. For years they had operated under the assumption that the companies they backed needed to be in the black for at least three years before the public would even consider buying the stock. That usually meant a long wait—seven to ten years on average—before they'd even stand a chance of making money on their original investment.

Suddenly the guy on the street was willing to put money down almost as soon as a venture was formed. They were even prepared to pay a handsome price for the additional risk. Venture capitalists were stunned by their good fortune and rushed to build and sell companies through initial public offerings (IPOs) as quickly as possible. The new format was such a break with the past that they created a new name for what they did: venture capitalists suddenly became "incubators," safe places where eggs could wait until the hatchling dot-coms were introduced to the outside world.

Investors' seemingly inexhaustible appetite for new issues led to a frenzy of IPO activity that turned many young entrepreneurs into paper billionaires overnight. At Akamai, an Internet infrastructure company, even students who had earned shares through part-time summer work were suddenly worth millions. Wall Street gurus such as Morgan Stanley's Mary Meeker and Merrill Lynch's Henry Blodget became household names. The fame of dot-com founders rivaled that of rock stars. In 1999 *Time* magazine named Amazon.com's creator, Jeff Bezos, Man of the Year.

Driven by the fear of missing out, some securities exchanges relaxed listing rules to enable start-ups with little prospect of near-term profitability to come to market just months after they were spawned. Wall Street justified sky-high share prices on nebulous new concepts of valuation.

The value of "first-mover advantage"—being first in any given area—was considered paramount. Staking a flag on Internet territory was thought to guarantee future riches. In the absence of profits, analysts measured companies' progress on the basis of page clicks—how many people entered the Web site. The business press was awash with Internet jargon. Investors talked up a New Economy that would break with the rules of the past. No longer would we be subjected to nasty recessions, or even business downturns.

Established companies, under pressure from investors, set out elaborate and costly Internet strategies. Like the securities firms, they were motivated by fear—this time of "disintermediation," another newly coined term that meant using the Internet as a distribution system to bypass middlemen such as bank branches and auto dealers.

To maximize their value as "pure plays," these ventures were often spun off as separate stocks. The dot-com side of the office supply store Staples became Staples.com, and the Web site of bookseller Barnes & Noble became BarnesandNoble.com. In an effort to be hip, Prudential, the UK-based financial group, dubbed its Internet bank sidekick "Egg." The online strategies of established groups were called "clicks-and-mortar." Experienced businesspeople who once wore their business suits as a badge of honor donned jeans and sweatshirts in an effort to appear to be on the cutting edge.

Ordinarily sensible business leaders announced their conversion to the religion of the New Economy. News Corporation's Rupert Murdoch—a self-admitted laggard of the Internet revolution—announced just before the crash that he had finally "got it" and would make a major dot-com commitment.

Some of these executives—including those at companies such as Reuters, Citicorp, and GE—gave up prestigious jobs to become Internet CEOs. In 1998 Pac Bell's CEO made the surprise announcement that he was leaving to head the newly formed group Pointcast, which aimed to deliver news and information to computer screensavers.

Others opted to join the swollen ranks of day traders, stock investors hoping to make a killing in a few days' trading. However high the price of the equity they were buying, there was bound to be a greater fool willing to pay even more. In words uttered by Federal Reserve Board chairman Alan Greenspan in early 1999: "What lottery managers have known for centuries is that you could get somebody to pay for a one-in-a-million shot more than the [pure economic] value of that chance."

The Internet crash was probably the most widely predicted in financial history. Books were written about the portending disaster. A full year before the boom ended, comparisons to the seventeenth-century tulip craze in Holland were common. At one point tulips were considered so valuable that a single bulb could be sold for four times the price of a town house. That mania ended badly when the bubble burst and the price of tulips plummeted.

The dot-com bubble ended no differently, and most of the participants in the dot-com lottery ended up losers. In March 2000, technology stocks—for little apparent reason—entered into free fall, destroying the billions of dollars in value that fleetingly resided in the superinflated stocks of dot-coms. In the aftermath, thousands of Internet companies have collapsed or been sold for a pittance. Others struggle on like the walking dead.

Instead of talking of future revenues and growth, dot-com executives began to measure their life span by "burn rates"—the rate at which they spent the cash they came by so easily. Workers who a few months before took their pick of fat-salaried jobs were suddenly throwing pink-slip parties to numb the pain of layoffs.

So what happened to the billions of dollars in real cash that was poured into Internet-related ventures? Did the end of Internet mania sound the death knell for the New Economy as well?

In the United States, which accounted for the lion's share of the investment in dot-com companies, the bulk of cash came from two main sources: venture capital and public stock offerings. According to data collected by PricewaterhouseCoopers, the accountancy firm, venture capital investments in Internet-related companies rose from just $176 million in 1995 to $19.9 billion in 1999, and totaled $26.5 billion over five years.

Yet venture capital funds and their investors—usually institutional investors and wealthy individuals—were not big losers. Their rates of return have merely fallen back from the supersonic (1,000 percent gains over a few years were not uncommon) to the perfectly acceptable. That's because many funds invested immediately before an initial public offering—a company's debut as a publicly traded stock—when the price was relatively cheap.

According to Dialogic, a New York-based investment bank research service, Internet-related companies raised $75.2 billion in the five years to December 2000, including $27.8 billion in 2000 alone. Follow-on offerings raised a further $51.6 billion. If those figures are added to the $26.6 billion raised in venture capital, they total just over $150 billion.

Of course, some of these funds never reached the dot-coms themselves. Wall Street investment banks took $5.3 billion of the money in the form of fees, says Dialogic. And almost half of the funds raised through secondary offerings—the sale of stock after the IPO—went to investors selling shares. These included the dot-com entrepreneurs cashing out some of their holdings and venture capital firms realizing the value of their investments.

Much of the money that reached the dot-coms—up to 80 percent in some cases—was spent on advertising and brand building, part of a race to grab a larger share of a market that hardly existed. Market research firms have calculated that Web sites spent several hundred dollars on marketing and promotion to attract a single customer.

The primary beneficiaries of this spending were the advertising agencies, media networks, newspapers, magazines, billboard owners, and—in the case of below-cost promotions—consumers themselves. E-toys, the online toy store, lost $4.04 on every order, according to McKinsey. Webvan, the online grocer, gave away $12.90 for every order delivered to a customer, and Drugstore.com lost $16.42 on every nonprescription order shipped.

There were other winners: the landlords who charged absurd rents to dot-com tenants, high-technology equipment makers whose sales soared on new demand from the Internet groups, headhunters paid handsomely for finding often ill-experienced executives to head the ventures, and others.

Alas, the losers of the Internet crash were also plentiful. The biggest victims were the wider public that was attracted to promises of big money. Mutual funds, pension funds, and others were badly hit, as were the people who entrusted the funds with their money. Workers who jumped on the dot-com gravy train only to find themselves pushed off a few months later now find themselves unemployed. Traditional companies found themselves out of pocket for the millions they sank into failed dot-com forays.

Given the extent of the losses, it is surprising there is not more resentment over Internet mania. Some of the explanation may lie in the perception, at least in America, that there is something of lasting importance in the creation of the World Wide Web. The Internet is here to stay. Between October 2000, well after the bubble burst, and February 2001, e-commerce growth actually accelerated. Seventeen million Internet addresses were registered over that time period.

Broadband connections from home—high-speed telecommunications that allow for rapid transmissions over the Internet—rose 150 percent in 2000 and are projected to continue growing fast. Worldwide, the number of people going online is expected to more than triple over current rates, reaching 1.5 billion by 2005.

Yet the Internet's impact on business is very different from original forecasts. Bricks-and-mortar companies, far from being disintermediated, continue to ply their wares on Web sites, even as pure plays drop away. And the flood of wealth the technology was expected to create is nowhere to be seen. In 1999 Goldman Sachs compared the Web to the invention of electricity: although the power source transformed people's lives and fueled economic growth, few individual companies profited much from the innovation.

Come to think of it, farmers still make money from tulips as well. The Internet is here to stay, and it will certainly change the way things are done. Yet money from the breakthrough will likely flow a little more slowly than it did in the technology's early heady years.

WHEN BAD THINGS HAPPEN TO GOOD PRODUCTS: WHAT YOU CAN LEARN FROM THE APPLE III FIASCO

Bill Pollack

The story of the development of Apple III is a cautionary tale of management ideals—such as the value of working in teams and the importance of working to an ambitious deadline—that can prove fatal in real life. After two years of development, the Apple III was announced on May 19, 1980, during the National Computer Conference (NCC) in Anaheim, California. With Apple's typical flair for spectacle, the company rented Disneyland for five hours the following night at a cost of $42,000, and transported an estimated seven thousand NCC attendees to the site in British double-decker buses.

Apple was proud of the Apple III because it represented many firsts for the company. Foremost, it was the company's first attempt at building a powerful business computer. It was also the company's first major departure from the tried-and-true Apple II architecture. It would prove the company's first bona fide failure. Unfortunately, instead of learning from the experience, Apple repeated many of the same mistakes with the Lisa and the Mac.

The Apple III was sold in two different configurations ranging in price from $4,340 to $7,800. At the heart of each was a microprocessor running at twice the speed of the Apple II. On paper, all the specifications were quite impressive, but implementing them proved a humbling experience for Apple.

Apple originally promised to ship the Apple III in July, but production problems plagued the product throughout the summer and into the fall. Unlike the Apple I and II, which were essentially the work of one man, Steve Wozniak, the Apple III was designed by a committee headed by Steve Jobs, who would demand one thing one day, then the opposite the next. The shipping delays threatened to mar Apple's initial public offering in December, so managers ignored the dire warnings of engineers who knew what would happen if they pushed the Apple III out the door before its time. As soon as units began trickling into distribution in late November, the worst fears of the engineers were realized.

On February 10, 1981, Apple announced that the Apple III would no longer contain the built-in clock/calendar features because National Semiconductor's clock chip didn't meet Apple's specifications. How the flaky parts got into a shipping product nobody was willing to say. Apple dropped the price of the Apple III to $4,190 and gave a $50 rebate to everybody who had purchased an Apple III up to that date.

When the first volume shipments began in March 1981, it became apparent that dropping the clock chip was just a finger in the dike. Approximately 20 percent of all Apple IIIs were dead on arrival, primarily because chips fell out of loose sockets during shipping. Those that did work initially often failed after minimal use thanks to Jobs' insistence that the Apple III not have a fan (a design demand he would make again on the Mac). He reasoned that in addition to reducing radio-frequency interference, the internal aluminum chassis would conduct heat and keep the delicate components cool. He was wrong.

Compounding the problem was that Jobs dictated the size and shape of the case without concern for the demands of the electrical engineers, who were then forced to cram boards into small spaces with little or no ventilation. As the computer was used, its chips got hot, expanded slightly, and slowly worked their way out of their sockets, at which point the computer simply died. Apple's solution was to recommend lifting the front of the computer six inches off the desktop, then letting it drop with the hope that the chips would reseat themselves!

The problems with loose chips were exacerbated by short cables between internal components and no-gold connectors that suffered from corrosion. To its credit, Apple didn't buy the problem; on April 15, 1981, Mike Markkula, president and CEO, admitted to the *Wall Street Journal,* "It would be dishonest for me to sit here and say it's perfect." Apple instituted a liberal repair policy, swapping brand new Apple IIIs for bad ones on the spot, no questions asked. To everyone's dismay, the replacements often failed too.

On November 9, Apple announced a revised Apple III with a base price of $3,495. The company steadfastly claimed that the original problems were linked to shortcomings in manufacturing and quality control procedures rather than the underlying design of the computer. Nonetheless, the new Apple III featured different sockets, updated software, memory expansion up to 256K, and an optional 5MB hard disk drive. Based upon the Seagate ST506 mechanism, the $3,495 ProFile was an important addition to the system since IBM didn't yet offer a hard drive for its PC, which had been introduced that August. Of the 7,200 original Apple IIIs that had been sold, 2,000 were replaced for free when the new version became available in mid-December.

Even after the Apple III had been revised, sales remained disappointing. Analysts estimate that Apple sold 3,000 to 3,500 units a month, just one-tenth the sales rate of the venerable Apple II. According to Info-Corp, a Santa Clara research firm, the Apple III had an installed base of only 75,000 units by December 1983, compared to 1.3 million Apple IIs. Potential buyers had been turned off by the bad publicity as well as by a lack of useful software that took advantage of the Apple III's unique Sophisticated Operating System. Industry experts openly referred to the operating system by its distress-signal initials, SOS, although Apple preferred the phonetic nickname "applesauce."

In a last-ditch effort to revive the product, Apple replaced the Apple III with the $2,995 Apple III Plus in December 1983. In addition to a lower price, the new model came standard with 256K of RAM, a built-in clock that actually worked, a new logic board, SOS version 1.3, improved peripheral ports with standard DB-25 connector, and a modified slot housing for easier card installation. It was a classic case of too little too late.

Although the Apple III Plus had helped boost the installed base to an estimated 120,000 units, Apple abruptly dropped the line on April 24, 1984. "While the Apple III is an excellent business computer," wrote David Fradin, Apple III business unit manager, in a memo to his staff, "it is a generally accepted view by Apple's product managers that Apple can best serve the future needs of our business customers by expanding the Apple II and Apple 32 (Lisa and Mac) product families, and by concentrating future development, marketing and sales efforts on those products. Therefore, we have decided that no further product development efforts shall be initiated and undertaken for the Apple III product line, effective immediately." After losing over $60 million on the Apple III product line, Apple quietly removed it from the product list in September 1985.

Said Apple employee number six, Randy Wigginton: "The Apple III was kind of like a baby conceived during a group orgy, and [later] everybody has this bad headache and there's this bastard child, and everyone says, 'It's not mine.'"

Notes

3. Finance and Accounting

FACT, NOT FICTION: FINANCIAL STATEMENTS FOR THE REAL WORLD

1. The SEC is the U.S. Securities and Exchange Commission, which is the federal government agency in charge of the U.S. securities markets.
2. *United States v. Arthur Young & Co.*, 465 U.S. 805, 817–818 (1984), emphasis in original.
3. Arthur Andersen, Deloitte & Touche, Ernst & Young, KPMG, and PricewaterhouseCoopers.
4. GAO Report to the U.S. Senate Committee on Banking, Housing, and Urban Affairs, October 4, 2002.
5. Deloitte & Touche.
6. Some of the Sarbanes-Oxley provisions are not new, but simply reiterate and codify existing laws.
7. For example, in 2000 Enron paid Arthur Andersen $25 million for audit work and another $27 million for consulting services. Also in 2000, Sprint paid Ernst & Young $2.5 million in audit fees plus $63.8 million for other services; General Electric paid KPMG $23.9 million for audit fees plus $79.7 million for other services; and J. P. Morgan Chase paid PricewaterhouseCoopers $21.3 million for audit work plus $84.2 million for other services.
8. One main reason for the separation of audit firms from their consulting divisions was pressure from the SEC.

TRANSPARENCY: SEEING THROUGH THE SEERS OF WALL STREET

1. Scott E. Stickel, "Predicting Individual Analyst Earnings Forecasts," *Journal of Accounting Research* 28 (1990): 409–17; or David Dreman and Michael Berry, "Analyst Forecasting Errors and Their Implications for Security Analysis," *Financial Analysts Journal* 51 (1995): 30–42.
2. Hsiou-wei Lin and Maureen F. McNichols, "Underwriting Relationships, Analysts' Earnings Forecasts and Investment Recommendations," *Journal of Accounting and Economics* 25 (1998): 101–27; or Roni Michaely and Kent L. Womack, "Conflict of Interest and the Credibility of Underwriter Analyst Recommendations," *Review of Financial Studies* 12 (1999): 653–86.
3. Benjamin M. Cole, *The Pied Pipers of Wall Street: How Analysts Sell You Down the River* (Princeton: Bloomberg, 2001); and Saul Hansell, "As Tech

Stocks Fall, Some Analysts Prosper," *New York Times*, online edition, March 4, 2001.

4. Harrison Hong and Jeffrey D. Kubik, "Analyzing the Analysts: Career Concerns and Biased Earnings Forecasts," *Journal of Finance* 58, 1 (2002): 313–51.

4. Strategy

THE FALL AND RISE OF STRATEGIC PLANNING

1. Michael Porter, "The State of Strategic Thinking," *Economist*, May 23, 1987, p. 21.
2. Philip Selznick, *Leadership in Administration: A Sociological Interpretation* (New York: Harper & Row, 1957).
3. George Steiner, *Strategic Planning: What Every Manager* Must *Know* (New York: Free Press, 1979), p. 9.
4. Peter Lorange, "Roles of the CEO in Strategic Planning and Control Processes," in a seminar on The Role of General Management in Strategy Formulation and Evaluation, cosponsored by E.S.S.E.C., E.I.A.S.M., and I.A.E. (Cergy, France: April 28–30, 1980), p. 2.
5. H. Igor Ansoff, *Corporate Strategy: An Analytic Approach to Business Policy for Growth and Expansion* (New York: McGraw-Hill, 1965), p. 44.
6. Mariann Jelinek, *Institutionalizing Innovation: A Study of Organizational Learning Systems* (New York: Praeger, 1979), p. 139.

THE SYSTEM: MEASURING AND MANAGING YOUR WAY TO SUCCESS
USING THE BALANCED SCORECARD

1. See http://www.schneiderman.com/The_Art_of_PM/what_is_the_BSC/what_is_a_BSC.htm.
2. Arthur M. Schneiderman, "Why Balanced Scorecards Fail!" *Journal of Strategic Performance Measurement*, January 1999, special edition, 6.

8. Marketing

THE TEN COMMANDMENTS OF MARKETING

1. For the importance and role of mental models, see Y. J. Wind and C. Crook, "Making Sense," Wharton School working paper, 2002.
2. See, for example, P. Shoemaker, *Profiting from Uncertainty: Strategies for Succeeding No Matter What the Future Brings* (New York: Free Press, 2002).
3. For a discussion of vision creation, see Y. J. Wind, "Creating a Vision," in *Technology Management Handbook* (Boca Raton: CRC Press, 2000).

4. For the importance of the emotional link, see Y. J. Wind and V. Mahajan, "Got Emotional Product Positioning? There's More to Positioning than Just Features and Benefits," *Marketing Management*, May–June 2002, 36–41.

5. R. Lauterborn, "New Marketing Litany: 4 P's Passe; C-Words Take Over," *Advertising Age*, Oct. 1, 1990, 26.

6. Y. J. Wind and V. Mahajan with R. Gunther, *Convergence Marketing: Strategies for Reaching the New Hybrid Consumer* (Upper Saddle River, N.J.: Financial Times-Prentice Hall, 2002), 262.

7. For a discussion of adaptive experimentation, see Y. J. Wind, "The Challenge of Adaptive Experimentation," Wharton School working paper, 2002.

FROM ZERO-SUM TO WIN-WIN: PERFORMANCE-BASED PRICING

1. The example is described in detail in Sherwood C. Frey and Michel M. Schlosser, "ABB and Ford: Creating Value Through Cooperation," *Sloan Management Review*, fall 1993, 65–72.

SPEND 90 PERCENT ON THE WHO, 9 PERCENT ON THE WHAT, AND 1 PERCENT ON THE HOW: THE ART AND SCIENCE OF BRANDING

1. This certainly isn't the only definition around. Don Sexton of Columbia University says he has accumulated seventeen. Generally speaking, the two most common are a narrow legal definition that says a brand is a trademark, and a more expansive one, used by advertising agencies, that defines brand as a "promise that exists in the minds of the consumer." Others, such as Scott Bedbury, have proposed even more expansive ones, e.g., "the central organizing principle of a company." However, for the practical purposes of brand building, the definition of a brand as a "relationship" is a particularly workable one.

2. Anjan Chatterjee, et al., "Revving Up Auto Branding," *McKinsey Quarterly*, 2001, 1.

3. Sam Hill, et al., "How to Brand Sand," *Strategy & Business*, 1998, 2.

4. Even the original consumer products brands were "natural" brands. The first modern brand logo was a star used by Procter & Gamble on its first soap product in the mid-nineteenth century. But P&G didn't create the star. Longshoremen on the Mississippi River chalked it on the side of Procter crates to denote that those were of better quality than competitors' products.

5. Not surprisingly, there is considerable variety in terminology for these two steps. For example, the core target market is also called the "bull's-eye consumer." The point of differentiation is also called the "unique selling

proposition," etc. In the main, these differences represent less true differences in approach than attempts by marketing service providers to brand their service offerings.

6. Home Depot is the king of spotting sleepers. They have also worked with Scott's fertilizer to create and sell a lawn tractor, and with GE to create a line of water heaters.

7. Sam Hill, *Sixty Trends in Sixty Minutes* (New York: Wiley, 2002).

8. Some differentiation claims to avoid: One stop shopping, Made in the USA, and claims of longevity.

9. Pui-Wing Tam, "Small Wonder," *Wall Street Journal,* June 25, 2001.

9. Communication

IT PAYS TO TALK RIGHT: THE POWER AND INFLUENCE OF CORPORATE COMMUNICATION

1. Aristotle, *The Art of Rhetoric* (Cambridge, Mass: Harvard University Press, 1975).

2. Mary Munter, *Guide to Managerial Communication,* 6th ed. (Upper Saddle River, N.J.: Prentice-Hall, 2002), 3–33.

3. Harold J. Leavitt, "Hot Groups," *Harvard Business Review,* July 1, 1995, 109.

4. Matthew Boyle, "The Right Stuff," *Fortune,* March 4, 2002, 85–86.

About the Contributors

PAUL ARGENTI, professor of management and corporate communication, has taught at Harvard Business School, Columbia Business School, and, since 1981, at the Tuck School of Business at Dartmouth. He has also taught as a visiting professor at the International University of Japan, the Helsinki School of Economics, and Erasmus University. He currently serves as faculty director for the Tuck Leadership Forum and has previously served as faculty director for the Tuck Executive Program (TEP), for Update 2000, and for Tuck's senior executive program at the Hanoi School of Business in Vietnam.

BERNARD AVISHAI is director of the Zell Entrepreneurship Program at the Interdisciplinary Center in Herzliya, Israel. An early leader in developing corporate knowledge strategy, he has consulted to such companies as Motorola, Coca-Cola, and Millennium Pharmaceuticals and was the founding chairman of Boston's Lunar Society. He has been international director of Intellectual Capital at KPMG, head of product development at Monitor Company, and technology editor of *Harvard Business Review.* He has written about business and politics for such publications as *The New Yorker,* the *New York Times, The New York Review,* and *Fortune.* He is the author of *The Tragedy of Zionism: How Its Revolutionary Past Haunts Israeli Democracy* and *A New Israel: Democracy in Crisis, 1973–1988.* Avishai has taught the humanities at MIT and was awarded the John Simon Guggenheim Foundation Fellowship in 1987.

WARREN BENNIS is a respected thinker and writer in the areas of management leadership and teams. He is a professor of business administration at the University of Southern California's Marshall School of Business, where he is also founding chairman of the Leadership Institute. Bennis has advised four U.S. presidents and over 150 corporations and has written a number of management books, including *Organizing Genius* and *Co-Leaders.*

JAMES A. CHAMPY is chairman of Perot Systems' consulting practice and also head of strategy for the company. He is responsible for providing direction and guidance to the company's team of business and management consultants. Champy is recognized worldwide for his reengineering and change management insight. He is coauthor, along with Michael Hammer, of *Reengineering the Corporation,* a best-seller that sold more than two million copies and was on the *New York Times* best-seller list for more than a year; it has been translated into seventeen languages. His follow-up book, *Reengineering*

Management, is also a best-seller and was recognized by *BusinessWeek* as one of the best business books of 1995. Champy is a leading authority on the management issues surrounding business reengineering, organizational change, and corporate renewal. He consults extensively with senior-level executives of multinational companies seeking to improve business performance. Prior to joining Perot Systems, Champy was chairman and CEO of CSC Index, the management consulting arm of Computer Sciences Corporation. He was one of the original founders of Index, a $200 million consulting practice that was acquired by CSC in 1988. Champy's latest book is *X-Engineering the Corporation, Reinventing Your Business in the Digital Age.* He received both his bachelor's and master's degree from the Massachusetts Institute of Technology and his law degree from Boston College Law School. He is a life member of the MIT Corporation, the school's board of trustees, and a member of the board of Overseers of the Boston College Law School. He also sits on the board of Analog Devices, Inc.

GEORGE CONRADES is chairman and CEO of Akamai Technologies, Inc., in Cambridge, Massachusettes. A technology industry veteran, Conrades joined Akamai in 1999 after serving for five years as CEO of BBN, a pioneering software firm, also based in Cambridge. Conrades engineered the 1997 deal in which BBN was acquired by GTE Internetworking. Prior to BBN, Conrades was an IBM senior vice president and member of IBM's corporate management board. There he ran many of the company's key businesses, including IBM United States, IBM Asia/Pacific, and two manufacturing and development groups. A graduate of Ohio Wesleyan University, where he majored in physics and mathematics, Conrades earned an MBA from the University of Chicago Graduate School of Business. He serves on the board of directors for Harley-Davidson and Cardinal Health. He also serves as a venture partner at Polaris Venture Partners, an early-stage investment company in Boston.

STUART CRAINER and **DES DEARLOVE** are writers and editors based in the UK. Together, they edited the *Financial Times Handbook of Management* and coauthored *The Ultimate Business Guru Guide.*

ROBERT G. ECCLES is president and cofounder of Advisory Capital Partners, Inc. (ACP) and a senior fellow of PricewaterhouseCoopers. Prior to founding ACP, Dr. Eccles was a tenured professor at Harvard Business School, where he was on the faculty for fourteen years. Dr. Eccles is a world-renowned expert in the field of corporate performance measurement and reporting. His most recent book is *Building Public Trust: The Future of Corporate Reporting,* which he coauthored with Samuel A. DiPiazza Jr., CEO of PricewaterhouseCoopers. He is also a coauthor of *The Value Reporting Revolution: Moving Beyond the Earnings Game* with Robert H. Herz (chairman of the Financial Accounting

Standards board), E. Mary Keegan (chairman of the Accounting Standards board), and David M. H. Phillips (partner at PricewaterhouseCoopers).

CARL FRANKEL, writer, journalist, and consultant, is a leading authority on sustainable development. He has edited environmental business magazines, such as *Tomorrow* and *Greenmarket Alert.* He is the author of *In Earth's Company: Business, Environment, and the Challenge of Sustainability.*

BILL GEORGE is the author of *Authentic Leadership: Rediscovering the Secrets of Creating Lasting Value* and the former chairman and CEO of Medtronic. Currently, he is professor of leadership and governance at IMD in Lausanne, Switzerland, and executive-in-residence at the Yale School of Management. He is a member of the board of directors of Goldman Sachs, Novartis, and Target Corporation.

VICTORIA GRIFFITH is the Boston bureau chief of the *Financial Times.* The national science and biotechnology editor for the paper, she has also written extensively about management issues.

WILLIAM HASELTINE is CEO of the biotechnology group Human Genome Sciences (HGS). A noted AIDs researcher, Haseltine's goal at HGS is to develop drugs to treat a wide variety of disease, including the autoimmune condition lupus and cancer.

RONALD A. HEIFETZ and **MARTY LINSKY** teach leadership at the John F. Kennedy School of Government at Harvard University. Heifetz is the author of *Leadership Without Easy Answers* and cofounder of the school's Center for Public Leadership. Linsky is faculty chair of many of the school's executive programs. Coauthors of *Leadership on the Line: Staying Alive Through the Dangers of Leading* (Harvard Business School Press, 2002), they are also partners in Cambridge Leadership Associates.

SAM HILL As president of Helios Consulting, based in New York and Chicago, Sam works with the top management of Fortune 500 companies on issues of growth and marketing. Prior to founding Helios he was vice chairman, strategy, at DMB&B, and prior to that a vice president and chief marketing officer at Booz-Allen & Hamilton. His work has appeared in *HBR, Strategy + Business, Fortune,* the *Financial Times, Context,* the *Wall Street Journal,* and the *Los Angeles Times,* among others, as well as in six books, including *Radical Marketing* (Harper Business, 1999), cowritten with Glenn Rifkin, and *The Infinite Asset* (Harvard, 2001), cowritten with Chris Lederer.

HARRISON HONG is a professor of economics at Princeton University, where he teaches courses in finance in the undergraduate, masters, and Ph.D. programs. Before coming to Princeton in 2002, he was on the finance faculty of Stanford University's Graduate School of Business, most recently as an associate professor of finance. He received his BA in economics and statistics with highest distinction from the University of California, Berkeley, in 1992 and his Ph.D. in economics from M.I.T. in 1997. Hong's research has covered a range of topics, including behavioral finance and stock-market efficiency; asset pricing and trading with market imperfections; social interaction and investor behavior; career concerns and herd behavior; mutual funds; and security analysts and investor relations. He is on the editorial board of the *Journal of Financial Intermediation* and has received various research grants and awards.

DEAN KAMEN is an inventor, entrepreneur, and business leader. His company, DEKA Research and Development Corporation, based in Manchester, New Hampshire, has developed a series of breakthrough medical devices. Kamen created the IBOT, a sophisticated mobility aid for the physically challenged designed to climb stairs and traverse uneven terrain. He also invented the Segway Human Transporter, a self-balancing personal transportation device. A firm believer in the need to motivate young people to pursue opportunities in science, technology, and engineering, Kamen created the FIRST robotic competition, which now includes six hundred teams and twenty-two thousand students from high schools across the United States and around the world.

ROSABETH MOSS KANTER holds the Ernest L. Arbuckle Chair as professor of business administration at Harvard Business School. She has been editor of *Harvard Business Review,* an advisor to leading companies and governments worldwide, the cofounder of a consulting firm, and a corporate and nonprofit director, and she has been named to lists of the most important women in the world. Among her award-winning, best-selling books are: *Men and Women of the Corporation, The Change Masters, When Giants Learn to Dance, World Class,* and, most recently, *Evolve!: Succeeding in the Digital Culture of Tomorrow.* Her forthcoming book, *Confidence: How Winning and Losing Streaks Begin and End,* will be published by Crown in the fall of 2004.

RANDY KOMISAR calls himself a "virtual CEO," because he is not tied to any single company. He incubates start-ups such as WebTV and TiVo. He was CEO of LucasArts Entertainment and a cofounder of Claris Corporation. Komisar was also involved in Apple in its early days. Komisar wrote a best-selling book, *The Monk and the Riddle,* about Silicon Valley at the height of the Internet boom.

AMIEL KORNEL is an independent business consultant based in Palo Alto, California. Since 1992, he has helped clients realize new ventures in emerging technology and online markets. Formerly a partner at a Silicon Valley strategy consultancy, The McKenna Group, where he headed the Innovation

Practice, Kornel advises chairmen, CEOs, and other senior executives of Global 1000 companies, as well as visionary entrepreneurs. Past clients include Sony, Reed Elsevier, Coca-Cola, HP, British Telecom, Motorola, and Lilly.

Kornel also has authored hundreds of articles for business and trade publications, such as the *International Herald Tribune*, the *Economist, Computerworld, Network World*, and *MIT Management.* In 1991 and 1992, he served as student editor for the *Sloan Management Review* while attending the MBA program at MIT's Sloan School of Management.

Over the past twenty-five years, he has reported stories and served clients around the world—across most of Europe as well as in Mexico, Canada, Japan, and Australia.

LES LIVINGSTONE earned MBA and Ph.D. degrees from Stanford University, with majors in accounting and economics. He is a CPA (licensed in New York and Texas) and a CVA (certified in business valuation). He is a qualified arbitrator, appointed to the American Arbitration Association panels on large commercial disputes and construction disputes. Les has been a frequent speaker at litigation service seminars of the American Institute of CPA's, the Florida Institute of CPA's, and the Texas Society of CPA's.

He has substantial professional experience, including five years in corporate strategy consulting, ten years in public accounting practice, and twelve years as a business school professor. He was a principal in the MAC Group, an international management consulting firm specializing in corporate strategy, with offices in Boston, Chicago, Los Angeles, San Francisco, Washington, D.C., London, Paris, Munich, Rome, and Tokyo. At MAC, he served major corporate clients and also the U.S. Postal Service, the SEC, and HHS agencies of the federal government. MAC has since been acquired by Cap Gemini/Ernst & Young Consulting. Les has also been a partner in the international accounting firm of Coopers & Lybrand (now PricewaterhouseCoopers).

Previously, he was the Arthur Young Distinguished Professor of Accounting at Ohio State University, Fuller E. Callaway Professor at Georgia Institute of Technology, and chairman of the department of Accounting and Law at Babson College, Wellesley, Massachusetts.

THORNTON MAY is a futurist, consultant, and trusted advisor to senior executives. His extensive experience researching and consulting regarding the design, structure, and operation of information technology organizations makes him the "first phone call" many boards of directors and "C" level executives make when confronting important technology management decisions. On average, he interacts with three CIOs in the Global 2000 every day. May served on the executive committee at Cambridge Technology Partners and founded the Director's Institute, a program to improve board-level technology decision making. He is responsible for creating the technology curriculum for executive education programs at the John E. Anderson Graduate School of Management at UCLA. He also teaches the strategic IT module in the Advanced Management Program at the Haas School of Business at the University of California at Berkeley. May has served as an advisor to the senior management teams at Toyota USA, American Express, Staples, and Cisco Systems. As a futurist, May speaks in the narrative tone of a native of, not a visitor to, the future. Known in the industry for being an astute chronicler of the technology-driven economy in which we live today, May is a sought-after voice about what comes next. A columnist for *ComputerWorld*, May has an MS in industrial administration from Carnegie-Mellon University and a BA in Asian studies from Dartmouth College. He also studied organizational design at Keio University in Tokyo.

TIMOTHY J. McMAHON is president and CEO at Adams, Harkness & Hill in Boston. In his current position, which he assumed in April 2001, McMahon has overseen the establishment of the firm's Wealth Management Division, the expansion of the Equities Group in the San Francisco office, and, most recently, the launch of offices for the firm in New York City. Prior to his promotion, McMahon served for seven years as the company's managing director and co-head of investment banking. During his tenure, McMahon was responsible for driving the expansion of Adams, Harkness & Hill's Investment Banking Division, growing it from three to thirty-five members, as well as spearheading the office opening in San Francisco. He first joined the firm in 1984 as an associate in the Corporate Finance Department, where he focused on underwritings, mergers and acquisitions, and private placements. McMahon began his career as an officer at Multibank, a commercial bank. Upon graduation from business school, he was hired as a consultant for Mitchell and Company, a management and financial-strategy consulting firm. McMahon currently sits on the board of advisors for Boston College Carroll School of Management and is a member of the Securities Industry Association's Institutional Brokerage Committee. He earned his BA in finance from Boston University and MBA from Babson College.

BOB METCALFE has always been ambitious. By the age of ten, his dream was to become an electrical engineer at the Massachusetts Institute of Technology, which he later attended. In 1979 Metcalfe founded 3Com to promote the revolutionary Ethernet networking standard he had invented a few years before. At 3Com he served as CEO, president, chairman of the board, division general manager, and head of sales. Metcalfe retired in 1990. In recent years, he has written columns for magazines, acted as a consultant, and served as a venture capitalist at Polaris in Boston.

MICHAEL MILKEN, one of America's leading philanthropists, is often said to have revolutionized modern capital markets, making them more democratic by innovating a wide range of financing techniques that previously were unavailable to most companies. This created millions of jobs. He cofounded the Milken Family Foundation in 1982 and now heads the Center for Accelerating Medical Solutions, the Milken Institute, CaP CURE and Knowledge Universe, Inc. He and his wife, who were married in 1968, have three children and live in Los Angeles.

JOSH MILLS, director of the Master's Program in Business Journalism, has worked as a business journalist for more than twenty years, half of that at the *New York Times* as an editor and reporter. He has written about technology for *Bloomberg News,* and he has written on a wide variety of subjects for *Esquire, Rolling Stone,* the *Village Voice, New York, TV Guide, Stereo Review, Columbia Journalism Review,* and other publications. He has also worked as a reporter or editor at the *Newark* (NJ) *Star Ledger,* the Associated Press, the *New York Post,* the *New York Daily News,* and *Newsday.* Mills frequently edits books about business. Among the subjects that interest him are the media business, international trade, the business of sports, the business of culture, and almost anything about ice hockey.

HENRY MINTZBERG is the Cleghorn Professor of Management at McGill University. His Ph.D. is from MIT and he is also a Visiting Scholar at INSEAD. Dr. Mintzberg has spent the past several years with colleagues from Canada, England, France, India, and Japan developing new approaches to management education. Dr. Mintzberg's books include *Why I Hate Flying, Strategy Safari, The Fall and Rise of Strategic Planning,* and *The Nature of Managerial Work.*

GEOFFREY E. MOORE is an author and communications consultant based in Santa Monica, California. Previously, he was senior vice president, strategic communications, for Dow Jones Markets. He served for twenty-two years in various communications management positions for IBM in the United States and Asia. Earlier, he was an assistant to New York Governor Nelson Rockefeller, press secretary to U.S. Senate Minority Leader Hugh Scott, and director of public information for the U.S. Equal Employment Opportunity Commission. A graduate of the University of Pennsylvania, he began his career as a broadcast journalist.

PAUL OSTERMAN is a professor of human resources at the Massachusetts Institute of Technology's Sloan School. His research explores changes in work organization within firms. He has written a number of books on the labor market, including *Securing Prosperity: How the American Labor Market Has Changed and What to Do About It* and *Broken Ladders: Managerial Careers in the New Economy.*

BILL POLLACK worked at Apple Computer in the late 1970s, when the company was wowing the world with its technological innovations. From this front-row seat, Pollack got a chance to see how a great company like Apple got things right—and, sometimes, how it got things wrong.

MICHAEL PORTER is one of the world's leading management theorists. He has authored sixteen books and more than one hundred articles about competitiveness and has served as consultant to numerous heads of government and corporations. As a professor at Harvard Business School, he leads the Institute for Competitiveness and Strategy, which studies issues of competitiveness around the globe.

PETER ROTHSTEIN is an expert in the area of entrepreneurship, strategy, business development, acquisitions, and general management in software, energy, and Internet-related markets. He has founded and built several software companies and has held various R&D management, general management, and strategy positions at Lotus and IBM. Rothstein was a partner at Kodiak Venture Partners and currently is founder and President of Allegro Strategy (www.allegrostrategy.com), an advisor to early-stage ventures, and a founding partner at Allegro Ventures (www.allegroventures.com), a seed-stage fund in the Boston area. He received his MBA from the MIT Sloan School of Management and his undergraduate degree from Clark University.

PETER SENGE is an MIT Sloan School professor and a sought-after consultant and speaker on change and learning at corporations. His best-selling book *The Fifth Discipline*, first published in 1994, changed management thinking and set out theories about "the learning organization."

ARTHUR M. SCHNEIDERMAN is an independent consultant on process management. From 1986 to 1993, Schneiderman was vice president of quality and productivity improvement at Analog Devices, Inc. He was responsible for planning, facilitating, and supporting Analog's worldwide implementation of Total Quality Management as well as its performance measurement and balanced scorecard systems. Schneiderman was also a senior examiner for the Malcolm Baldrige National Quality Award and served on the conference board's U.S. Quality Council II. He is a visiting fellow at the Centre for Business Performance at Cranfield University's School of Management in the UK and a tutor in the University of Limerick's Master of Quality Programme in Ireland. Schneiderman has published many articles concerning quality goal setting, quality costs, performance measures, and the balanced scorecard.

Before joining Analog Devices, Schneiderman was a consultant with Bain & Company, the Boston-based international consulting firm specializing in strategic planning and implementation. He is a graduate of MIT with a BS and MS in mechanical engineering and an MS in management from MIT's Sloan School of Management.

BEN SHAPIRO is a well-known authority on marketing strategy and sales management with particular interests in pricing, product line planning, and marketing organization. He is also the Malcolm P. McNair Professor of Marketing Emeritus at the Harvard Business School, where he taught full time from 1970 to 1997. He continues to teach there in several executive programs, including the CEO Program, the Young Presidents' Program, and Business Marketing Strategy. Since 1997, Professor Shapiro has concentrated his professional time on consulting, speeches, boards of directors, and writing.

During his twenty-seven years on the full-time Harvard faculty, he taught a wide variety of MBA courses, including industrial marketing, sales management, creative marketing strategy, integrated product line management, and participated in many executive programs. Professor Shapiro has also held various administrative positions, including senior associate dean for publications, research director, head of the required MBA marketing course, and faculty chair for strategic marketing management, a two-week program for senior marketing executives. Professor Shapiro is the author, coauthor, or editor of fourteen books and nineteen *Harvard Business Review* articles, including "Leveraging to Beat the Odds: The New Marketing Mind-Set," "What the Hell is 'Market Oriented'?," "Manage Customers for Profits, Not Just Sales," and "Staple Yourself to an Order." Two of his most recent books, both coedited, are *Seeking Customers* and *Keeping Customers* from the HBS Press. He has served as a consultant to more than 260 companies, including start-ups, medium-size firms, and large international corporations. He has participated in more than one hundred executive education programs outside of Harvard for corporations and associations. Professor Shapiro holds a BSE (chemical engineering) from the University of Michigan as well as MBA and DBA degrees from Harvard.

ADRIAN J. SLYWOTZKY is a managing director of Mercer Management Consulting and the author of six highly acclaimed management books, including *How to Grow When Markets Don't, The Art of Profitability, How Digital Is Your Business?, Profit Patterns, The Profit Zone,* and *Value Migration.* In his role as a consultant, he has provided advice and counsel to senior executives of companies in a broad range of industries on issues relating to new business development and value growth.

JEFFREY SONNENFELD is the associate dean for executive programs at Yale University's School of Management as well as the founder, president, and CEO of the Chief Executive Leadership Institute of Yale University. The Institute is dedicated to the advancement of top leadership education through scholarly research and peer-driven educational programs. Previously he was a professor at the Goizueta Business School of Emory University. There, he founded the Center for Leadership and Career Studies, which he ran for eight years. Prior to this, Sonnenfeld spent ten years as a professor at the Harvard Business School. His research, publications, and consulting address issues of top leadership development, executive succession, and board governance. Sonnenfeld received his AB, MBA, and DBA from Harvard University. Sonnenfeld has published five books and numerous articles in the areas of chief executive leadership, corporate governance, CEO succession, executive careers, and the management of corporate social performance. His articles have appeared in the *Wall Street Journal* as well as *Administrative Sciences Quarterly*, the *Academy of Management Journal*, *Academy of Management Review*, *American Psychologist*, *Social Forces*, *Organizational Dynamics*, *Human Resource Management*, *The Journal of Organizational Behavior*, *Harvard Business Review*, and *Human Relations*. A frequent speaker before executive audiences, his consulting work and research activities reflect a continued interest in chief executive succession and board governance along with corporate culture and strategic change. A regular commentator on PBS's "Nightly Business Report," and NPR's "Marketplace," he is a frequently cited leadership expert appearing on CNBC, CNN, FoxNews, ABC, NBC, and CBS as well as in such publications as the *New York Times*, the *Wall Street Journal*, *BusinessWeek*, *Fortune*, *US News & World Report*, *Newsweek*, the *Financial Times*, and the *Economist*.

Sonnenfeld's book *The Hero's Farewell: What Happens When CEOs Retire* (Oxford University Press) was designated as "the stand-out new management book of the year" in 1988 by *BusinessWeek*, and it earned the executive search community's "Golden Baton Award."

PAUL TAYLOR is a freelance business and technology journalist based in New York. He was born in Liverpool, England, in 1953 and has spent most of his writing career covering business and technology issues for the *Financial Times*.

Paul, who has a BA in economics, politics, and philosophy from Oxford University and a postgraduate diploma in journalism from Cardiff University, currently writes weekly columns for the *Financial Times* on personal technology and global investing issues, and he also contributes regularly to a number of other financial and business publications.

After completing his graduate journalism course, he worked for a number of local and national newspapers in Britain before joining the *Financial Times* as a reporter in 1978. During his twenty-two years as a staffer at the *Financial Times,* he held a wide range of jobs, including New York correspondent in the early 1980s, foreign news editor from 1986 to 1990, South East Asia business correspondent based in Bangkok, and was the *Financial Times'* IT editor based in London for most of the 1990s. Paul launched the *Financial Times'* monthly IT section and covered many issues, including the application of technology to business, e-commerce and the Internet technology bubble, and the growth of the offshore outsourcing market in India and elsewhere. Paul left the *Financial Times* early in 2000 to move back to New York and start up a Silicon Alley online technology analysis service followed by a technology mergers and acquisition service. In 2002, he launched a new weekly personal technology column for the *Financial Times,* which he continues to write. Paul, who describes himself as "a bit of a geek," has been a regular speaker on IT, communications, and business issues at conferences and on radio and television. He was named Online Editor of the Year in Britain in 2001.

He lives in Westchester county, New York, with his wife, two dogs, and five cats. They have four children.

YORAM (JERRY) WIND is the Lauder professor and professor of marketing at the Wharton School. He joined the Wharton faculty in 1967, after receiving his doctorate from Stanford University. Since 1988, he has served as the founding director of the Wharton "think tank"—the SEI Center for Advanced Studies in Management—and is currently leading the development of the X-Functional Integration initiatives of the school. He is also the founder and academic director of the Wharton Fellows Program. From 1995 to 1997, he led the development of the globalization strategy of the school. Dr. Wind chaired the Wharton committees that designed the new MBA curriculum (1991–1993), and WEMBA, the Wharton Executive MBA Program (1974). Dr. Wind was the founding director of the Joseph H. Lauder Institute (1983–1988) and cofounder of the Wharton International Forum (1987).

Dr. Wind has served as editor in chief of the *Journal of Marketing,* area editor of *Marketing Science,* and has been on the editorial boards of most major marketing journals. He has published more than 250 papers and articles and more than twenty books. His recent books, *Driving Change,* with Jeremy Main, and *Convergence Marketing,* with Vijay Mahajan, have received wide acclaim.

Dr. Wind has consulted and conducted research for more than one hundred companies. In addition, he has served as an expert witness in various intellectual property and antitrust cases. He is a member of the advisory boards of a number of entrepreneurial ventures and a trustee of the Philadelphia Museum of Art. He is the recipient of major marketing awards, including the Charles Coolidge Parlin Award (1985), AMA/Irwin Distinguished Educator Award (1993), and the Paul D. Converse Award (1996). He is the current recipient of the 2003 Elsevier Science Distinguished Scholar Award of the Society for Marketing Advances.

JAMES WOMACK is founder and president of the Lean Enterprise Institute. He has coauthored a number of notable management books, including *The Machine That Changed the World* and *Lean Thinking*. In *The Machine That Changed the World*, written with Daniel Roos and Daniel Jones, Womack analyzed Toyota's highly successful production system.

SIMON ZADEK is in high demand as a consultant, lecturer, and writer on sustainable business. He is founder of the Institute of Social Ethical AccountAbility and has written a number of books on the subject, including *The Civil Corporation*.

Acknowledgments

Good ideas don't just fall from the trees, as the saying goes. They have progenitors, to be gender-neutral and politically correct. In this case, the progenitor was John Mahaney, my editor at Crown Books. Some time ago, I was in a meeting with John, trying furiously to sell him yet another idea for a book about turning business lead into business gold. As I finished my pitch and searched his face for signs of a sale, he said to me, "I think I have another idea. Would you like to hear it?"

This book is the culmination of John's *other* idea. What John had in mind was a book about business that would be edgy, interesting, different, and irreverent. A book that would connect the reader to the subject matter in a very direct and deliberate way. A book that would convey personality, along with information, insight, and some useful tools. In other words, as usual, John sold *me*—and I am grateful.

A book like this could—and should—never be undertaken alone. It was really the work of friends, all of whom were excited about the idea of writing about business from a personal point of view. In fact, as I recall, I did not have to twist any arms or send Fred the Barbarian over to call in favors. All I did was describe the project to a few dozen people and wait for their pieces to roll in. They were happy to contribute.

Joining me in this effort was Victoria Griffith, a reporter for the *Financial Times*, who talked to many people, helped them craft their pieces, and give those pieces a real voice. Victoria and I have worked together on many projects, and she has never failed to make the final product better.

Also joining me in this endeavor was Glenn Rifkin, a writer and journalist of many talents and a good friend. Glenn and I worked together at the *New York Times*, the *Harvard Business Review, Strategy + Business,* and at Knowledge Universe. We collaborated on a previous book and—surprisingly—we never came to blows. At least physically. His contributions to this tome were in the *he-man* category.

In addition, Jacqueline Collette helped the cause by neatly tying together all the loose ends. She tracked down authors, located their bios, and searched through copyrights. She made certain that everyone was properly identified and that every article and section was in the correct order. Jackie and I have worked together for years, beginning at Harvard.

I am also indebted to my agent, Helen Rees, for her excellent ideas and strategies, and for her funny e-mails. I first met Helen when I had to negotiate against her. Poor me! It only took me a few short minutes to realize I was more than bested. When those negotiations concluded, and we were both free of any conflicts, I asked Helen to represent me, which she graciously agreed to do. I am very glad she said yes.

I could not complete this acknowledgment without thanking my wife, Karen, for putting up with me during the writing and editing process. The only regret I have is that now that the book is finished and in the stores, I no longer have a convenient excuse for my grouchiness, ill temper, or coal-black moods. Oh, well. I suppose I'll just have to write another book.

But most of all, I am indebted to each person who contributed to this book and for their willingness to put their ideas into print.

My job was easy. All I had to do was look up at the stars, grab the rudder, and bark a few orders. It was the contributors who actually had to row. It was the contributors who had to distill new wisdom from a lifetime of experience. Each contributor to this book did an outstanding job. Each of them gave me their best thoughts. Each of them contributed happily. For the excellent work of all the contributors to this book, I am very much indebted.

JOEL KURTZMAN
Concord, Massachusetts

Index

About the Authors

JOEL KURTZMAN is global lead partner for thought leadership and innovation at PricewaterhouseCoopers and chairman of the Tangible Group. Mr. Kurtzman has been an editor and columnist at the *New York Times,* the editor of *Harvard Business Review,* and is the founding editor of *Strategy + Business.* Mr. Kurtzman is the author or editor of eighteen books, including *How the Markets Really Work,* and hundreds of articles. He has consulted to some of the world's largest companies. Mr. Kurtzman has lectured and hosted television and radio programs globally. He has been a speaker and moderator at Microsoft's CEO Summit and at the World Economic Forum held annually in Davos, Switzerland. Mr. Kurtzman is chairman of the Global Growth Summit at Pebble Beach and the author of numerous studies on growth and the capital markets.

VICTORIA GRIFFITH is the U.S. science, biotechnology, and management correspondent for the *Financial Times.* She has interviewed many of the top CEOs and management thinkers in the country, including Peter Senge of MIT, Jim Kilts of Gillette, and Art Levinson of Genentech. Victoria has also made lunch for Julia Child and profiled Teresa Heinz Kerry. She lives in Boston with her husband and two young daughters.

GLENN RIFKIN is an author, business journalist, and human interest columnist. He has written extensively for the *New York Times* for more than a decade. He has contributed to dozens of publications, including the *Harvard Business Review, Technology Review,* the *Boston Globe,* and the *Wall Street Journal.* His books include the bestselling *Radical Marketing: From Harvard to Harley, Lessons from Ten That Broke the Rules and Made It Big* (HarperBusiness, 1999), which was chosen as one of *Fortune*'s "Best Business Books," *The CEO Chronicles: Lessons from the Top on Inspiration and Leadership* (Knowledge Exchange, 1999), and the bestselling *The Ultimate Entrepreneur: The Story of Ken Olsen and Digital Equipment Corporation* (Contemporary, 1988). His latest book, *The CEO and the Monk: One Company's Journey to Profit and Purpose,* will be published by John Wiley & Sons, January 2004.